Researching the Margins

Researching the Margins

Strategies for Ethical and Rigorous Research with Marginalised Communities

Edited by

Marian Pitts

and

Anthony Smith
Australian Research Centre
In Sex, Health and Society

First published in 2007 by
PALGRAVE MACMILLAN
Houndmills, Basingstoke, Hampshire RG21 6XS and
175 Fifth Avenue, New York, N.Y. 10010
Companies and representatives throughout the world.

PALGRAVE MACMILLAN is the global academic imprint of the Palgrave
Macmillan division of St. Martin's Press, LLC and of Palgrave Macmillan Ltd.
Macmillan® is a registered trademark in the United States, United Kingdom
and other countries. Palgrave is a registered trademark in the European
Union and other countries.

ISBN-13: 978–1–4039–1811–6 hardback
ISBN-10: 1–4039–1811–2 hardback

This book is printed on paper suitable for recycling and made from fully
managed and sustained forest sources. Logging, pulping and manufacturing
processes are expected to conform to the environmental regulations of
the country of origin.

A catalogue record for this book is available from the British Library.

A catalog record for this book is available from the Library of Congress.

10 9 8 7 6 5 4 3 2 1
16 15 14 13 12 11 10 09 08 07

Printed and bound in Great Britain by
Antony Rowe Ltd, Chippenham and Eastbourne

For the two Ds

Contents

List of Abbreviations

ABS	Australian Bureau of Statistics
ACASI	Audio Computer Assisted Telephone Interview
ACT	Australian Commonwealth Territory
AFAO	Australian Federation of AIDS Organisations
AHEC	Australian Health Ethics Committee
AIDS	Acquired Immune Deficiency Syndrome
AIHW	Australian Institute for Health and Welfare
AIVL	The Australian Injecting and Illicit Drug Users League
ANCAHRD	Australian National Council on HIV/AIDS, Hepatitis and Related Diseases
ARC	Australian Research Council
ARCSHS	Australian Research Centre in Sex, Health and Society
ASHR	The Australian Study of Health and Relationships
ASSDA	Australian Social Science Archive
ATPA	AIDS Treatment Project Australia
ATSI	Abroginal or Torres Strait Islander
AZT	Azidothymidine
BBV	Blood Borne Virus
CASI	Computer Assisted Self Interview
CATI	Computer Assisted Telephone Interviewing
CHC	Community Health Centre
CLO	Community Liasion Officer
CTARC	Clinical Trials and Research Committee
DUO	Drug Users' Organisation
ESDS	Economic and Social Data Service
HCV	Hepatitis C
HIV	Human Immune Deficiency Virus
HIV/AIDS	Human Immune Deficiency Virus, Acquired Immune Deficiency Syndrome
HSOP	The Health Status of Older People
IDRS	National Illicit Drugs Survey
IDU	Injecting Drug User
JJ	Juvenile Justice
MACASHH	Ministerial Advisory Committee on AIDS, Sexual Health and Hepatitis

MELSHA	Melbourne Longitudinal Studies on Healthy Ageing Programme
MSM	Men who have sex with men
NAPWA	National Association of People Living with HIV/AIDS
NCHECR	National Centre in HIV Epidemiology in Clinical Research
NHMRC	National Health and Medical Research Council
NSP	Needle and Syringe Programmes
NSW	New South Wales
NSW OPHS	The New South Wales Older Person Health Survey
NT	Northern Territory
OATSIH	Office for Aboriginal and Torres Strait Islander Health
OPHS	New South Wales Older Persons' Health Survey
PLWHA	People Living with HIV/AIDS
PREP	pre-exposure Prophylaxis
QuAC	Queensland AIDS Council
RA	Research Assistant
RDS	Respondent-Driven Sampling
SSAY	Same-Sex-Attracted Youth
STD	Sexually Transmitted Diseases
STI	Sexually Transmitted Infections
TRIPS	Trade-related aspects of intellectual property rights
WHA	Women's Health Australia
WTO	World Trade Organisation
WHO	World Health Organisation
VACCHO	The Victorian Abroginal Community Controlled Health Organisation

Acknowledgements

The editors would like to thank the contributors to this book for their willingness to contribute and their frankness and involvement in the research process. We would also like to thank other members of the Australian Research Centre in Sex, Health and Society (ARCSHS) who have supported the researchers throughout the writing process. We owe particular thanks to Robert Myall, Jacqui Randall, Emma Ashmere, Maureen Lockhart, Sunil Patel and Alina Turner, all of whom have helped at various stages in various ways.

We would like to acknowledge the support of Victorian Health Promotion Foundation (VicHealth) for the centre over a period of years that has allowed this innovative research to take place. The Commonwealth Department of Health and Ageing has supported the centre's work on HIV over a long period.

We would like to thank the editors at Palgrave Macmillan for their patience throughout this process and to Jon Reed for his encouragement at the early stages of this work.

Notes on Contributors

Colette Browning is Professor of Healthy Ageing in the Monash Institute of Health Services Research at Monash University, Australia. She is Co-director of the Melbourne Longitudinal Studies on Healthy Ageing and Convenor of the Health Ageing Theme in the Australian Research Council Research Network in Ageing Well. Professor Browning has published widely in journals on ageing and was recently a contributing editor of the book *Behavioural Change: An Evidence-based Handbook for Social and Public Health*.

Peter Canavan is the HIV Living Programme Coordinator for the National Association of People Living with HIV/AIDS (NAPWA), Australia. He has worked as an advocate for HIV positive people since 1988 and has been awarded life membership of NAPWA in recognition of his contributions to governance and treatments advocacy work. Peter is the Convenor of the AIDS Treatment Project Australia (ATPA) and is currently coordinating a national audit on the changing care and support needs of people living with HIV/AIDS (PLWHAs) in Australia for NAPWA.

Sue Dyson is a Research Fellow and Doctoral Student at the Australian Research Centre in Sex, Health and Society (ARCSHS), Australia. She has a background in nursing, education and women's studies and has practised for many years in women's health and lesbian health before becoming a researcher. The focus of her doctorate is on the ways in which the lesbians in her project produced and managed their own health, as well as how they engaged with and experienced services. Her work interrogates the concept of lesbian invisibility, and argues that lesbians are agents in clinical spaces, whether they choose to be out or conceal their sexual orientation from health care workers.

Jeffrey Grierson is a Senior Research Fellow with the ARCSHS, Australia. A psychologist by training he has worked in the community sector, government and academia in the HIV sector for 18 years. He leads the Living with HIV projects at ARCSHS and has presented his work at major international conferences.

Lynne Hillier is a Senior Research Fellow at ARCSHS, Australia, and the recipient of a Vic Health Public Health Fellowship which she commenced in 2006. Lynne has been involved in research on the sexuality, health and well-being of marginalised people for the past 12 years. Her researches with same-sex-attracted young people and people with an intellectual disability each were awarded Victorian Public Health Awards for innovation and excellence in research.

Philomena Horsley is currently undertaking a PhD at the University of Melbourne, Australia. She has been involved with numerous projects at ARCSHS that include women's health and lesbian health; social and cultural politics of gender; sexuality and health, particularly for marginalised communities such as lesbians, women living with HIV/AIDS and people with intellectual disabilities.

Michael Hurley is a Senior Research Fellow and Postgraduate Co-ordinator at ARCSHS, Australia. He writes mostly about gay men, HIV and contemporary gay cultures. He was a member of the Gay Men's Health International Thinktank 2001–2002, Researcher in Residence at the Australian Federation of AIDS Organisations (1999–2000) and Writer in the Community at the AIDS Council of New South Wales (NSW) (1995) . His research reports include *Then and Now. Gay men and HIV* (2003); as editor, *Cultures of Care and Safe Sex amongst HIV-positive Australians* (2002) and *Strategic and Conceptual Issues for Community-based HIV Treatments Media* (2001). His book *A Guide to Gay and Lesbian Writing in Australia* (1996) is in over 40 libraries internationally. He also co-authored *TwoTiming. Sex, writing and the writing of sex* (1991).

Kelley Johnson is currently a Marie Curie Fellow at the National Institute for Intellectual Disability, Trinity College Dublin, Republic of Ireland. Kelley has worked extensively with people with intellectual disability over a period of 15 years as a researcher and an advocate. She has written a number of books which focus on issues of concern to people with learning difficulties in particular deinstitutionalisation, women's lives and researching with people with learning difficulties.

Annie Madden is the Executive Officer of The Australian Injecting and Illicit Drug Users League (AIVL), Australia. She has worked as an advocate for drug users for more than 15 years in a variety of positions. She provides advice and advocacy on behalf of people who use drugs to the State and Federal Government and a number of research institutions. Mary O'Brien and Annie have worked together as co-investigators on a number of research projects, and have each served in formal and informal advisory roles on projects within each others' organisations.

Shelley Mallett is an Anthropologist. In March 2005 she was awarded a five-year VicHealth Research Fellowship to examine the governance, content and implementation of cross-sectoral early intervention programs for vulnerable young people and their families. Before commencing this fellowship Dr Mallett was the Research Director of Project i, a five-year longitudinal study of homeless young people in Melbourne and Los Angeles. Shelley has also worked for over ten years in homelessness service provision.

Anne Mitchell is a community development worker and an adult educator with over fifteen years experience in the field of sexual health. As Manager of the Community Liaison and Education Unit at the ARC-SHS, Australia, she has worked on research and research-into-practice projects, particularly those with hard-to-reach groups. This includes work on gay men and HIV, lesbian health and the safety and well-being of same-sex-attracted young people in schools. She has published widely in the field of gay and lesbian health and has considerable experience in advocacy and community development work in this community. She is currently Deputy Chair of the Victorian Ministerial advisory Committee on Gay and Lesbian Health and for the past two years has been Director of Gay and Lesbian Health Victoria.

Mary L. O'Brien is an Australian Research Council (ARC) Postdoctoral Fellow at the Youth Research Centre, Faculty of Education, University of Melbourne, Australia. She is currently Chief Investigator on an ARC-funded study examining the effects on the subjectivity of young adults of health promotion strategies about injecting, smoking and exercise. She was formally a Research Fellow at ARCSHS.

Marian Pitts is Professor and Director of the ARCSHS, Australia. She is a Health Psychologist and has published more than 100 articles in the areas of women's health, sexually transmitted infections and preventive health. She is the author/editor of three books including *The Psychology of Health*, now in its second edition. She has researched and taught in the United Kingdom and the United States and southern Africa and was involved in the founding of the British Psychological Society Division of Health Psychology.

Mark Saunders is a Community Liaison Officer and researcher at ARCSHS working on projects with Indigenous men and People Living with HIV/AIDS (PLWHA). He was previously Chair of the National Indigenous, Sistagirl and Transgender committee of the Australian Federation of AIDS Organisations and was a member of the Indigenous Sexual Health Committee (IASHC), a subcommittee of Ministerial Advisory Committee on AIDS, Sexual Health and Hepatitis. He has worked extensively in Queensland and the Northern Territory and is currently working with incarcerated Indigenous men.

Susan Quine is a social scientist with a background in sociology, social anthropology, social psychology, education, demography and social epidemiology. She has been working in public health education and research at the University of Sydney, Australia, for over twenty years. Susan is a recognised expert in survey and questionnaire design, and qualitative methods. She has wide experience working in multidisciplinary health research teams and is an invited conference and workshop speaker on the benefits of combining qualitative with quantitative methods to enhance health research projects. In the past decade she has concentrated on the area of healthy ageing and prevention of disability, investigating psycho-socio aspects of ageing, including the prevention of hip fracture, measurement of social support needs, service and access needs and use, medication use, self-efficacy and socio-economic and cultural variation.

Anthony Smith is Professor and Deputy Director at ARCSHS, Australia. He was one of the founding staff of the Centre and has played a key role in the development of the research agenda there. He carried out the first, large-scale national survey of sex, health and relationships in Australia. Anthony is the author of more than 110 refereed articles in the area of sexuality and sexual health.

Rannveig Traustadóttir is a Professor and Director of the Centre for Disability Studies in the Faculty of Social Science at the University of Iceland. Her academic work is in the areas of disability, gender, lesbian and gay studies, ethnicity and qualitative methodology. She has published her work widely in books and journals. Rannveig has been active in disability studies internationally and is the current president of NNDR, Nordic Network on Disability Research.

Jon Willis worked as an anthropologist for the Pitjantjatjara people of Central Australia from 1985–1997. From 1988 to 1989 he worked as a consultant to the Northern Territory (NT) and Commonwealth Health Departments, evaluating health programs in remote Aboriginal communities throughout central Australia . He has a PhD in Tropical Health. He has worked as a Lecturer in Indigenous Health at the University of Queensland and as a Research Fellow at ARCSHS since 1999. He is a fluent speaker of Pitjantjatjara language, and is conversant in a number of other Central Australian languages including Yankunytjatjara and Ngaanyatjarra. He has published a number of significant journal articles on Pitjantjatjara health culture, including in the areas of renal disease, palliative care, accidental death and male sexual culture.

Part I
Setting the Scene

Researching the Margins: An Introduction

Anthony Smith and Marian Pitts

Introduction

This book brings together the collective experience of a group of researchers who have spent their careers working with communities and populations too often neglected or understood to be too hard to reach or to work with. Many of the authors included in this book work at the Australian Research Centre in Sex, Health and Society (ARCSHS). The Centre is dedicated to the advancement of knowledge and applied skills in sexual health research and education locally, nationally and internationally. Through our research, teaching and community activities we have developed and sustain a direct and organic link with the wider community. As well as carrying out high-quality research and the teaching of postgraduate students, ARCSHS provides a variety of services to government and non-governmental organisations locally and internationally. Consultancy services have been provided in the areas of programme design, implementation and evaluation; formative evaluation; and curriculum design. ARCSHS seeks to be responsive to the community's need for assistance and expertise in research, evaluation and policy advocacy. Staff at the Centre have been awarded research grants from the National Health and Medical Research Council (NHMRC), the Australian Research Council (ARC), National Institute of Mental Health (United States), World Health Organisation (WHO), Ford Foundation, Family Health International, the Bertarelli Foundation and various State, Territory and Federal government departments. The success in attracting grants is attributable to the combination of academic rigour in the research with the assurance of delivery on time and a commitment to disseminate our results widely.

Nearly all the studies and data presented in this book are drawn from Australia. The policy response of consecutive Australian governments to issues relating to the communities dealt with in this book have been at times very different from those in many other countries. While this may mean that researchers operating in other contexts will face different and perhaps greater challenges in working with these communities, the book provides general as well as sometimes specific guidance on how to deal with many of the challenges a researcher may experience in the field.

Our purpose in commissioning the chapters in this book was not to provide a manual on how to do research that is rigorous and ethical. Instead, we wanted to share experiences of working with communities usually understood to be marginalised, to identify challenges and obstacles, risks and benefits, and modes of engagement with communities and the processes that underlie the formation of long-term research partnerships with communities and community organisations. This is a book about how to be a researcher with marginalised communities rather than a book about how to do research.

What is research?

Most of the time we take research for granted. Increasingly, policy and practice require an evidence base, and research is the means by which this evidence base is generated. Research breeds research; it is a truism that most research papers end with the exhortation that further research is required. Having begun using the word 'research' without definition, it is important to understand what we mean by this term. For the purposes of this book we define research very broadly: research is purposive knowledge generation. That is, we set out explicitly to create knowledge in relation to a specific set of problems or challenges. Given such a broad definition of research, we consequently include in the pool of those we consider researchers: students, practitioners, academics, and other gatherers of information. These groups share the need to develop research skills.

Many people in the academy have a formal model for the research process. It begins with a review of extant literature on the specified topic; the formulation of a research question based on the literature; the design of a research protocol to address that question; and then the recruitment of participants, the collection of data and the analysis of data. Finally, there is a requirement to disseminate the findings – often to fellow researchers via academic writing, to the communities involved in the research, and to the policymakers.

We hate research: under and over researching

Probably the most researched group anywhere in the world are first-year psychology undergraduates, who, as part of their research training, are often recruited (voluntarily or not) into research studies. However, it is increasingly apparent that they do not reflect society in all its glory and diversity, and university ethics committees are increasingly uncomfortable about a requirement that undergraduates must be participants in research. That said, there is still considerable variation among universities in their approach to undergraduate participation in research. The central tension is between the views of some psychologists that in order to understand the research process, students must experience research from the perspective of a participant and the countervailing view that consent can never be mandated as a requirement of course completion. Thus many ethicists would view the requirement of participation as inherently unethical because consent cannot be freely given, refused or withdrawn.

Some of these dilemmas also occur in the wider community. This is particularly in relation to contexts in which individual consent is problematic and can be understood to be overridden by a collective or community consent, or where consent appears to be unnecessary.

For example, a researcher interested in crowd behaviour may undertake observations of a football crowd, including interactions among members of the crowd and videotaping interactions between crowd members. What are the obligations for this researcher to gain individual, or indeed group consent? Recently, at an airport we observed a sign stating that an airline was making a promotional video and that members of the public would be videotaped, any one objecting to this was advised to contact an airline staff member. Both of these examples show the fine line between opting in and opting out of any process, including a research process.

If we were members of the crowd, either at the airport or the football ground, what expectations might we have about consenting to participate in research? A simple response might be that we would never take part in research without having given formal written consent and without having the purpose of the research explained to us. However, a crucial consideration in the ethical deliberation about whether individual consent was required is the relationship between risk and benefit. In situations such as those described so far, it is entirely possible that the conduct of the research offers benefits through the creation of knowledge that far outweigh the ethical costs associated with failing to obtain consent. Such a calculus should only be permissible where the potential risks to participants are fully understood and the likelihoods of any particular risk can be specified. Not as easy as it sounds though. Let us suppose that the airline video becomes a television advertisement and I am seen to be boarding a plane with someone other than my partner – or that the football match took place during working hours, or that the football crowd became violent and the police made use of the observations to identify and charge segments of the crowd.

While these outcomes may seem unlikely, they are nonetheless foreseeable and would need to have been taken into account in any ethical review of the research activities. We hope that we have already raised sufficient problems to convince you that research is never simple or straightforward.

While we have illustrated with fairly simple examples the ways in which apparently straightforward research can have potentially serious ethical and other implications, when we move to consider research with marginalised communities and populations, the challenges and risks increase exponentially. So, who is marginal?

Who is marginal?

Being central or peripheral to a particular concern or issue is by definition relative. It depends not so much on an objective reality but on the power of the people or institutions framing the concern to position specific populations or groups in specific ways. For example, analyses of the abstracts from a number of international HIV/AIDS conferences have demonstrated an apparent absence of research on heterosexual men in relation to HIV. Clearly this does not reflect the reality of the HIV epidemic, which in much of the world is a heterosexual epidemic affecting both men and women more or less equally. One interpretation of this would be that the absence of research on heterosexual men is a reflection of their marginality in the epidemic (it is the absence of a body of research that often leads to a claim of marginalisation). An alternative and perhaps more compelling reading of the apparent absence of research on heterosexual men is that the agenda is largely framed by heterosexual men who, in common with other groups in society, locate risk elsewhere.

The groups that we will be discussing in the second part of this book are characterised broadly as 'marginalised'. The list, which includes gay and lesbian people, Indigenous people, people living with HIV, injecting drug users, people with intellectual or physical disabilities, older people and younger people, is not intended to be comprehensive or definitive. No list could be. Rather, we have chosen groups that we have personally worked with over a number of years and who can act as exemplars to illustrate particular ethical or practical issues. We will seek to find commonalities and differences that can allow for a reflexive consideration of problems, challenges and opportunities of researching with these groups.

In what ways are these groups marginalised? For some, it is a consequence of history. Until fairly recently, in most societies, homosexual activity was illegal. In some societies it still is. Powerful institutions such as the law and the church prosecuted and persecuted individuals who engaged in such activities. Where the law has been reformed to remove the legal sanctions against homosexual activity (within certain age-specified limits) gay men and lesbians remain the subjects of legalised discrimination in a number of areas of their lives. It is this combination of historical and contemporary discrimination that leads to the recognition that gay men and lesbians are marginalised communities.

The marginalisation of Indigenous communities is a worldwide phenomenon of a scale that dwarfs most other forms of marginalisation that we address. In Australia, the history of dispossession, disease and the denial of basic human rights have a profound legacy. For example, the current life expectancy of an Aboriginal man in twenty-first century Australia is approximately twenty years less than that of his non-Aboriginal counterpart. An unlikely but foreseeable outcome of this marginalisation has been a heightened research interest in Aboriginal communities; that has sometimes led to particular communities being severely 'over-researched' with little or no consent or benefit. Research such as this has sometimes been characterised as 'helicopter research' where well-meaning researchers arrive, collect data, often of a descriptive kind, and leave. The community awaits the next round of research.

We have worked with People living with HIV/AIDS (PLWHA) for many years. They are a group who are marginalised not because of what they do, or what their ancestry may be, but because of the highly stigmatised nature of their disease. When HIV was recognised in certain Western countries it was associated in the public imagination with particular groups who were already subject to social sanctions. These included sexual minorities, injecting drug users and particular cultural or ethnic minorities. Even in settings where the prevalence of HIV is high (more than 30 per cent), being HIV positive largely remains a private matter because of the continuing stigma derived from the early associations.

One of the groups perceived to be at increased risk of HIV are those people who inject illicit drugs. In most countries the possession and use of certain drugs, most notably heroin, is illegal and one of the most common routes to incarceration. Beyond the obvious marginalisation that flows from engaging in illegal activities, common representations of those who inject drugs include people who survive through illegal means, abuse the welfare system to support their drug use and are the cause of most burglaries. The notion that a person who injects drugs is incapable of self-control is widespread.

Over the past 20 years, many countries have engaged in a process of de-institutionalisation for people with intellectual and physical disabilities. While this was a well-intentioned attempt to integrate people with disabilities into mainstream communities, under-resourcing of such programmes has failed to achieve the desired goals. People with disabilities have often been regarded as incapable of self-determination, including providing consent (or not) for research participation and have been the subject of institutionalised human rights abuse through strategies such as forced sterilisations. Alongside the programmes of de-institutionalisation we have seen the rise of advocacy and activism among people with disabilities. Largely, this has rested on an assertion of human rights, particularly the right of self-determination.

Old people and young people, two groups apparently part of the mainstream, may seem unlikely candidates for marginalised communities. However, as we have already noted, marginalisation is not necessarily an objective fact but a reflection of power in particular circumstances. Depending on the setting, young people can be deemed incapable of providing informed consent before the age of 15, before the age of 16 or before the age of 18. Frail elderly people may be excluded from studies because of concerns about their ability to provide informed consent. As with young people, they are not central to the process of framing issues and hence their concerns are often not reflected in research priorities and programs. A particular example of this is the way in which old people and young people are presumed not to be sexually active and hence there exists a culture of silence around research with older people about sexuality.

The problem of naming

Already we have had to face how to characterise those people with whom we research. Naming is never a straightforward or neutral issue. Choosing to name one's sexuality as 'gay' is a political act. Identifying as of Aboriginal or Torres Strait Islander (ATSI) descent is similarly political, although with potentially different consequences. Identifying as both gay and of ATSI descent brings with it consequences that demonstrate that the cumulative effect of such political acts is multiplicative rather than simply additive.

The problem of naming arises in two ways. First it can involve the location of a specific 'problem' within a particular community. Thus for many years, it was difficult to have open discussions about the high levels of recreational drug use among gay men as this was seen to demonise gay men. Similar concerns have constrained the ability of some Indigenous communities to address the issue of sexual violence.

The second problem of naming involves the identification of specific communities and groups in a manner that draws them to the attention of the state when previously they were 'invisible' or overlooked. A recent example from Australia would be the attention given to people who use the drug methamphetamine (crystal or ice) in such a way as to portray a looming crisis giving prominence to particular subcultures in a way that characterises all users of crystal meth in particular ways and as particular sorts of people.

The issue of naming leads to the issue of identity. Whilst I may choose to identify myself as gay, or as a PLWHA, can I similarly identify myself as an old, or a young person? Groups such as 'young people' are the product of an externally applied definition, rather than the common adoption of a shared identity based on community or practice. Some young people may indeed see themselves as sharing practices and cultures, but for others their identity as Indigenous or gay, may override these other affiliations. Often it is the State that determines who is young or old – by constraining freedoms, by demarcating entitlements and by enhanced surveillance.

A simple example is the State's attempt to restrict or regulate young people's sexual activity through the promulgation of age of consent laws (that vary in different jurisdictions by as much as seven years) and the requirement in some jurisdictions that certain classes of people are required to report underage sexual activity.

Issues of naming and language generally go beyond identity or ethnicity politics. Researchers need to be mindful that their choice of words can signal implicit values. We have frequently encountered research that reports that men *admit* to unprotected anal sex, or that they *confess* to drug use.

Researching oneself, one's own

As we indicated earlier, decisions about who are members of communities, and which of those communities is marginalised is an expression of power. Traditionally research has also been an expression of power where the researchers are viewed as being in a position of authority or power over the research participants. More recently, there have been significant challenges to the notion of researching *down* towards a more egalitarian framework based in researching *with* rather than *on* communities. This has been especially reflected by feminist researchers and by the paradigm of feminist research.

At its most pure form this approach has been taken to mean that research is best carried out by researchers who are themselves members of the communities or groups of interest. Importantly, these moves should not be understood to mean that only members of particular groups are authentic researchers who must, by definition of their group membership, have a 'better' understanding of the issues of that community.

In commissioning the chapters for this book we have been mindful of the value of researching with communities and the trap of applying an essentialist notion that only members of those communities can give authentic insights about them. Throughout the book there are authors who have multiple identities that may or may not be of particular relevance to the chapters they have written. All, though, have had extensive experience of researching with the communities they discuss.

As for us? While both of us were once young and with luck will one day grow to be old, one of us is unlikely to be a gay man.

The problem of rigour and the hierarchy of evidence

We set out in this book to explore the twin notions of ethical and rigorous research with marginalised communities. This means, of course, that we must develop a clear understanding of what constitutes rigour in research. As one might expect, rigour is a contested concept in research.

In a climate where evidence-based policy and practice is becoming more commonplace, it is salutary to recognise the importance of what is known as the hierarchy of evidence. In contemporary practice there is a clear graduation of evidentiary weight of data from case series (low), through description studies of various types (medium), through to randomised controlled trials (high). In simple terms, it is a widely held presumption that the only form of evidence suitable to inform policy and practice are the results of randomised controlled trials.

The thinking behind this revolves around notions of causation. A case series, for example, offers a series of observations that might suggest an association between a particular exposure and an outcome – the supposed link in the 1980s between AIDS and use of amyl nitrate is an example of a case series that was plausible but ultimately mistaken. Descriptive studies such as surveys and case-control studies are viewed as stronger forms of evidence than case series, but because they cannot demonstrate the direction of causation between exposure and outcome, they demonstrate associations only. A stronger claim to evidential status is made by cohort studies where the temporal association between exposure and outcome can be directly observed. However, the randomised controlled trial is still considered to be at the pinnacle of the evidence hierarchy because it is the method in which the true effect of interventions can be observed.

In keeping with our somewhat inclusive definition of what constitutes research, we do not agree that the hierarchy of evidence is an adequate description of the ways in which we can make sense of the world and do so in a systematic and meaningful way – a way that is rigorous.

Dictionary definitions of rigour often emphasise strictness and harshness. Our view, however, is that rigour in research is achieved not through harsh or strict or slavish adherence to a particular set of rules; rather it requires the application of appropriate research tools driven by the need to ensure that all ethical principles are adhered to at each stage of the research process. Rigour in this sense is the application of the best possible method to a research question. While we address some specific ethical issues in relation to particular forms of research, the reader needs to review carefully the current literature on research methodologies to ensure they are employing the most up to date and thoroughly proven techniques.

Confidentiality and anonymity

As a rule, participating in research involves individuals disclosing personal or otherwise private information about themselves and others. When a person decides to take part in research, it represents an exercise of trust; explicit in that exercise of trust is the requirement that any information provided as part of the process will not be disclosed to others except within the agreed terms of research. Confidentiality extends to all elements of the research process including the fact of participation itself. It is inappropriate to disclose to a third party the fact of participation, as well as the content of that participation. In practice, however, this is not easy to achieve. If we collect data in a public place, for example, a football match, or gay Pride event – then participation is public. In a small number of studies, the requirement for confidentiality has been waived and the participants are formally identified in the publication produced. For example, one of us carried out a study of the Australian research response to HIV. It involved interviews with the major players in the field, and their comments were attributed to them in the published paper. They were made fully aware of this at the point of interview and it was incorporated into the process of gaining consent – in this way, their comments were understood by both the researcher and the researched to be 'on the record'. The participants were able to make comments 'off the record' during the interview process. Before the material was published the selected quotes were shown to their authors for approval.

The primary strategy for ensuring confidentiality of research material is to restrict access to both physical and electronic copies. Simple strategies such as always keeping consent forms or other printed material in locked filing cabinets or cupboards are undoubtedly effective. Similarly, ensuring that access to electronic files is restricted through passwords can also work well. An area that people sometimes overlook is in ensuring the security of backup or portable copies of electronic data. It is unwise to work on confidential material on public access computers, such as those available at airports, or at Internet cafes. The chances of saving to the hard drive or leaving a disk in the machine are surprisingly high. Similar concerns exist in relation to backup copies on CD, DVD or USB drives.

Sometimes in research, it is important for members of the research team to be debriefed or have the opportunity to discuss with others their experience of undertaking the research. In these circumstances, there may be a number of people who potentially could identify research participants; this is especially an issue when working in small networks, or in a very specific geographical location. Therefore it is very important to ensure that all people who participate in such conversations recognise and are bound by the need for confidentiality. Undertaking research involves trying to find out things about the larger world. Sometimes researchers are surprised to discover that their research participants wander into their larger worlds beyond the research context. For example, encounters may happen in the supermarket, the pub or a party. In this event, the confidentiality relating to the fact of participation is likely to force the researcher to dissemble.

Another complexity that can arise is the participation in research of people already known to the researcher. Here, the issues can be much more complex. It may not always be possible for the researcher actively to forget information they acquired during the research process. This possibility should lead to substantial reflection on the part of both the participant and the researcher about how to manage these possibilities and whether the values of participation outweighs the changes that may occur in their relationships as a consequence of participation in research. These dilemmas become particularly apparent when working with a unit of participation that is greater than an individual, for example, when interviewing partners or friends together, or members of a family, either together or separately.

Anonymity can sometimes be confused with confidentiality, even though they are conceptually very different. Whereas confidentiality concerns restricting access to research material, anonymity concerns ensuring that the identity of research participants can never be determined from the public research material. Easier said than done. In the case of quantitative research this is usually achieved. As a rule, only aggregated data are published; we are not interested in representing individuals through quantitative data. In situations where the raw data are in the public domain, the issues are more complex. Many datasets are now required to be lodged in publicly accessible data archives, for example, Economic and Social Data Service (ESDS) in the United Kingdom and Australian Social Science Archive (ASSDA) in Australia. When this happens researchers pay particular attention to geographic information such as postal codes or addresses. Most commonly, data are aggregated to a higher level of geography, for example, state or region to minimise the possibility of individual identification. Similar concerns exist in relation to sites at which research takes place, such as a particular university (difficult to disguise) or school or community. Even when such steps have been taken, some researchers require third parties accessing the data to sign a confidentiality agreement which covers the possibility that they will learn the identity of an individual or site of research. The agreement would require that the third party immediately notifies the researcher should this transpire.

Qualitative research brings additional challenges in regard to anonymity. It is not uncommon in qualitative research to provide a word sketch of individual participants. Researchers disguise aspects of the participants in order to attempt to maintain the participants' anonymity. When working with particularly small or closed networks or communities the identity of participants may be more readily apparent to other group members than to the researcher. For this reason, it is important to ensure that the advice obtained from members of that community about how to edit the word sketches to achieve anonymity is applied carefully. Given that age and gender are often important axes of analysis there are clearly some constraints on the liberties which may be taken in this regard.

Sometimes individuals occupy such specific and public roles that even disguising some of their characteristics is insufficient to guarantee anonymity. For example, in a study of managers of national football teams, it would be virtually impossible to sustain anonymity – and probably neither useful nor desirable. In these circumstances, the strategy outlined above, where individuals are named explicitly is the preferred option. To have undertaken the study of managers of national football teams on the basis of sustaining anonymity would reflect poor research design.

Legal issues

Information collected as part of a research project does not have any special standing in relation to the law. Thus, research materials can be seized or taken through the application of a search warrant, or they can be subpoenaed. Given this, it is important to ensure that participants understand your commitment to protecting the confidentiality and/or anonymity of research participation and material, and the limitations outlined above. It is extremely rare for research materials to be obtained in these ways; however, researchers do need to be mindful of this possibility particularly in regard to the documenting criminal acts.

The law also restricts the type of research that is possible. For example, to access online child pornography for the purposes of research is illegal. Research in this area is difficult although one researcher has actually managed to carry out a study of online pornography without actually viewing any of the images and being restricted to an analysis of the text accompanying the images.

A further way in which legal issues may impinge on research is being in the wrong place at the wrong time. That is, for example, when carrying out ethnographic research and being present unintentionally at the commission of a crime. Simply being there for research purposes offers no protection under the law.

Researchers may have a duty of care in relation to the disclosure of certain experiences. This can be particularly problematic when working with young people. In some jurisdictions, researchers may have a legal obligation to report certain behaviours. Most commonly, this concerns sexual activity involving children, but may also include domestic violence. It can be difficult for researchers to ascertain their reporting obligations. Where possible, it is advisable to avoid collecting information that may place others, especially research participants, at risk of prosecution. Sometimes this is unavoidable, or perhaps undesirable; for example, little research would be carried out with illegal immigrants, paedophiles, abortion providers in setting where abortion is criminalised or other groups where we may need to know more.

Research that lingers

In some forms of research it is possible that strong bonds will emerge between the researcher and the researched. In long-term ethnographic studies, these are very common. Managing these relationships can be challenging and may require the researcher and/or the researched to re-evaluate participation. It may be that the researcher and the researched value the emerging relationship above the continuing research process.

Particular issues may arise in studies of sexual behaviour that can be erotically charged. Inappropriate behaviour or the development of relationships within the research process is perhaps ill advised. Existing relationships, however, need to be respected and, more importantly, need to be acknowledged. The integrity of the research process and the meaning of informed consent may each be jeopardised by inappropriate interactions between the researcher and the researched.

Who owns the data and who owns the knowledge?

Many people and agencies are partners in the process of research, and with those partnerships can come issues of ownership of data. This can be relatively straightforward, or extraordinarily tricky.

Probably the researcher is the person who would lay primary claim to ownership of the material generated through research. Certainly they are likely to have primary responsibility for the safe and ethical collection and storage of data. Most frequently however, the researcher (investigator) is not a single individual; most frequently there are multiple researchers. A research team might include two principal investigators, and a more junior (less experienced) researcher, and two research assistants might be employed specifically to work on the project. Then there may be a team of interviewers. Does each member of this research team have equal ownership of the data? Certainly they will not have equal responsibility for the safe and ethical conduct of the research. In both instances it may be that the primary researcher is a student carrying out the research as part of their undergraduate, or postgraduate study. In this case, what responsibility and ownership of those data does their supervisor have? There are few clear-cut answers to these questions, and in particular, issues of data ownership may not arise frequently. But when they do, the situation can become fraught very quickly. It is probably best policy to discuss ownership with all team members and to record agreements for future reference. However, teams change, and relative contributions to research can also change, so there must be the possibility of renegotiation further down the line.

Issues of data ownership, however, are broader than simply the research team. To what extent do participants in the research have ownership over their data? Some of the answers here will relate to the nature of the informed consent obtained before the research began, and to whether there are possibilities for participants to withdraw their 'own' material from the research study at a later date. Again, clear agreements need to be in place prior to data collection. What about the communities from which the participants are drawn? To what extent do they have ownership of the material, particularly if they have played a key part in facilitating recruitment of study participants? Managing the expectation that community members might have access to the materials generated by the research is essential.

Who else might claim ownership of the research? Two likely candidates are the funding agency and the host institution. In the case of the funding agency, there is usually a contract or clear set of agreements about ownership, including issues of intellectual property. In the case of the host institution the issue may arise when one or more members of a research team, for example, leaves one university to go to a rival university. Can the researcher take all the data generated from his or her first workplace to the next workplace? There are international conventions that address intellectual property in specific contexts, for example the World Trade Organisation (WTO) convention: TRIPS (trade-related aspects of intellectual property rights). However, much of the regulation of intellectual property occurs at the state or national level. Therefore researchers will need to acquaint themselves with the regulations concerning the ownership of intellectual property in their local setting.

Often those responsible for recruitment and data collection may be members, or potential members of the communities from which they are gathering their participants. This can raise significant ethical challenges for the research as a whole and for the principal researchers. If we are employing people who inject illicit drugs as recruiters and interviewers on a project concerning injecting drugs, what are our obligations and responsibilities towards these people? We need to set some clear boundaries and guidelines. No research team can sanction illegal activities as part of the research process. Boundaries become critical to the well-being and safety of both the researchers and the researched. Whilst community membership may be advantageous to the research process, it also carries risks.

The research process

The literature review – of value and values

Earlier we referred to a classical model of research which is premised on a literature review with everything flowing from that. It is important to realise that literature reviews can and should be legitimate research activities in themselves. This is particularly the case when they are used to identify gaps in knowledge, or particular forms of bias underpinning research in ways which inappropriately restrict the scope of potential research. The rigour associated with a literature review concerns the scope and specificity of the search strategies used. Most literature reviews are carried out electronically these days, using electronic data sets such as Medline, Current Contents and others to identify a body of research work published within a specified time period. These slick methods can generate many thousands of references concerning a particular topic and the task then becomes one of systematically reducing this body of work to manageable proportions that can be analysed. It is unlikely that any current literature review can be totally exhaustive, and so the decision of what to include becomes testing – being explicit and consistent are two of the better techniques. Paying particular attention to the context in which the research study has been conducted is also valuable in ensuring that the research that is analysed has the potential to be relevant to the current research setting. This can particularly be the case with national obsessions. For example, most social research that emanates from the United States will have *race* as a major axis of either recruitment or reporting. In other countries, *race* does not loom so large to play out in the same manner; instead, class or religious affiliation may be important.

A special case that underlines the sometimes limited value of the literature review is where there simply is no relevant published research. In such a case it becomes difficult to justify a research question except by corollary or analogy from other research topics. This also highlights one of the traps inherent in an over-reliance on literature reviews. The searches can only recover research that has been done. Thus, it will reflect the overarching view of how the field of research is constituted, the range of questions that can be validly asked, the methods thought appropriate and the analytic methods useful. The nature of the trap is that a slavish devotion to the literature review may simply reproduce existing understandings and constrain the possibility of original research that actually challenges received wisdom.

Publication bias is an important issue to be mindful of when conducting a literature review. This refers to the fact that certain sorts of results, particularly negative results, are less likely to be published. Thus, the use of databases such as Medline and Current Contents will paint only a partial picture of completed research. As more and more information becomes available on the World Wide Web, access is improving to the so-called grey literature which has been defined as: the quasi-printed reports, unpublished but circulated papers, unpublished proceedings of conferences, printed programmes from conferences, and the other non-unique material which seems to constitute the bulk of our modern manuscript collections (Hirtle, 1991). Given that research published in journals has generally been subjected to peer review, whereas grey literature usually has not, particular care must be used in evaluating the import of grey literature.

Developing research questions – is small better?

When framing a research question we are sometimes so committed to a particular area of research or community that we develop a question the answer to which will change the world. Rarely can one piece of research achieve this. Instead, one must be more modest in one's aims for at least with modesty comes some chance of actually achieving the aims. So what are the features of an achievable research question? Such a research question has two important features: specificity and feasibility. The nature of specificity is such that the research question is rather narrowly defined in such a way to make clear the boundaries of the enquiry. Thus, a simple question such as 'what can I learn about the health of lesbians?' lacks boundaries and specificity – which lesbians, what aspect(s) of their health are we interested in, is it physical health, emotional health, access to assisted reproductive technologies? A research question that would meet the criteria for specificity might be, 'what are the reproductive health needs of lesbians in inner Melbourne?'

The notion of feasibility of a research question can be thought of as 'doability' – just how practical is the attempt to answer the research question given the resources that are available, the chosen mode of data collection, the sample size required and the characteristics of the community of interest. One common problem for graduate research students is that they are encouraged to develop the best possible, as opposed to the best feasible, research proposal. They are then left needing to address a range of issues around fund-raising and project management that often require operating with a skill set beyond that which they can reasonably be expected to have at the beginning of a research career.

Often, the range of issues that need to be addressed in assessing the feasibility of a research question can be numerous and require extensive experience in research to anticipate and answer accurately. Most commonly those questions include how many interviews/surveys/focus groups do we need to do; what is the unit cost of each of those activities and how many of them need to be undertaken by outside agencies and at what cost; how long will it take to recruit participants and collect data; what costs are associated with data entry or transcription and how long will that take; what will be involved in analysing the data collection and again how long will it take. Increasingly, graduate students are completing a suite of studies rather than a single, large study and thus the need to address all of these questions in relation to each of the studies can constitute a significant burden. In part, our preference for smaller research questions reflects a desire to lessen this burden.

Agenda and tensions that shape research questions

Sometimes the research questions, including the specific ways in which they are asked, may be the subject of tensions between the researched communities and those who fund the research. Many of us apply for targeted research grants, where the brief and even the research questions may be set by the funding agency. Often the agencies are health or service related and that reflects their interests in any given group. For example, most research on sex work focuses on issues of regulation and of preventing people from entering, or assisting people to leave the occupation. In contrast, during interviews with sex workers, they have often raised questions about occupational health and safety and about managing clients. Similar tensions can be seen in research with other marginalised groups.

The broader research agenda is heavily influenced by funding agencies. Most of the research on gay men's health has focused on their HIV risk, yet we know that gay men face many similar health challenges to the wider community of men, have specific health needs associated with high rates of smoking and alcohol use, and with mental health. But the research that gets funded, and consequently gets done, is almost exclusively concerned with gay men, risk and HIV (Pitts, Couch and Smith, 2006).

It is not always possible to accommodate the suggested research questions that may emanate from community groups or key stakeholders – they may be too ambitious in scale and scope, or they may not be research-able in ways that would generate meaningful information. The sugges-tion or the demand that research produces evidence to order and is tailor-made to fit a concern of the moment may not be possible, or desirable.

Funding agencies may also require rights over the research material. They may require an in-confidence report and may wish to manage or restrict which data are published or made more available. It may then become a matter for the researcher(s) to decide whether the restrictions make the research worth doing at all, or whether restricted information is preferable to none.

Through whose lens?

Related to the issue of choice of research questions are the issues associ-ated with what is regarded as relevant or ethical for different groups and communities. As sex researchers over a number of years we have become fairly inured to asking anything of almost anyone. Little fazes us. However, others involved in the research process may not feel quite so at ease. It is commonly supposed that gay men will be comfortable with detailed questions of who they have had sex with, where, in what cir-cumstances and the exact nature of the sex acts they engaged in (in sequence). In contrast, we have struggled and failed to persuade other research teams to include a single question to middle aged and older women concerning whether they have ever felt attraction to another woman. There are similar discrepancies between what is regarded as acceptable to ask older and younger people, Aboriginal and non-Aboriginal people.

Just don't go there

A further issue in relation to what can or cannot be asked of participants is the potential for the confronting or depressing findings that research can sometimes produce. Whilst researching with a community what are our obligations about bad news findings? What are the responsibilities around reporting negative or stigmatising findings, evidence that might offer apparent reinforcement for prejudice or stereotyping, or indeed around reporting on behaviours that are unethical or illegal?

Research methods and their particular ethical issues

From different study designs flow different methodological options. For example, it may be equally valid to use interviews and/or surveys and/or focus groups in our study of the reproductive health needs of lesbians in inner Melbourne. It may equally be valid to rely in part on ethnographic studies of a lesbian *in vitro* fertilisation support group. Each method has its strengths and weaknesses but more importantly it has its appositeness. By this we mean the fit between the research question and the chosen method. Different research methods generate meaning in different ways – a survey consisting only of closed choice questions can generate a numerical description of the question of interest – it cannot usefully explain how people construct meaning. Similarly, focus groups and interviews are poor tools if we are interested in what proportion of people experience particular things. It would rarely be possible to undertake enough focus groups or interviews to estimate a proportion with any reliability.

So what are the particular issues of ethics and rigour that are associated with different choices of method? We will discuss the particular concerns about rigour in relation to qualitative approaches later in this chapter.

With each method come specific ethical issues

Probably the most common research technique is the survey. Surveys can be delivered in a number of formats including self-completed printed surveys – often thought of as a questionnaire, face-to-face structured interview, telephone or Internet structured survey, computer-based methods including Computer Assisted Self Interview (CASI) and Audio Computer Assisted Telephone Interview (ACASI). Features of these techniques are that the data can readily be anonymised and, depending on the mode of delivery, can offer higher degrees of confidentiality. However, these potential benefits can also bring drawbacks. If data are anonymous at the time of collection, then participants cannot have their responses removed from the database. Some survey methods have a reputation for poor quality – self-completed postal surveys in particular are characterised by low response rates and incomplete responses. An ethical issue to be aware of concerns the use of printed surveys. It is impossible to tailor the questions presented to participants to reflect their personal history or experience. The other survey research methods have at least the capability of ensuring that questions are only asked when appropriate – for example, if the participant reports no history of drug use, then further drug use questions are not asked. It is not possible to make contact with a specific participant if an anonymous self-completed questionnaire is employed. This can have potentially serious consequences. For example, you are unable to exercise your duty of care appropriately should a young person report an intention to self-harm. A related concern is the inclusion of a standardised screening instrument as part of the survey. Quite commonly the purpose is to identify mental or physical health conditions or concerns. The researcher needs to be clear what the purpose and consequences would be of identifying a mental or physical health condition. Should that information be fed back to the participant, should referral be suggested or even undertaken?

Semi-structured or unstructured interviews with individuals are commonly used in qualitative research. As a rule they are recorded and subsequently transcribed. Sometimes the transcripts are returned to participants for comment and/or correction. Conducting an interview foregrounds a number of issues. Duty of care is usually the overriding ethical concern and plays out in particular ways. First relates to disclosure; this might be disclosure of intention to harm oneself or others, to report current or past criminal behaviour or to disclose a physical or mental health condition that may warrant intervention. There needs to be a clear protocol to cover these contingencies which may include referral to appropriate agencies or the notification to a third party. This is a research interview and not a counselling or therapeutic session. The boundaries need to be clear to both the interviewer and the interviewee. The protocol must be shared with the interviewee before the interview begins. See the section on confidentiality for a further discussion of issues relating to transcribed qualitative data.

Group interviews usually involve bringing together between six and eight individuals who may or may not already know each other. Usually, group interviews are chosen to obtain information about social or cultural environments or contexts: they are not appropriate to elicit individual behaviours or experiences. The benefit of group interviews is to devise or achieve some element of consensus or to test where opinions diverge. Because a group interview involves guided interaction between participants and the facilitator, it is impossible to know in advance what might be generated in the interview. Some of the issues pertaining to group interviews are the same as those pertaining to individual interviews. But there are additional areas for concern. Whereas in an individual interview confidentially is more easily guaranteed, in a group interview establishing the need for confidentiality must always be a clearly stated and agreed condition of participation. A second ground rule that must be established and agreed upon is the need to respect the views of others in the group, whilst being able to express disagreement. When the group interview deals with topics about which participants might have strong opinions, for example, football or politics, the facilitator needs to pay particular attention to deploying strategies that can disrupt tension in the group.

People participate in research for many reasons, most commonly from altruistic motives. However, motivations can at times reflect a personal issue, crisis or concern relating to the topic of the research. This may drive them to participate when it is neither in their best interests, nor the best interests of the researcher or other participants. The participation of people who bring these issues to a group will, at its most benign, be a tendency to dominate or to direct the discussion towards their own particular concern. In these cases, the facilitator needs to redirect conversation and to encourage greater participation from the other group members. Duty of care concerns may also play a part here. Participants in group interviews sometimes later regret either what they have said or even their participation in the group – one of us has experienced a personal threat of violence subsequent to a group interview – a rare but not impossible outcome. A consequence of choosing group rather than individual interviews is that should a participant subsequently request that their contribution to the interview be deleted, this can only be done in a way that may render the rest of the interview of questionable value. Given the nature of group interviews, it is often not possible to identify individual speakers from the audio record; where this is possible and an individual's contribution is deleted it is extremely difficult to understand other contributions made in response.

Diaries and other forms of self-documentation are increasingly commonly used research methods. Alternative forms of self-documentation can include audio, photographic and video diaries. Self-documentation raises a specific issue of confidentiality. It becomes the participant's responsibility rather than the researcher's to maintain the confidentiality of the material while it is being collected. This requirement needs to be fully understood by the participant, and a comprehensive recognition of the implications of a failure to maintain confidentiality must be demonstrated. There are also issues, particularly in photographic and video diaries, of the inclusion of individuals who are not direct research participants and hence who have not consented to be part of the research process. These issues of third-party representation are particularly fraught in marginalised communities where happenstance identification could have serious consequences. Being videoed at a football match during working hours could be a problem but being videoed injecting illicit drugs could be a record of a crime. Unlike the transcripts of interviews, editing of photographs and videos to disguise the identity of individuals can be a technical challenge.

Ethnography typically refers to the conduct of field work involving the researcher living with or interacting with those being studied, usually over an extended period of time. It also includes formal interviews, casual or day-to-day interaction with research participants, documenting or examining physical localities and the minutiae of everyday life. It is an advanced research strategy which should only be employed with considerable sophistication. The practical and ethical issues surrounding the deployment of ethnography are considerable and we recommend that you address specialist texts if you are interested in using ethnography.

Size matters

The size of a research study with communities is often quite small, for example around thirty respondents. Does this matter? It largely depends on the use to which the research findings will be put. Whilst interviews (particularly if they are rich, in-depth interviews) with 30 people can shed much light on the personal stories of the individuals, it is unlikely to generate the kind of information that will persuade policymakers or, say, health practitioners to change the ways in which they work with communities. For the purposes of advocacy, size matters. To tell policymakers that more than 1000 people living with HIV in Australia experience this, or know that, is powerful evidence indeed. To communicate with teachers that 68 per cent of a sample of 2,000 same-sex-attracted secondary students had experienced discrimination in the classroom makes the point that this is an issue that potentially affects every class in every school.

Sampling and recruitment

Sampling implies that we can know the size and nature of the population from which we are deriving our sample. One of the characteristics of hidden, marginal or hard-to-reach populations is that we cannot know their size with any certainty. For example, how can we estimate the number of individuals engaging in sex work in Melbourne, how can we know how many people identify as gay or lesbian in a given population? There has been some progress made towards gaining good estimates in certain circumstances. National sex surveys of the kind carried out twice in the United Kingdom (in 1990 and 2000) and once in Australia (in 2002) give us population estimates for the number of Australians between the ages of 16 and 59 who identify as gay, straight, bisexual or other sexual identities (Smith et al., 2003). Similarly, national surveys of drug and alcohol use can tell us how many randomly surveyed individuals have injected illicit drugs in the past six months (AIHW, 2005). However, in both these examples it is likely that populations vary in different parts of the country and consequently the number of people who identify as gay in, say, Melbourne, remains difficult to estimate.

Choosing the size and nature of the sample then cannot rely simply on population size estimates. Clearly the context of recruitment can have an important effect on the numbers and nature of people who have been recruited. Household surveys are rarely relevant to reach the kinds of population we are concerned with here. Instead, more informal and contextualised methods need to be considered. Recruiting from known sites where individuals of interest might be found is possible, but can seriously bias the kinds of individuals recruited. We will find different people in gay bars, gay pride events and sporting events. The notion of community connectedness becomes relevant – for some groups there are evident communities; similar people occupy similar spaces; for other groups however, there may be less obvious communities.

Recently there has been a move towards respondent-driven sampling to provide an estimate of the size of a hidden or hard-to-reach population and an understanding of mobility. Three kinds of sampling techniques are described here with sex workers in Melbourne as the notional hard-to-reach population to be studied.

The first is known as Capture-Recapture. This technique has been used for a number of 'hidden' or 'hard to reach' populations. The basic concept relates to an age-old-method for estimating the number of fish in a pond. A large fishing net is thrown into the pond and all captured fish are counted and marked. They are then put back into the pond and after a short while the same method is employed. This second time, the total number of fish caught comprises both those fish captured for the first time and those previously captured. The total number of fish in the pond can be estimated from these figures. Of course, sex workers in Melbourne are not all located in a single 'pond'; nevertheless it is possible to identify certain areas where sex workers might be found and the capture–recapture methodology could be used to estimate the total number of sex workers operating in metropolitan Melbourne.

The second method is known as Respondent-Driven Sampling (RDS). This has recently been applied to hidden populations such as injecting drug users and men who have sex with men (MSM). RDS has two main components: a subject recruitment method that is participant driven and that can achieve lengthy referral chains, and a theoretical model of the sampling process that allows population estimates to be achieved.

A number of 'seeds', that is, in our example, sex workers in Melbourne, are recruited; they in turn recruit others, who recruit others, and so on. It has been shown that every person in a country as large as the United States is indirectly associated with every other person through approximately six intermediaries. This is known as 'six degrees of separation'. Therefore everyone could hypothetically be reached within six waves of respondent-driven recruitment. In practice, for a study such as that envisioned here, the number of waves of respondents is likely to be fewer than six.

The third sampling method is time space sampling. This is a probability-based method for recruiting members of a target population at specific times and venues. We could potentially identify important times and spaces where sex workers might be found through interviews with key informants. A randomly stratified sample of venues and times could be drawn up and sex workers to be found there will then be counted.

Finally, but of increasing relevance to many hard-to-reach populations, the Internet provides a variant of time and space sampling. In the case of sex work it would be possible to identify town-specific sex sites and recruit through them. We will discuss later further issues associated with Internet-based research.

Often our sampling methods are less systematic than those discussed so far. Key informants from a community can provide good information about how best to recruit to a study, but issues of representativeness, and indeed representation, remain. Context is clearly relevant to many of our marginalised or hard-to-reach groups, and only too often we recruit where it is easiest to recruit. Hence young people are frequently recruited through the formal educational institutions such as schools – they are in many ways a 'captive' sample. Whilst in many countries most young people below the age of 16 will be in school, there will always be a proportion who are not – and these may be the very people that we are most interested in studying: see the chapter on young people for a further discussion of young homeless people. At the other end of the age spectrum, studies of old people that simply recruit from aged care facilities will inevitably under-represent those old people who live independently, or with their families, or who are in acute care facilities. In a similar vein, recruiting people who inject illicit drugs through a needle and syringe exchange program, or a safe injecting clinic may offer access only to certain kinds of people who inject; others who acquire their needles through private means will not be included in the sample.

Reporting the research

Research findings need to be widely disseminated. There are many ways of achieving this dissemination – a refereed journal article or book chapter is unlikely to be sufficient. We have adopted numerous strategies to achieve effective dissemination of our research findings. These include community reports, broadsheets, workshops or feedback fora, websites, and probably the most useful of all: media coverage. Use of mass media increases the likelihood that many members of a community will receive some feedback or information concerning the research findings. See the section on ethical principles for further consideration of the importance of respectful language and representation of research participants and communities.

The problem of time

One of the key challenges when undertaking research with any community is educating your community partners about the nature of the timescale of academic research. This can be particularly vexing for marginalised communities if they have less experience of research than other communities or because they perceive their research needs to be more urgent than those of other communities.

Academic research can be experienced as an excruciatingly slow process. While there are no hard and fast rules about timescales, it is not uncommon for researchers to spend three to six months developing a research proposal. That proposal must then be funded and many funding agencies take 10–12 months to consider a request for funding. If the request for funding is successful, the fine detail of the project must be specified and ethical approval sought. These processes can take a further three to six months. So, researchers can be up to two years into the process and not a shred of data might have been collected.

This rate of progress may, or more probably will, appear glacial to a concerned marginalised community who perceive their needs as real and urgent. It is therefore vital to communicate very clearly and unambiguously with communities about the timescales involved and the inherent uncertainties involved in seeking research funding.

Once data collection has been initiated the process may continue for months if not years. Again, clarity in your communication with the community about the nature of the data collection process is important. Perhaps most challenging is the need for the communities to understand the intricacies involved in data analysis. People who have little experience of research may think that once data have been collected they are analysed by the push of a button.

While it is true that some sorts of statistical analysis can be done at the press of a button, the act of data analysis is an act of interpretation. Done properly, analysis is an extremely measured and nuanced activity that goes from what the data might say to what the data might mean. The set of potential meanings need to be tested and the most likely candidates put under the most serious of scrutiny.

It is common academic practice to break large, complex questions down into smaller, more manageable, questions that can be answered more or less unambiguously. An outcome of this process is that there is no single analysis but instead a number of them, perhaps a large number. As a result, the research will not generate a single answer to a large question but a series of answers to smaller questions. Unfortunately, the synthesis of those smaller answers to smaller questions into a larger answer for a larger question is yet again an act of interpretation that is far beyond a simple mechanistic activity.

While there can be no hard and fast rules about how long research will take, it always takes longer than you think it will. Being realistic in your dealings with communities about the time and complexity of research is an important strategy to prevent the development of unrealistic expectations about the research.

Managing expectations

Research can move mountains. There are numerous instances when research has provided the evidence to achieve social change. However, not every piece of research can make a difference. There are numerous reasons for this. The research may not seem relevant to policymakers and practitioners, its timing may be less than opportune, its sample may be regarded as 'unrepresentative', or major political/cultural or social forces may not be in line with the findings. Under these circumstances it would be unrealistic to expect a single body of evidence to effect change. The promise that research may reap benefits either for the participants themselves or for their communities may be empty. Nonetheless, much research is predicated on the hope that the findings will be of use to the researched communities. At the very least, there is a reasonable expectation that the findings will be widely and appropriately disseminated.

Dealing with the sometimes unrealistic expectations associated with participation in research is part of the research process. Ensuring that participants are enthusiastic about their participation needs to be balanced with the understanding that not much might change as a consequence of the research. Hidden voices may remain hidden.

Dealing with ethics committees

The principal objective of a system of ethical review is to ensure that all research involving humans is conducted to high ethical and scientific standards so that the duty of care to the safety and dignity of research participants is met, research of potential benefit to humans is not impeded and the community trusts and supports the research endeavour.

University, hospital and other ethics committees are an important part of the research process. Any research involving people and primary data collection will usually require ethical review. The purpose of ethical review is to achieve an appropriate balance between the risks and benefits associated with the specific research project. No research project will be free of risk: no research project will be entirely beneficial. Generally, ethics committees include people from specified backgrounds. Usually, there is a minister of religion, a lawyer, a doctor with research experience and community members, sometimes referred to as lay members. The rest of the committee is made up of individuals who are either active in research or who have research experience in the areas that the committee is likely to review.

The choice of expertise is rarely stated explicitly. However, it would appear to draw on notions of relevant subject area expertise, ethics, legal issues and consumer opinion. The role of religion is rarely explicitly discussed and it is often taken for granted that this implies Christian affiliation. It is difficult to understand the rationale for the inclusion of ministers of religion on ethics committee. It may be that they are expected to function as a lay ethicist given that most religions have a clearly articulated ethical framework. They may also be seen as guardians of cultural norms. It is also possible, given the influence of the American procedural approach to ethical review, that the place of ministers of religion on ethics committees in other countries is an artefact of copying committee membership from a setting where religion is an important part of public life to one where it is not.

Regimes of ethical review have changed from a relatively narrow focus on clinical medicine to a framework that captures all research that involves human participants. As such, this has created considerable difficulties for various types of social research where issues of consent look very different from those which exist only within doctor–patient relationships. The struggle to make the processes of ethics review more generic in order to accommodate different paradigms of research has only served to make the process even more cumbersome.

The purpose of the national guidelines for the ethical conduct of research is to protect the welfare and rights of participants in research and to facilitate research that is, or will be, of benefit to the researcher's community or to humankind.

There are four essential ethical principles described in the national guidelines – these are respect for persons, research merit and integrity, balancing benefits and risks in research and justice. They may also contains specific guidance for different types of research such as research involving covert observation and epidemiological research, and guidance for particular kinds of participants such as children and people in dependent relationships.

It is important to accept that ethical review is much more than simply ticking boxes to indicate that a research proposal complies with some general code of conduct. Instead, ethical review must ensure that with appropriate safeguards in place the potential benefits of the research outweigh the potential risks.

Before turning to research ethics, it is important to distinguish between human rights and ethics. Over the past decade, there has been enormous progress in articulating the relationship between health and human rights. Indeed, the language of human rights has become an important and effective tool available to those communities most affected by HIV. Human rights, their language and the advocacy they engender are primarily legalistic. Resting on international covenants such as the Universal Declaration of Human Rights in 1948 and the International Covenant on Civil and Political Rights in 1966, human rights provide a language with which communities can address the state to press for legislative protection.

Ethics has no such global covenants or legally enforceable entitlements. Instead, ethical frameworks provide guidance for the practices of individuals and groups of individuals in specific settings. In a strict sense, ethics is actually a branch of moral philosophy. As such, expertise in research ethics does not naturally lie with practitioners of the law but instead lies with ethicists and philosophers as the theoreticians of ethics and with researchers themselves as the practitioners of research ethics.

Research ethics

The ethical framework currently most commonly employed in research is derived from bioethics. While the ethical framework for research does share some similarities with the clinical ethics that guide the interactions between clinicians and their patients, the relative emphases of clinical and research ethics are different. The clinical ethical framework evolved with the development of the healing arts and sciences in the Western world. It can be traced back to the Hippocratic Oath and has been extensively influenced by Judeo-Christian ethical traditions. The clinical ethical framework guides the interactions of doctors and patients and has at its heart a notionally unproblematic good – the best possible outcome for the patient. The need for the continued development of clinical ethics is a reflection of the fact that what actually constitutes the best possible outcome for the patient is not always unproblematic. In research, unlike clinical practice, there is no notionally unproblematic good. The purpose of research is the generation of knowledge, which of itself has no intrinsic value. Thus, the ethical safeguards pertaining to research must have a different focus and different emphases from those that guide clinical ethics.

The research ethics framework was largely codified in the Nuremberg Code and the Declaration of Helsinki in the years after World War II and came about directly as a result of medical experimentation undertaken by the Nazis. Since the 1960s the procedures for assessing the compliance of research with these and related codes of practice have become increasingly formalised and enshrined in law. However, it would be a mistake to believe that these procedures themselves ensure the ethical conduct of research or to believe that the conduct of ethical research requires slavish adherence to the particular procedures of one particular country or culture. The central issue of the ethical nature of research is adherence to the principles – a judgement that can only be established empirically through careful examination and consideration of the precise nature and context of the research.

Within this framework, the four key principles of ethics are respect for persons, avoiding the causation of harm, providing benefits and balancing benefits against risks, and justice in the distribution of benefits and risks. It is important to recognise that these are principles used to judge the ethical nature of specific actions. As such, they do not expressly forbid any action. Thus, while it is accepted that to take another person's life would breach these principles, the taking of another's life can be ethically justified in specific circumstances such as in self-defence or in the conduct of a just war. Of course, the circumstances that may constitute self-defence or the conduct of a just war are themselves subject to debate.

Similarly, there is debate as to the nature of the activities that constitute research involving human participants that require ethical approval through some type of formal process. Regardless of whether a formal process is required, all research that involves human participants requires ethical consideration. That is, the researchers must examine their activities with regard to the four ethical principles. They must consider whether the research shows respect for persons through obtaining appropriate informed consent to participate, respect for the confidentiality of the information acquired through research, and respect for a person's decision not to participate. They must also determine that the research will not lead to the participants being harmed without careful consideration of the risks and benefits of the research not only to the participants themselves but also to society more broadly. The researchers must also consider issues of justice in their research in that the participants in the research may not unduly suffer the burdens of the research without opportunity to gain from the benefits of the research.

There are different ways to describe the ethical principles that underlie good research. The basic ethical principles are four: non-malfeasance; beneficence; respect for persons and justice. Some authors treat non-malfeasance and beneficence as two components of a single principle but it is better to treat them separately. This is because the principles when applied to a specific research proposal could be in conflict.

Non-malfeasance is the ethical principle of not doing harm. Clearly, one would prefer not to conduct research that harms or injures participants but sometimes it will not be avoided. An interesting example is the use of dummy or sham surgery. Patients are given either a general or a local anaesthetic and an incision is made but no surgery is actually performed. The outcomes are compared with those for people who were actually given surgery. Clearly, to anaesthetise someone and then make an incision contravenes the ethical principle of doing no harm. How then can it be viewed as ethical?

The rationale for sham surgery is that many surgical procedures have been developed and introduced over the years without having been subjected to a randomised trial to establish their effectiveness. Thus, it is possible that many surgical interventions have either no effect or are actually harmful. Because of this the use of sham surgery could be justified as administering an anaesthetic and performing an incision may actually be *less* harmful than the surgery that would otherwise be performed. The benefit derived from such studies is the evidence about the utility, or otherwise, of specific surgical interventions.

The second ethical principle is to do good. At face value, this seems a very simple principle to recognise in a research proposal. However, the question must be addressed – doing good for whom and who judges what counts as good. For the researcher, being able to complete the research is probably a favourable outcome. It is often less clear that the participants in research experience their participation as a positive and rewarding experience. When working with marginalised communities it is often the case that the opportunity to take part in research is highly valued simply because the community has been overlooked in the past and the research gives voice to that community and their experiences. This can sometimes expose the community to harm because it may draw the attention of powerful others to the community and their social practices – an issue we have already explored under the problem of naming. Often, communities have unrealistic expectations about the good that might be derived from research.

Too often the principle of respect for persons is treated as simply ensuring that informed consent be obtained. However, it is a more broad-ranging principle than just consent. First, respect for persons requires a careful assessment of all aspects of the research process from research design to the language used in documents, the process of informed consent, and the ways in which research participants and their communities are portrayed or understood in the research findings when disseminated. It is this notion of portrayal or representation that is often crucial in maintaining long-term research partnerships.

Sometimes it is very challenging to ensure that all research participants are treated with respect. Recently, we were involved in a survey of people from the Australian gay, lesbian, bisexual, transgender and intersex communities. The research proposal required a large sample and the most timely and cost-effective means to obtain such a sample was to administer the survey on the Internet. Because it was a structured survey instrument, participants at a number of points in the survey needed to respond to specific questions in order to proceed. Their responses to those questions determined the branch of the questionnaire they then completed.

An early question required participants to specify the gender with which they identified. This was necessary in order to ask subsequent questions that were of relevance to one gender but not another – for example, women's experience of pregnancy or childbirth. For some participants, being asked to specify the gender with which they identified was the end of their involvement in the study. Some had a stated gender identity that was neither male nor female and thus they could not tick an appropriate box and felt excluded from the research. Clearly, this was a case where research participants were not accorded the respect that they should have been.

The issue of respect most commonly comes into play in the process of obtaining informed consent. It is important to note that obtaining informed consent is a process; it is not simply obtaining a signature on a form. Valid informed consent requires that the person is competent to understand what their involvement in research entails. It also necessitates that the procedures involved are understood and that the potential risks and benefits are also clear (see Chapter 3 by Hillier, Johnson and Traustadóttir). If we have established that the potential participant is competent, we must provide a description of the research including all procedures involved; the time commitment that participation represents; the likely benefits to themselves, if any, and the likely benefits to humanity more generally; how any data they provide will be managed, stored and disposed of; whether the findings are likely to be published and whether participants will be identifiable from the published work and how the confidentiality of the results will be ensured and anonymity preserved where appropriate. Clearly, this can sometimes be a long and quite involved process. It is vital that potential participants are provided with that information, have the opportunity to ask any questions they might have and are also provided with the contact details of the appropriate person to inform if they are unhappy about the research process or the actions of the research team.

One of the risks that can emerge in research is the report of illegal behaviour. In most countries, research data has no special protection under law and so the potential always exists that data can be obtained by police for the purpose of prosecution. Over the years we have asked more than 30,000 people about illegal drug use and the possibility has always existed that our data will be subpoenaed. It has not happened yet, but if we held identifying information along with the reports of drug use our data could represent a risk to the liberty of many people. Researchers adopt a range of strategies to ensure that this risk is minimised. Most commonly, researchers ensure that the participants in research remain anonymous – thus their identity is protected. Where this cannot be achieved, participants are either invited to identify themselves with pseudonyms or their identities are obscured as soon after the point of data collection as possible if not at the point of data collection.

Once someone has had the research explained fully to them, their consent must be recorded. People may assume that this means that the participant must sign a consent form. There is no ethical requirement for a signature and consent can be recorded in a variety of ways. If your chosen method of data collection is a self-completed survey, then the act of completing the survey can constitute informed consent provided that the participants are appropriately informed. Similarly, participation in an interview or a focus group can constitute informed consent. With another form of research, ethnography, informed consent can be provided by simply choosing to remain at the site of research and be included in the observations that are taking place.

Informed consent need not be an individual act. When working with some communities and in some cultures, decisions made about participation in research occur at a collective level, for example the family or the community. However, this does not mean that collective consent can override an individual refusal to consent. A situation where research has both a collective consent and an individual refusal represents a particular challenge and needs to have been foreshadowed in the research design in such a way that data collection can proceed but the privacy of the individuals who decline individual consent can be respected.

The final ethical principle is justice – an issue of particular concern to many marginalised communities. The principle of justice is concerned with the distribution of the risks and benefits of research within the community. Thus, the principle of justice would be in jeopardy if one particular segment of society was consistently participating in research that benefited society as a whole. The general rule with the principle of justice is that fairness should obtain in relation to the research burden.

A recent set of circumstances have drawn particular attention to the issue of justice. Some clinical trials of anti-HIV medications have been undertaken in some low-resource countries using formulations of the drugs which have been superseded and are not the current standard of care in richer countries. It would be clearly unethical to expose people to those drug regimes in low-resource countries simply because the regimes could not meet the current standard of care. Can those formulations be ethically tested in low-resource countries? And how do we understand the benefits that might flow to rich countries from the results of those trials when they could not be ethically conducted in those countries?

This is an extremely contentious question about which there has been considerable debate and about which there has been no clear resolution. The current accommodation rests on the local circumstances in which the trial takes place. If the proposed clinical regimes meet or exceed current standards of care, then the trial might be viewed as ethical. However, safeguards need to be in place to ensure that a reliance on local standards do not become an excuse to experiment on people in poor countries in such a way as to have the benefits largely accrue to rich countries.

Another component of the principle of justice is that people should have a right of participation in research. Marginalised communities often argue that they have particular needs that are unmet by standard research and sometimes find it valuable to couch their concerns in the language of justice.

A further ethical principle described in the Australian National Statement on the ethical Conduct of Research involving Humans is research merit and integrity. This is at times a very vexed issue and researchers sometime take affront when challenged by an ethics committee about the design of their research. The core of the ethics committee's concerns often rests on the question of whether bad research is also unethical. For example, if a study sets out to demonstrate some difference between two groups of participants but has too small a sample size to reach statistical significance, is this bad research that should not be allowed?

As with most ethical issues, there is not a simple answer to the question. Instead, we must consider the potential benefits of the research to the researcher, the participants and humanity more generally, and weigh these against the risks, if any, and the burden that participation represents. Oftentimes, research can be approved even though it is unlikely to be subsequently published (usually a measure of the research merit) because the risks and burden are extremely low and the benefits to the parties involved are sufficiently substantial to warrant the research being conducted. Note, however, the ways in which the previous sentence contains many qualifiers and statements about relativities.

Some commentators might argue that poorly designed research should never be allowed but this position would fail to take into account the varied purposes of research. While we have argued that research is purposive knowledge generation, the notion of purpose has a dual nature. It relates to the way in which knowledge generation is addressed and also to the intent underlying the entire research enterprise. Many higher degrees require that student undertake original research, but the constraints on those students and their projects are such that the research needs to be extremely modest in scale and constrained in ways that makes the research less than current best practice, most commonly through the use of small samples or samples which are far from the ideal. It is in these situations that the qualifications and relativities about risks, burdens and benefits must come into play.

Ethics and the problems of non-participants I

There is a little acknowledged but nonetheless ethical problem that relates to a large body, perhaps the majority, of social research. Suppose you are interested in the eating habits of a household. You might choose to interview one household member and ask them to report on the choice of breakfast cereals of each family member. No ethical dilemmas here surely? But let's examine a more complicated situation; when, for example, you ask people to provide information about their most recent sexual experience, they will most commonly report on an experience that involved another person – usually another person who is not actually a participant in the research. Let's now ask three common questions in sex research: did vaginal intercourse occur? (Let's for the moment assume a heterosexual couple); did the participant experience orgasm? and, did their partner orgasm?

Clearly we are dealing with three different sorts of information. We could, for example, argue that the participant's report of their own orgasm was their personal information to provide to whomever they wanted, under any circumstances of their choosing. The status of the report that vaginal intercourse occurred is a little different as it clearly cannot be the experience solely of the participant but one that is only possible as a shared or joint practice of the participant and non-participant. The final question relates to the experience of the non-participant, and although the participant may have a role in the outcome it is difficult to argue that they were solely responsible for the orgasm and in some sense owned it.

The ethical issue arises when we stop to consider the role of the non-participant in this research. Clearly, information about them is being obtained without their consent and it is unclear the extent to which the decision to provide information about shared experiences is solely within the gift of one participant to impart. While it is clear that a research participant should have right to have data pertaining to them deleted, it is less clear that a non-participant should have the right to have information deleted about them when provided by a participant.

While we have no clear guidance to offer on this topic it is one that will increasingly challenge researchers. In many countries, stringent privacy legislation is being enacted. At some point it is almost certain that the collection of information relating to non-participants in research will be found to breach privacy legislation. Resolving this tension between research and privacy will require robust public debate.

Ethics and the problems of non-participants II

Just as data collection may involve the accumulation of information about people who have never consented to take part in research, so may the conduct of research have effects beyond those who choose to take part. One clear case of the way this might happen is in the case of intervention research.

There have been a number of clinical trials around the world of vaccines to prevent the acquisition of HIV infection. One of the key features of those trials has been the need to ensure that participants are aware that the effectiveness of the vaccine is unproven, is at best likely to be partial, and should not be allowed to erode safe sex or safe injecting practices. A further issue is that the fact that a vaccine is being trialled cannot be contained solely within the group of people who are actually participating in the trial. The diffusion of information about the trial to the broader community from which participants were drawn is inevitable. However, the information provided to participants may not diffuse to non-participants in its entirety or without some translation or miscommunication.

In such a situation it is clear that there may exist risks to non-participants through the conduct of the research. What is less clear is the extent to which the researchers should be held accountable for the risks experienced by non-participants and the resources it may be sensible or reasonable to ask to be committed to minimise the risks to non-participants.

Participant payments

Paying people to take part in some forms of research is extremely common, for example trials of medicines. In social research, however, the role of participant payment is more problematic. It is important to ensure that payment or other forms of recompense are not sufficient to constitute a significant inducement to take part. If this were to occur the requirement for a consent freely given would be violated. On the other hand, how reasonable is it to presume that people will give their time freely for research purposes?

Some people will not participate in research because of the opportunity costs involved. Put simply, what they must forego in order to take part in research, for example an hour's paid work, may represent too great a cost to bear. In these situations, paying participants for income foregone can be justified, for example, in the case of sex workers. However, we observe that there are few studies that opportunistically include high court judges or media magnates.

One strategy allows the offering of a high-value reward for participation. The use of raffles or lotteries for high-value prizes are generally not construed to constitute inducement.

Participant and researcher safety

There are ethical and legal requirements regarding the safety of both researchers and participants. It is important that participants are not exposed to unnecessary physical or emotional risks as a consequence of their participation in research. For this reason it is essential that all possible risks are clearly identified during study design and ethical review to ensure that the likely benefits of the research clearly outweigh the potential risks involved.

Researcher safety can easily be overlooked. Key issues include maintaining the physical safety of the researcher through ensuring that they operate only in controlled environment or if in an uncontrolled environment such as a participant's home or perhaps a pub, the whereabouts of the researcher should be known and they should have a means of exit and should be able to communicate with colleagues at all times. The emotional well-being of the researcher should also be considered carefully.

About the rest of the book

We have chosen the subject matter of the chapters in Part II to reflect the many and diverse ways in which people or communities can be construed as 'marginal'. Particular attention has been paid to ensuring that duplication and repetition between the chapters has been kept to a minimum. Also, in an attempt to minimise 'reader fatigue' the style, presentation, and voice of each chapter is unique. While some readers may find this a curious editorial decision, we stand by it and hope that the diversity of Part II underlines and reinforces the variety of challenges associated with working at the margins.

What follows is a collection of essays exploring in more detail and with particular emphases on many of the topics we have already raised. Part II begins with a discussion of knowledge relationships and identity in research on drug use. Mary and Annie consider a number of ethical issues that have particular consequences when working with drug user organisations. The fact that their focus is on research relationships between such organisations and researchers should already flag for the reader their commitment to working towards models of co-research. They reflect on the political and social consequences that flow from research studies. Also they provide examples of foreseeable and unforeseeable consequences of research for the researchers, the researched and the wider community.

In Chapter 2, Philomena and Sue have chosen to consider research with lesbians. They highlight the lack of research directed at lesbians and the relationship between feminist and women's health movements as they pertain to research on lesbians. A particular issue addressed by Philomena and Sue is that of researching one's own community. Lesbians commonly fall under the rubric of gay and lesbian, gay or lesbian or bisexual, gay or lesbian or bisexual or queer, gay or lesbian or bisexual or questioning, gay or lesbian or bisexual or transgender, gay or lesbian or bisexual or transgender or intersex. The history of these communities forms an important backdrop to researching with this community or communities. For the purposes of this book we have chosen research with lesbians, but it does not act as an exemplar of all research concerning sexual and gender minorities.

In Chapter 3, Lynne, Kelley, and Rannveig share their experiences of working with people who have an intellectual disability. They draw on two research projects, one dealing with the sexual lives of people with an intellectual disability, and the second on mothers who have an intellectual disability. In both research projects particular attention has been paid to the active engagement of the researched in the research process.

The challenge for Jon and Mark in Chapter 4 was to consider whether research could be harmful to a disenfranchised community. The challenges associated with documenting the history of research engagement with Indigenous communities and whether it is possible for non-Indigenous researchers to carry out ethical and rigorous research with Indigenous communities in a way that does not reinforce the colonial experience are outlined. They offer particular practical guidance on the strategies that have worked and crucial advice on the nature of the research process that needs to be constructed in order to engage Indigenous communities and ensure research that is relevant and useful to those communities.

Chapters 5 and 6 are written by researchers who have worked with young and old participants on a range of projects. In Chapter 5, Lynne, Anne and Shelley consider the practical and ethical issues involved in research with three groups of young people: those in schools, those who are homeless and those who are attracted to their own sex. In addition to advice on research with young people in general, they offer particular suggestions about working with young people who may be characterised as 'vulnerable'. They detail strategies for engaging gate keepers and institutions in the research process. They consider practical issues concerning informed consent and duty of care and, importantly, they offer advice on insuring the results of research matter. Susan and Colette in Chapter 6 offer a wealth of practical advice on working with older people. Drawing on their own research and that of others they explore sampling and recruitment, the strengths and weaknesses of particular research methods as they apply to older people.

Jeffrey and Peter decided to hold a structured conversation as the basis of their reflections on working with PLWHA. We have annotated this conversation to flag the range of issues they cover. They are particularly concerned with the nature of representation, what it means to speak or act as a member of a community and how representation can shape research questions and research findings. Given the emphasis through-out the book on establishing and maintaining research relationships, it is particularly appropriate that this chapter is presented as a conversation, reflecting the many conversations that all the researchers have had in the course of research and of constructing this book.

Part II ends with a reflection on the nature of marginality. We asked Michael Hurley to write that chapter in a way that would encourage readers to reflect again on the larger purpose of the book – while at the same time to engage critically with the assumptions, both explicit and implicit contained in each of the chapters.

Part II
Case Studies

1
Knowledge, Relationships and Identity in Research on Drug Use

Mary L. O'Brien and Annie Madden

Introduction

It is often assumed when researching at the 'margins', that people are marginalised because of their identity. This chapter begins from a standpoint that views identity as a contingent concept that is negotiated and constituted through relationships with individual and collective groups of people who use drugs. Research is a key knowledge-making practice when it comes to what can be said about drug use and people who use drugs. The relationships that people who use drugs and drug users' organisations (DUO) have with researchers are closely tied to the ability to articulate and perform the identity of drug user. These relationships are also an important factor in drug users and DUO being able to engage as knowledge-makers themselves in both public and policy arenas. This chapter articulates the significance of this by reflecting on a range of issues. The first section deals with some ethical issues specific to research in the area of drug use, such as data protection, consent and participant payments. The second section deals with broader research issues such as who determines what research questions get asked and the influence of methods and sampling. The final section examines, how do we define 'people who use drugs', the importance of recognising research as a knowledge-making practice and issues such as representation, capacity building and mutual benefit. This chapter is not an attempt to be prescriptive about approaches to working with people who use drugs; rather, we seek to reflect on a range of experiences that have arisen in several years of overlapping and collaborative work together. While mostly we are able to speak with one voice on issues, there are occasions when our own individual experiences within DUO or as a researcher require that we speak from our individual positions. Throughout, when we use the terms drugs, we are meaning 'illicit drugs'.

Ethics

Data protection, confidentiality and anonymity

One of the most significant issues for both qualitative and quantitative research work on drug use is that data collected by researchers are not legally privileged. This creates the possibility that information collected during research may incriminate participants thus causing them harm. This potentially endangers a primary ethical principle guiding researchers, beneficence, or the responsibility to do no harm. Moreover, it means that if a researcher was subpoenaed in court to reveal information and refused, they themselves could be subject to legal sanction. Actual instances of this occurring are rare, but the possibility has led to a number of changes in research practice over the past 10 years.

Some countries have a process where researchers can apply for their data to be 'protected', but this type of process largely does not exist in Australia (some provisions in the Australian Capital Territory (ACT) are the exception) and the United Kingdom. Others have covered some of these issues in Australia (Fitzgerald and Hamilton, 1996; Israel, 2004) and in the United Kingdom (Coomber, 2002) in more detail.

In light of the legislative and legal limits to confidentiality, our main strategies to protect participants have been first to not collect identifying information (even when gaining consent) and second to warn people that the information they provide can only be held confidentially 'subject to the usual legal requirements'. This then requires an explanation that while it is extremely unlikely to occur, information given in a research context can be accessed in legal proceedings and that we want as little detail about illegal matters as possible. This has not impacted greatly on our research where the focus has largely been on social and health outcomes, but it may be a less useful approach where illegal activities (e.g. drug dealing) are the core issue being examined.

Research adopting cross-sectional designs, where follow-up information is not required is also a way of reducing the risk of research participation for people using drugs. However, as we will discuss later, this has implications for the types of questions that are explored by researchers.

Anonymity is relatively easy to maintain with cross-sectional designs or survey-based work. However, in ethnographic research where the method of data collection is to engage over a period of time in the social world of those of interest, it is impossible to not know (even if one does not record or write down) identifying information about participants. Here researchers are able to protect participant anonymity only by refusing to disclose information if subpoenaed. Researchers who are not part of a particular community or network need to acknowledge that they may not know (especially in small networks) what information may identify a participant to a third party. What seems like a non-identifying piece of information to a researcher may be revealing if one knows the scene, or combines it with other knowledge such as police intelligence.

It is not just ethnographic or other social research that can place research participants at risk. In the United Kingdom a blood sample collected from a prisoner to investigate an outbreak of HIV, later contributed to the prisoner being convicted of recklessly causing injury to another through the transmission of HIV (see Bird and Brown, 2001). The question raised by the authors on whether doctors and scientists could '... continue to appeal to patients, especially prisoners, to contribute samples for molecular studies when there is a risk that incriminating evidence will be discovered' (Bird and Brown, 2001: 1176) needs to be equally considered by researchers in the current legal context.

Consent

Many drug researchers have adopted a modified process of gaining consent in order to try to protect participants. These include consent forms being signed with a pseudonym, a first name, or in some cases not requiring participants to sign a form at all. In the latter example, the researcher may sign the consent form as a declaration that they have gone through the consent process. An additional strategy if conducting formal interviews is to make an audio tape recording of the informed-consent process. Rather than ensuring that a written *document* recording consent to participate exists, the focus is on documenting the consent *process* itself. This requires some degree of trust in the professionalism of the researcher from ethics committee. While quite common now, our experience was that initially ethics committees were concerned at these modifications to the usual consent process.

Of course the real issue here is that a potential research participant is provided with detailed and appropriate information and an opportunity to discuss the research before they become involved. DUO have been involved in research projects where the participant information sheet has been little more than a 'cut and paste' from the project proposal rather than information that has been specifically developed for participants. This type of approach highlights that despite developments in methods of gaining consent, some researchers are still focused on documenting consent over considerations of appropriate and sensitive informed-consent processes.

In different contexts, people using drugs are often asked to sign similar forms to guarantee both their rights and confidentiality, only to see those rights routinely violated or ignored in the context of service delivery. One example of this is the often negative experiences that people who use drugs have when signing forms related to accessing drug treatment services such as methadone (see Thomson and Morgan, 1999). Breaches of confidentiality, poor treatment and a lack of adequate complaints processes are frequently experienced by people on methadone programmes and this can then result in a lack of trust in the 'safety' of signing other agreements such as consent forms for research (for more on this see AIVL 2003: 13).

Even while cognisant of these issues, unanticipated events can occur. In a qualitative study of women living with hepatitis C (Gifford and O'Brien, 2001) a research assistant (RA) who had been interviewing at a community health centre (CHC) was asked to identify a participant, as the staff suspected her companion was responsible for the theft of a CD player from the building. The RA referred this request to the Senior Investigator. While neither the police nor the CHC formally followed this up, a number of things were highlighted. First, the assumption that, in this public place it would be 'the drug user' that stole something underlines the sort of discriminatory attitudes that our research has repeatedly highlighted people who use drugs face. Second, on later filing the consent forms, we found that indeed one of the participants had written out a full name and address (despite our request for only a first name). Finally, it highlights the *unintended* scrutiny that people who use drugs can be exposed to through our research.

Payment

In most of our research on drug use we have adopted the practice of paying participants. This is common practice in most Australian studies of drug use. The current Australian human ethics guidelines specifically prohibit offering an inducement to participate in research that would impair the voluntary nature of consenting or refusing to participate (see 1.10, NHMRC, 1999: 12). In our experience there is a general inclination to assume both that drug users would participate in research just to acquire money, and a concern that money paid for research participation would necessarily be spent on drugs.

While the level of social disadvantage experienced by many people who use drugs means that payment for participation in research is likely to be received favourably, like others in the community, people who use drugs agree to participate in research for many reasons. Many do so prior to being informed that a payment is available. Further, DUO have always found people to be very willing to participate in peer-based research projects that are often unable to offer payment. This willingness reflects the fact that many people who use drugs are motivated by factors other than personal financial gain, including the relevance of the research question to their daily lives.

Notwithstanding that some research cannot or does not pay participants, our position is that withholding payment or providing vouchers rather than cash payment to people who use drugs on the basis that they might spend it on drugs is not only patronising but unethical.

Ritter et al. (2002) examined some of these issues after a Coroners Court heard evidence that a person died of a heroin overdose may have participated in research on the day he/she died in order to obtain money for drugs. While in fact the person had not participated in the study on that day, Ritter et al. concluded that payment of injecting drug users (IDU) was consistent with the ethical principles of equity, respect and justice, but that greater discussion of the issue was warranted.

Similarly Fry and Dwyer (2001) examined Australian IDU motivations for becoming involved in research. They concluded that for their sample of IDU, motivations for research participation 'are often multidimensional, rarely to do with economic gain alone, and not necessarily defined by direct benefits or gains to themselves' (1324). While other issues may also be relevant in considering whether to pay research participants or not (see Mc Keganey, 2001); this study was an important contribution to considering the issue of payment.

An unresolved dilemma for us has been what to do when not all of your participants are (current) drug users – such as in our research on people with Hepatitis C. This is difficult both ethically and practically. Even in the context of being prepared to pay all participants, we have for example had resistance from hospitals who will not allow patients recruited at outpatient liver clinics to be paid (in part because of the precedent it sets). Thus, a person who is asked to complete a questionnaire at a hospital liver clinic would not be paid, but if he/she were approached at a primary care facility for people using drugs they may well be. Similar difficulties have arisen in wanting to interview a subset of people living with HIV who are also co-infected with Hepatitis C (which would necessarily have a higher proportion of people who had used drugs) when the broader study protocol did not routinely pay compensation for participating.

Our approach in surveys has mainly been to pay people who in essence are asked to complete something 'on the spot' at a service (except in a hospital). Those receiving a mail survey who are asked to complete it in their own time are not offered payment. This is a less than equitable solution.

The issues we have just considered in brief here speak to two overarching principles. First, researchers working with people who use drugs need to consider the specific and often changing conditions in which that work is occurring, whether that be legislative or cultural. Second, given the marginalised social location of many drug users, researchers have a duty of care to actively ensure that the dignity and autonomy of individuals who use drugs and their communities are respected.

Research

Who sets the research agenda?

While it might sound strange, researchers often do not have a great deal of choice about what gets researched. There are often topics that one would like to examine that simply would not be funded, under even 'investigator initiated grants'. However, researchers can and should exercise judgement on how to go about examining an area of interest. Studies examining the risk of blood borne virus (BBV) transmission for example tend to focus on how individuals place themselves at risk rather than on how this risk is socially and structurally produced. An illustration of how a research question can be reframed occurred when we were asked to examine the high rates of BBV spread in Juvenile Justice (JJ) detention contexts. Initially this was conceived as a study of BBV prevalence in inmates. After some initial consultation, we decided to reframe the research question by making two key decisions. First, rather than focus on how young people *individually* place themselves at risk, we examined the *social and structural contexts* which enabled such high prevalence rates to occur by studying the JJ system itself. Second, we chose to include both custodial and non-custodial contexts in the study. The final research project interviewed government and non-government workers about how health and risks were managed within the system. This enabled us to examine, for example, broader factors during post-release (such as the prohibitive cost of methadone dispensing) or indeed factors outside the JJ system (such as difficulties in finding accommodation for young people) that place young people at risk for BBVs (see O'Brien, 2001; and O'Brien and Greenwood, 2003). For us this had the politically important role of focusing on broader social and cultural contributions to risk for young people who use drugs rather than simply focusing on how the actions of individuals contribute to risk.

The question 'who sets the research agenda?' is one of the key issues of concern for peer-based DUO. Over the past ten years DUO have lobbied to have a much greater say in all stages of research involving people who use drugs. Beyond their right to do so, drug users can make a significant contribution to the research.

Drug user 'consumer representatives' have access to unique information, experiences and relationships that can have real benefits for research. In recruitment, DUO have access to networks that are often unavailable to researchers. In designing research questions, consultation with those who will benefit (or suffer) from the outcomes of the proposed research can be critical in helping to refine research objectives and therefore the focus and scope of the project. DUO commissioning research through established research organisations and DUO being *funded* to undertake partnership roles within research projects are just two of the ways that collaborative relationships have been developed. While DUO can play a key role in assisting researchers to identify research questions, refine methodologies that will work and interpret and disseminate findings, they can also conduct research on their own communities. More support from researchers for research conducted by DUO is needed. This type of research helps to build up a picture of the consumer perspective and identify issues that may otherwise remain undocumented and under-researched.

Methods

Methods are always a source of debate for researchers, but we intend to say little on it here. Regardless of the approach adopted, no one method or paradigm is inherently more valuable for researching drug use, nor is one approach less likely to cause harm than another. Longitudinal research can examine questions that cross-sectional studies are not equipped to look at, and vice versa. For us different research methods have been used for different purposes. Our small-scale qualitative study in 1999 of women's experiences of hepatitis C we think was part of a number of pieces appearing at that time that told a human story from the perspective of those people effected by Hepatitis C (Gifford and O'Brien, 2001). Other large-scale quantitative studies (Gifford et al., 2003, 2005) enabled us to examine whether drug users with Hepatitis C reported more experiences of discrimination than those who were not drug users. This work does not so much humanise this experience; rather the combined sample size of over seven hundred can give readers more confidence in accepting how wide spread this problem is. These different methods and questions can speak to different outcomes.

Sample

One of the most obvious starting points in discussing research with people using drugs is the lack of an identifiable starting point from which to draw a random sample, which tends to be the 'gold standard' in medical and health research. This means that unlike research on populations that are known and enumerated (or indeed what is referred to as the 'general population') sampling decisions can be critical in terms of the results collected and the political implications that follow. Researchers in this field – and in particular qualitative researchers – find it frustrating that what are perceived as inadequacies with the sampling frame are an impediment to publishing work particularly in journals with a biomedical or public health focus. Some of our work (Gifford et al., 2003, 2005) which has employed carefully managed stratified quota sampling on the basis of age, gender, and drug use history in order to minimise bias have been rejected by some journals because the sample was considered a 'convenience sample'. Our view is that this displays a lack of understanding of the difficulties of random large-scale cross-sectional studies with people using drugs or those living with hepatitis C. It also disregards the value of in-depth knowledge that we and our research partners have acquired in the social worlds of both people who use drugs as well as people with hepatitis C. Leaving aside debates about research paradigms, we also argue that researchers need to acknowledge the limitations of their samples while attempting to explain how the research is still valuable, as trying to 'fudge' the inherent limitations in any sample simply fuels scepticism about the merit of such data.

There is still a vast gap between the numbers of people that are estimated to use drugs and those that are researched. For a range of reasons most of our information about people who use drugs still comes from people who have in some way got into 'trouble' through their drug use in a social, health or legal sense. For this reason, sampling issues are critical because sampling choices influence the findings of a study. If researchers only ever contact people who use drugs through agencies, support networks and the legal system, then they are more likely to conclude that people who use drugs inevitably end up with health or legal difficulties. As Hough stated '[i]f the best available information about illicit drug use relates to uncontrolled or problematic drug use, there is a risk that policy – or at least political rhetoric equates *illicit* drug use with *problematic* drug use and criminality' (2001: 429, original emphasis). An Australian example of how sampling decisions may influence findings was illustrated in Lenton's (1997) study that surveyed IDUs by sampling from those who purchased syringes from pharmacies (in 'Fitpacks'). Although achieving a low response rate of 20 per cent, this study found for example that 70 per cent of those buying their syringes at pharmacies were employed, thus challenging a range of stereotypes about people who use drugs.

Much of our own efforts to contact people using drugs who are not undergoing drug treatment (such as pharmaco-therapies or detoxification) has focused only on people attending fixed site or outreach Needle and Syringe Programmes (NSP). This in itself produces bias. This is illustrated by a finding in the Australian Research Centre in Sex, Health and Society (ARCSHS) random population survey of nearly twenty thousand adults. Of those who had injected in the last year (1.2 per cent of men and 0.5 per cent of women), 60 per cent reported usually obtaining their needles and syringes from pharmacies, 34 per cent from NSP, 5.5 per cent from hospitals or doctors and 5 per cent from friends (Grulich et al., 2003). These sorts of studies remind us that our starting points in recruiting people who use drugs may significantly influence what we have to say about drug use.

In a similar vein, if interviews occur between 9–5 p.m. Monday to Friday, then people who use drugs who are working or studying may be excluded. In this example if the research is looking at needs or barriers to service delivery, it may end up developing service models that only suit people experiencing problems. Thus those who are managing but could be doing even better if they had access to services that meet their needs are not catered for. Researchers need to reflect on how their decisions about sampling may perpetuate stereotypes about people who use drugs and contribute to the development of services that do not meet their needs.

Sampling drug users outside of the usual profile is not easy but it is also not impossible. It takes more time and commitment to find a range of people but ultimately it comes down to using innovative strategies rather than the same old services and networks. This is one area where peer-researchers and recruiters have not been utilised enough. Peers not only know individuals who may be suitable for the study but they will also know where people hang out, what they do in their spare time, the times they are likely to access any services they do use and other strategies for appealing to the sample population. (For a discussion on the notion of 'Peer', see Madden, 2005.)

The point here is not to advocate one approach over another or that sampling one sub-population of drug users is more authentic than another. These sorts of common sampling issues need to be considered when designing research and discussed when reporting research findings. Beyond good research practice, this is part of researchers acknowledging that they actively participate in the problems of representation that drug users and other marginalised communities endure.

Collaboration

Throughout this book, a number of recurring themes arise in relation to how researchers represent and collaborate with particular communities. In this section we will explore the complex issue of what is and who defines a 'drug user' and how this shapes collaboration, research as a knowledge-making practice, representation, capacity building and mutual benefit.

Who are 'drug users'

One of the difficulties in thinking about representing drug users, either as a researcher reporting on findings or as a DUO, is of course that 'people who use drugs' are not a single category, but rather a series of contingent categories depending on context. Our research-funding bodies and our health-promotion frameworks tend to conceptualise people and practices into population groups such as 'gay men', 'IDUs', 'young people' and so forth (see Bartos 1994 on the creation of 'men who have sex with men') and this in itself produces certain types of effects, both positive and negative.

One positive effect of a categorisation on the basis of identity or practice in relation to drug use in Australia is that it allows the funding of state and national peak bodies to represent drug user issues and perspectives. As a researcher this affords an opportunity to at least attempt to be either collaborative or at least consultative in designing and conducting research. But at another level this can also let researchers 'off the hook'. It can encourage a culture where DUO are involved after research is designed and funded allowing little opportunity for meaningful input into this important part of the research process. It can also encourage a tokenism where the presence of a representative from a DUO lessens the imperative to consider matters of representation and collaboration in a more meaningful way (see AIVL, 2003 for a discussion on consulting with both DUO and individual drug users).

Another issue of course is the extent to which funded DUO are able to represent a category as broad as 'people who use drugs'. As a researcher, Mary takes a stance that it is important to remain critical of all 'truth' claims, including those of 'identity' that inevitably involve essentialised notions of 'the subject'. Part of the researcher's role is to interrogate or reflect on when and by whom a particular identity is invoked and to ask what does this stance allow or silence and what effects flow from this. However, this does not mean that one can ignore the need to engage respectfully with individuals and collective communities of people who use drugs.

In our experience the 'problem of representation' is largely undiscussed in the academic literature of drugs (though often hotly debated at the community level). Our many discussions of this issue are partly how we came to co-author this chapter. Annie's position is that the important issue is not whether or not one identifies as a drug user but rather the fact that people have a social connectedness that leads them to feel an 'identification' with common issues and experiences. These include for example experiences such as discrimination, poor treatment, police harassment, doing jail time, marginalisation, encountering certain health problems or conditions, knowing the rituals, fun and connections that you can make with people you use drugs with, and knowing the sense of being outside 'the system'. It is a form of identification, but with issues, experiences and values rather than some notion of an essentialised 'identity' as a drug user.

In terms of the issue about the 'representativeness' of DUO, Annie's reflections are that this has been problematised more in relation to drug users than other 'representative' groups. It may be that the thought of an organised collection of drug users is seen as politically threatening. There are many groups that 'represent' what are really highly diverse communities, some of which do not identify as 'communities'. One could equally ask how community-based AIDS organisations in Australia are able to represent a category as broad as 'gay men'. It is interesting that on the one hand the ability to 'represent' all drug users is questioned and that on the other hand drug users are told that they need to get better at speaking as one 'voice' as gay men's advocates have done. The fact is that no 'consumer' type organisation ever truly represents anyone other than their own experiences and perspectives. There are however well-recognised and accepted strategies that such organisations have historically employed to consult with members, represent 'issues' and 'needs' and raise awareness of key concerns. DUO employ all of the recognised strategies that are used by other consumer-based organisations but the bar seems to be raised higher for people who use drugs. In fact AIVL (The Australian Injecting and Illicit Drug Users League) states that it is 'the peak organisation for state and territory DUO and represents *issues* of national significance for people who use illicit drugs'. AIVL has never claimed to represent all people who use drugs, but as an organisation it has a good understanding of the range of issues, needs and concerns that affect people who use drugs through a range of participatory and consultative mechanisms including peer representation. One of the other strategies AIVL uses is having a commitment to self-determination within the peer model so that wherever possible it has people who are using heroin representing the issues for heroin users, people who use crystal representing the issues for crystal users, people on buprenorphine representing the issues for people on buprenorphine, Aboriginal injectors representing the issues for Aboriginal injectors for example. AIVL feels it does a lot more to address the problem of identity and representation than many more respected and legitimised consumer organisations.

There is a double edge sword when speaking as a 'drug user'. On the one hand there is an authority derived from specialist knowledge that is linked to this identity. On the other hand this identity is heavily stigmatised. In those (albeit few) environments where the identity of a drug user is a legitimate one, we need to acknowledge that this can silence those speaking from other positions (researchers, service providers) as well as those who may also have specialist knowledge as drug users, but who choose not to publicly identify themselves as such.

This highlights that the identity of being a drug user like all identities is a performative one. While others contest that drug users have a sense of community (see later discussion of Dowsett (1999)), in the same way that there is a performative effect for individual drug users in invoking an identity, when collectives of drug users speak of themselves as communities, they are communities.

In the absence of the capacity to have a truly representative body, many individuals will stand up and say they represent drug users or can speak authentically on their behalf. It can be particularly uncomfortable for a researcher presenting findings or discussing an issue when individuals use the implied authority taken from the speaking position of 'I am speaking as a drug user' or 'I am speaking as a parent of a drug user who has died' to criticise your standpoint or findings. Scott's (1993) excellent examination of the 'evidence of experience' is useful in reflecting on this issue. While not examining this in detail, we should also note here that often it is ex-drug users or 'recovering' drug users (those in treatment or abstinent) who are given the media, social and policy space to talk with authority on what it is like to be a drug user. This has a tendency to frame drug use itself in ways that we find problematic. Our view is that precisely who does or does not represent drug users is a question of politics and performance rather than one of fact. This sets up a complex arena in which to negotiate 'collaboration'.

Knowledge making

Reporting on research, whether quantitative or qualitative is a process of telling stories about people and issues. Most importantly it needs to be recognised that researchers make choices about the stories they tell about the people they research. These choices are fundamental in the representations that are made available to both the public and policymakers.

Researchers need to consider the moral and political effects of the types of stories they tell, or allow to be told using their findings. Sometimes in our work we collect information, but make a choice not to actively highlight it. For example the HIV Futures surveys of people living with HIV/AIDS (PLWHA) conducted by ARCSHS consistently find very high rates of illicit drug use by PLWHA. While this information is detailed in reports and provided to organisations working with PLWHAs, we have chosen to not feature these findings in press releases and general community briefings. Our concern has been that by drawing unnecessary attention to PLWHAs level of drug use we may reinforce stigma and encourage portrayals of PLWHA as irresponsible.

In this sense our concern is reminiscent of Harwood's (2004) insights that much commentary about queer young people (both by researchers advocating for them as well as others vilifying them) unproblematically equates being queer with 'woundedness' in the form of damage, injury or assault. She argues that what this produces is a 'dangerous irony' that it is only acceptable to talk about queer truths to young people in schools when those stories themselves are 'truths infected with woundedness' (468). This is a balance that researchers are always managing particularly when dealing with people who are socially marginalised. The tendency in past research on drug use has been to tell stories of social, psychological or medical deficit and thus to create an image of people who use drugs as fundamentally wounded. This can be avoided, and strong collaborations with people who use drugs can assist to sensitise researchers to these kinds of issues.

However, omissions can also cause harm. A lack of comment or failure to 'shape' the story told about drug users in a way designed to minimise their vilification may lead to more harm if findings are reported in a damaging manner in the tabloid media for example.

Recently in Australia research by Day et al., (2004) has concluded that a reduction in heroin supply has been associated with reduced drug injecting. This is a significant and controversial finding given the implicit support that law enforcement and particularly prohibitionist approaches to drug use may draw from such a finding. Other Australian researchers such as Higgs et al., (2004) cautioned that this finding should be contextualised by other research findings (such as Maher and Dixon, 1999) that documented the negative impacts of intensive policing. Further, Higgs et al., (2004) concluded that given the problems with the data measures used, there was insufficient evidence to link reductions in heroin supply and NSP distributions to either heroin usage or Hepatitis C (HCV) infections.

The stakes in this kind of controversy are not just those of researchers who have differing opinions. The political and material effects of such a finding for people who use drugs could be profound. Findings like these have already been used to increase funding to law enforcement initiatives and have been used by governments to support the further strengthening of the existing drug laws and harsher penalties in relation to illicit drug use and supply. At the end of the day, increases to law enforcement and harsher drug laws translate directly into increased harms for people who use illicit drugs. This is not just an 'academic' debate. Research affects policy and practice which in turn can have a direct impact on the lives of people who use drugs including increased levels of incarceration, poverty, unemployment, social isolation and increased health issues such as the transmission of BBVs and risk of overdose. We are not arguing that only 'good' stories about drug use should be told. We are arguing that it is beholden on researchers to consider these effects when reporting data and show particular concern to contextualise findings by caveats about the sample or in the context of other work in the area.

Recently peer-based DUO in Australia and researchers have discussed the potential for research data and findings to be used to support actions and outcomes that may have negative health effects for people who use drugs. These discussions have included issues such as: how do DUO make decisions about the relative benefits of research projects? and should there be a community endorsement process for research proposals involving people who use illicit drugs? Discussion of these issues has been motivated, at least in part, by the increasing practice of research data/findings being used to support and inform police operations and changes in government policy that DUO do not believe are in the best interest of people who use drugs. In fact peer-based DUO in the

Northern Territory recently withdrew from participating in the National Illicit Drugs Survey (IDRS) after they discovered that data had been used by police to target people injecting methadone and to seek support for increased funding to the Australian Federal Police.

Research does not merely report on a world that exists *a priori*, rather it actively constructs that world through defining objects of interest, asking particular questions and adopting particular methodological approaches.

Capacity building

The rhetoric of collaboration and partnerships with 'affected communities' is strewn throughout the latest state and national HIV and Hepatitis C strategies and applies equally to researchers as well as clinical and social support services. The realities of meaningfully engaging in collaboration in our experience are not easy.

DUO have extremely limited resources and most are not funded adequately to participate in all of the research projects that they are expected or invited to participate in. Researchers need to consider supporting the participation of DUO by providing them with adequate notice and information about the project, building in adequate resources to support consumer participation into the project budget and respecting the right of DUO to set their own priorities in terms of their level of participation in research. People who use drugs are researched a great deal and small DUO can easily experience 'research fatigue'. This can be a particular problem with smaller organisations where researchers tend to form a relationship with one or two individual consumer representatives and constantly approach those individuals to be involved in their projects. A better approach to working with DUO is to enable them to identify the appropriate level of participation for the particular project; from a letter of support through to contributing to the design, direction, conduct and dissemination of findings, depending on the needs and issues for consumers.

The other important factor is the capacity of the organisation to provide adequate training and support for consumer representatives involved in research collaborations. Consumer representatives are often expected to be both 'authentic' consumers and highly skilled professionals without appropriate training and support in research. Individual drug user representatives on advisory committees can feel very isolated. It often falls to them to raise complex and difficult issues that may not be fully understood by other members of the committee. This can lead to the drug user representative being cast into the role of 'trouble maker' or being seen as 'difficult'.

Because of a lack of formal research training, consumer representatives often feel unconvinced about their skills and capacity to participate as active members of research advisory committees. This can result in consumers opting to 'remove' themselves from the process through absence or by not actively participating in meetings. Sadly in the area of drugs this can simply serve to reinforce the stereotypical views of people who use drugs as unreliable and not able to offer anything of significant value. There needs to be recognition that research collaborations with DUO must include resourcing and support to build the capacity of the DUO to undertake such work.

The additional weight that consumer representatives carry because they often have direct and personal links to the research topic should also be acknowledged by researchers through the provision of adequate mechanisms and resources to support individual consumer representatives in their roles. These include feedback loops with their own communities so that they are not isolated, remuneration for their work, debriefing opportunities and other support strategies.

Too often, researchers who are developing projects or attempting to establish research collaborations with DUO overlook the fact that their project is only one of many research projects that the organisation is likely to be involved in at any given time. AIVL is a community-based organisation with five staff to carry out education, policy and advocacy work on all issues affecting people who use illicit drugs at the national level. One component of this work is participation and collaboration in research. Between July 2003 and June 2005 AIVL had involvement in over twenty separate research projects including being a major partner with a funded role in at least five of those projects. This does not include input into proposals that did not receive funding, participation in Scientific Advisory Committees and/or working groups for National Centres, presenting on research-related issues at conferences and events, and developing AIVL's own National Statement on Ethical Issues in Research.

Sometimes research even that which involves drug users can serve to undermine the capacity of DUO to build research capacity. The involvement of a group of users or indeed DUO does not necessarily produce good outcomes for drug users. Dowsett's (1999) work on IDU and Hepatitis C community organisations was done in partnership with a DUO. However, many of his conclusions, including the argument that IDUs 'lack a deep sense of community' (75), were criticised by the sector that was subject to the research. Many felt that this view reflected the author's experience as a researcher/activist in the gay men's/HIV community sector. This sector has long held that drug users did not constitute a community in the way that gay men did (see for example the 1998 AFAO manual conclusion that ' ...the idea of an injecting drug user "community" was meaningless' (124)).

One of the major political impacts of the promotion of the idea that there is no such thing as a drug user community has been in relation to the response to Hepatitis C. In this case, people who inject drugs, the group most affected by Hepatitis C, have been marginalised and silenced within the response to the epidemic because it has been viewed that in the 'absence' of an identified community there is no need to provide major funding to peer education initiatives. HIV affects a range of groups in the community but the fact that gay men are most affected by HIV within the Australian community has been used to support gay men taking the 'lead' role in the response. This same logic has not been applied in relation to the response to Hepatitis C where it has been characterised as a disease that affects a diverse range of groups with no particular group empowered to 'lead' the response on behalf of the affected communities. AIVL has argued that this has a direct relationship to the notion, articulated and perpetuated by research, that people who inject drugs do not constitute a community in the way that gay men do.

While working with the community sector has major benefits for research, as a researcher, collaboration with those in the usually underfunded and under-resourced community sector has at times been difficult. Mary has had two formal examples of paying a community sector/service organisation (one DUO and one not) to collect research data on the basis that they were better placed to sensitively recruit people. On one occasion the person at the organisation was to conduct qualitative interviews. After several months, while paying the organisation for a portion of the worker's time, few interviews had been conducted and in the end most of the data was not usable. In the second instance, we paid an organisation money for their workers time and participant payments in return for collecting survey data. In the end again we were not able to use the data collected.

While it is difficult to reflect on general principles from very specific circumstances (and we have certainly had positive and productive experiences too), several issues arose. The first involves the strain that community sector workers are under. Often individuals work in such organisations because they have a personal commitment to the area (this also applies to researchers). Researchers need to be aware that they are often negotiating with professional and personal stakes, and this may in itself lead workers at community-based organisations to be more vulnerable to things going awry.

The second is that the rhetoric of collaboration is often easier than the practicalities of a researcher overseeing or supervising a person in another organisation who is doing work on an outside project. Sometimes it is too late by the time one discovers that what you thought was happening was not. Our experience is that it is difficult to supervise and appropriately support someone that you do not have an already existing relationship with. Other authors in this book have devised more successful strategies for working with community organisations, and there are certainly lessons to be learnt for us in their experiences.

A third issue here is that researchers often manage *funds* as a proxy for managing *relationships* with community stakeholders. They do this through unit costed, output-based funding strategies (payment per interview or survey). While we believe it is important to pay organisations for their time and expertise, we worry that this type of funding strategy can have negative effects. It can mean that researchers employ or 'poach' individuals with expertise to work directly with them (casually or on secondment). This allows more direct supervision and support of the 'community researcher', but may have the effect of undermining the community sector by not allowing the sector to develop and retain research expertise. By reinforcing a fee for service model we move further away from an ideal of collaboration where there is mutual benefit for both parties. In particular, it is likely to work against the building of research capacity in community organisations, which we believe researchers should be concerned with.

Our experience suggests that researchers and the community organisations they are working with (drug user based or not) need to have formal discussions about internal processes in place to manage money, clarifying whether training is going to be needed and how workers will best be supervised and supported. While the same standards of accountability and professionalism should be applied across the board, collaborators need to work together to minimise the opportunities for things to go wrong, and for people who are vulnerable to be set up to fail.

Mutual benefit

In most productive relationships mutual and equal benefit to all parties is important. In research relationships we have to ask what do drug users (individually or collectively) get out of the equation.

At a minimum one of the ways for drug users to benefit is to at least be able to access the results of research. It is very difficult (particularly with anonymous surveys of people) to ensure that participants and the sector that provide services to them get access to the research results. An example of the range of strategies we employed in one project we provided a number of individualised oral and written briefings to local community organisations and services (drug user and Hepatitis C specific) prior to academic publication. We also separately collected names and addresses of people who wanted to receive a brief summary of results in an attempt to enable participants to hear about results. These were returned separately from surveys, and being on the mail-out list did not imply one was a participant as it contained service providers, other researchers, students and so forth. However, we recognise that many people with hepatitis C – and perhaps especially current drug users may not want to leave names and addresses in this way. To try to reach this group we also undertook specific analysis and made posters of results for display at NSPs and DUO that assisted us with recruitment. Finally in this project, further dissemination of results beyond academic publications occurred at community conferences on Hepatitis C, policy forums (such as the New South Wales Enquiry in to Hepatitis C related discrimination) and through the official publications of the Australian Hepatitis Council ('Hepatitis Chronicle') and AIVL ('Hepatitis See'). We have not always had the resources to try many dissemination strategies for one project, and despite this even in this project we feel that a majority of research participants would never have seen the results of their input.

There is an urgent need to create a better balance between the pressure on researchers to publish their research findings in peer-reviewed journals and the need for consumers to gain access to research findings that have a direct bearing on their lives and health. AIVL believes that this balance can be achieved through the implementation of ethical standards that create incentives for researchers to engage with consumers in the dissemination of research findings. Although we have outlined a few strategies that have been tried to provide more consumer access to research findings, there is still a great deal of work to be done to ensure effective access for the majority of consumers to research findings.

Conclusion

We thought we would end this chapter by briefly reflecting on our relationship. Good collaborative relationships between researchers and people who use drugs are difficult to achieve. We have both had some very good and some not so good experiences.

Researchers and the communities and individual drug users they are working with have different things at stake, and at times conflicting sets of accountabilities. This is no different from researcher relationships with other individuals or communities who do not identify as drug users. However, researchers do need to acknowledge that the broader social and cultural context of being a person that uses drugs often increases one's vulnerability to ill health, poverty and social stigma. Much of this is not inherent to the use of drugs but rather it occurs through the current regimes that regulate drug users. We need to acknowledge that researchers are part of these regimes.

Our positive experiences of working together over the years are based on respect for each other's professional and personal politics. Sadly it seems that there are many barriers to that sort of relationship becoming institutionalised beyond us as individuals within our own workplaces. We believe that is a loss for the community and the academic research sector as both arenas ultimately fail to fully draw on each others expertise.

We do not find the rhetoric of 'equal partnerships' between researchers and researched particularly useful. In a sense it obscures that we are always engaged in a series of relationships or moments characterised by different access to power and knowledge. There are times when those power imbalances run in both directions. In this sense power is more than a 'zero-sum equation' where for one to gain another must necessarily lose.

The fact that we are writing this chapter together makes it easier to acknowledge two key things. The first is that at times researchers struggle to see that they contribute to the public story of drug use as essentially problematic and they therefore participate in marginalising people who use drugs. The second is that individual drug users and the collectives that represent them sometimes act in ways where they position themselves in damaging roles such as powerless victims or 'addicts' compelled without choice.

Researchers and drug users need to speak about and reflect on the nature of their relationships. We hope this piece has offered something to that endeavour.

Acknowledgements

Thanks to our community and academic-based colleagues and collaborators, in particular the AIVL state and territory peer-based member organisations and Sandy Gifford for her role as Principal Investigator in the National Health and Medical Research Council (NHMRC) funded hepatitis C research projects. We would also like to acknowledge Nicky Bath, John Fitzgerald, Craig Fry and Tamara Speed for engaging in debate on many of the issues raised in this chapter.

2

From the Outside Looking in – Illuminating Research with Lesbians

Philomena Horsley and Sue Dyson

Introduction

In this chapter we trace the origins of the lesbian health movement and address some planning and preparation issues to be considered when researching lesbian health, including who to include, how to recruit, methodological issues and some pitfalls to be avoided. We are limiting our discussion to survey and interview-based methods while recognising that other methods such as ethnography and participatory action research offer rich and valuable data.[1] We also discuss ethical and responsible approaches to researching lesbian health and working with lesbians, and the dissemination of research. In doing this we hope to identify some of the key themes and challenges for the researcher inherent in this kind of work, as well as providing insight into how to engage a broad range of participants with rigour and sensitivity.

We write this chapter as two lesbians who have worked in the field of health as practitioners, community researchers, health educators and activists, and who have come to academia later in our careers. As we reflected on the themes involved in researching the margins we were conscious that the issues we raise in this chapter are salient for us as researchers as well as for those with whom we would carry out research. The issue of marginality is central to research with, by and for lesbians; it is also central for us as Australian researchers. Until relatively recently, most (published) research on lesbian health has been dominated by North American perspectives. In the early days of the lesbian health movement there was a tendency to rely heavily on US research and extrapolate the findings to all lesbians, regardless of where they lived, or their cultural or social differences. While there are similarities in the contemporary and historical nature of lesbians' life experiences across these continents, there are also significant differences. For instance, the issue of lesbians' 'access to health services' focuses upon the implications of health practitioner attitudes to, and knowledge about, homosexuality. In North America the access discussion is dominated by the structural injustices created by the lack of a free and universal health care system, a system available to all Australian lesbians. Similarly, the comparative level of homophobia in Australia is less,[2] and the legislative protections offered to lesbians, gay men and transgender people are more widespread.[3] Nevertheless, the themes and nature of evidence from the United States can be seductive; in our early days as lesbian health activists we probably fell into the trap of translating the US data into the Australian context without question. In the past few years lesbian health research in Australia has created new knowledges that have informed other projects. Findings from countries such as New Zealand, Canada and the United Kingdom have also contributed to the picture and have created understandings that are both specific to one country or area, and able to be generalised across geographical boundaries.

In writing this chapter we are aware that there are many issues that present challenges to researching lesbian health, not the least of which is related to the ways in which we are positioned as lesbians, as activists and as researchers. The issue of power is central for any researcher, whether she is a member of the community she is researching, or an outsider to that community. Feminist researchers have for some time attempted to recognise their position of power in relation to their participants and equalise it in some way (Kirkman, 1999; Smith, 1987). Feminist theory applied to research methodology has led to increased acceptance of the personal as a starting point for research and addresses the position of the researcher as an 'insider'. Feminist theory suggests that being an insider to an experience positions the researcher in ways that make it possible to understand what others in a similar position have to say, and in ways far less accessible to outsiders. This has been called a new 'epistemology of insiderness' that sees life and work as intertwined (Reinharz and Davidman, 1992) and can be seen as an advantage for a lesbian when working with other lesbians. As Waite (1996) states, 'Who designs, conducts and controls the research raises issues of ownership. There is often a need for lesbians to conduct research with lesbians because from the very outset of identifying the problem, the insiders (lesbians) have more knowledge and sensitivity to the issues than and outsiders (non-lesbians).'

Another way of conceptualising the position of the lesbian carrying out research with other lesbians is as the researcher being 'embedded' in the community she is researching. This is not without risk however: 'In the hands of relatively privileged researchers studying the experience of those who have been marginalised ... the potential to silence subjects is of particular concern. It is easy ... to slip into ... a "compulsive extroversion of interiority" ' (Denzin, 2000).

Denzin refers here to the risk of over-identifying with, or even becoming hypercritical of those with whom you plan to research, to the detriment of the research. It is possible to silence subjects in many ways. For example, there are many different ways to 'be' lesbian, but at times one way is privileged over another. In privileging one way it can be implied that this is the 'true' way, and others may find it difficult to tell their stories if they feel they will be de-legitimised because they are different. As embedded researchers it is important to be cognisant of the pitfalls as well as the advantages of working with our own communities. Ensuring that these are addressed in research plans includes maintaining sufficient flexibility or adaptability.

Our positioning in relation to those we are researching must be continually addressed in the research process. We believe that this can be done through rigorous reflexivity, including constant attention to ethical process. This is a process by which we critically reflect on ourselves and how we are positioned as researchers, as well as on ourselves as instruments of research.[4] This critical engagement with the self is an ongoing process, a dialogic that focuses on the researcher, the context, data and materials, the people with whom we plan to carry out research and the historical process of knowledge production. There are four phases in which reflexivity is important: in the design phase, in the relationship between existing knowledge and what it is you seek to understand, in the ways in which you choose to carry out your research and finally, in data analysis and writing and disseminating the results. It is helpful to ask at each phase of the research, what is my reflexive position?[5]

Why research lesbians?

Health is a complex field that has been influenced by a number of social and political changes since the middle of the twentieth century, and arguably the most recent influential shift occurred as a result of the 1948 World Health Organisation (WHO) definition of health as: '... a state of complete physical, mental and social wellbeing, and not merely the absence of disease or infirmity' (World Health Organisation, 1978).

This statement has influenced the ways in which health has been conceptualised and services have been delivered ever since. The construction of health as being not only about the absence of disease, but also promoting well-being and preventing illness, has played an important role in carving out territory for previously unrecognised or marginalised groups, although it was not until 2000 that the WHO formally acknowledged sexual rights (Tiefer, 2002). According to Tiefer this occurred as a result of the AIDS epidemic as well as the second wave of the women's movement and the gay rights movement.

By the early 1980s these social changes led to the emergence of the women's health movement. Until that time women's health had been seen as similar in most ways to that of men, with exception of reproduction (Dyson, 2001). Many lesbians were active and worked to establish a broader social view of women's health, but gradually it became clear that lesbian health issues were not being addressed by the women's health movement:

> Lesbian health activism grew out of the women's health movement and employed many of the strategies developed in the wider context of feminist health care politics. The women's health movement was, by definition, part of a long lasting social and political struggle for rights. Not only did lesbian health activists cut their teeth on such issues, they also had to fight within feminism, against the heterosexual majority who thought lesbian issues unimportant or who believed that to include lesbians would bring feminism into disrepute.
>
> (Wilton, 2002)

Seminal early work from the United States (Stevens, 1991; 1992) traced a genealogy of the ways in which lesbians had lived for centuries under heavy moral, legal and medical penalties, forcing many to lead hidden, isolated lives. It also identified the concomitant health effects of these pressures. This and other early research sparked increased activism by lesbians, many of whom were also health workers, which led to an escalation of research about lesbian health over the ensuing decade. While some early lesbian health research has been criticised because of sampling and methodological problems, the territory has been refined and expanded and the specific body of knowledge has grown.

Although lesbians have much the same physical health concerns as heterosexual women there has been a tendency for lesbian health research to focus predominantly on reproductive, sexual, emotional and mental health. The 1999 report from the US Committee on Lesbian

Health Research Priorities described existing research on lesbian health under headings of mental health, cancers, sexually transmitted diseases (particularly HIV/AIDS), and substance use (including alcohol, tobacco and illegal drugs) (Solarez, 1999). This narrowly focuses lesbian health to reproductive or mental health concerns. Contemporary literature on lesbian health has started to take a more holistic approach however, with connections being identified between general health, and mental and sexual health (Bradford, 1994; Solarez, 1999). These priorities still fall short of meeting the WHO's criteria for an holistic approach to health for lesbians. Perhaps a more relevant way to conceptualise health when planning research with lesbians is as follows:

> Health is a state which individuals and communities alike strive to achieve, maintain or regain, and not something that comes about merely as a result of treating and curing illnesses and injuries. It is a basic and dynamic force in our daily lives, influenced by our circumstances, our beliefs, our culture and our social, economic and physical environments.
>
> (Health Canada, 2003)

We believe that this social view of health is far from being achieved with regard to lesbian research. As Rosier (1993) asserts, issues such as homophobic discrimination, rejection by family and friends, internalised homophobia and the stress of living a double life must be addressed as health issues.

Methodological challenges

It has been posited that prospective, longitudinal studies are essential for understanding the vulnerability, resilience and well-being of lesbians across their life span (Solarez, 1999). One of the challenges in reaching lesbians lies in defining who is to be included. In this chapter we use the term 'lesbian' in an inclusive manner to take account of all women who relate primarily to other women either sexually or emotionally. Who and what constitutes a lesbian continues to be a shifting and contested territory, and is largely defined by women themselves. This is important to take into account when planning research with lesbian populations. There are many assumptions and preconceptions about what constitutes a lesbian, yet we are as diverse as the general population of women. We are represented in all racial and ethnic groups, all socio-economic strata and all ages. There is no single-type characteristic of family, community, culture or demographic category that typifies a lesbian, which can obscure health issues for (or even the existence of) many minority groups within lesbian populations. Over time, across cultures and between individuals, definitions shift and change and the consequent population included in studies can vary, which makes comparisons over time difficult.

Questions and debates also continue over categories of 'lesbian': for example, can a woman be a lesbian if she also relates or is attracted to men? Is lesbianism only about sex or identity or does it have other dimensions? In the past decade there has been an increasing shift towards recognising three dimensions of sexual orientation to include identity, behaviour, and/or sexual attraction (Laumann, 1994). Some studies define sexual orientation as a form of identity and include only self-identified lesbians, while others include women who are sexually active with women but do not necessarily identify as lesbian and others include multiple components of identity, attraction and behaviour (Sell, 1996). When researching with lesbians these factors are important whether you are planning to compare findings with other studies or to investigate new territory. Some interesting approaches can be seen in recent Australian research. One study investigated the transmission of sexually transmitted infections (STIs) and blood born viruses among women who have sex with women, who attended a sexual health clinic in Sydney (Fethers, 2000). Another investigated self-identified lesbians' experience of menopause (Kelly, 2005). The differences in these two projects illustrate some of the complexity concerning inclusion criteria and offer examples of rigour in planning and recruitment. Both Kelly and Fethers had very different research aims, and thus identified different potential participants to achieve their respective aims. From our point of view, clarity regarding inclusion criteria, coupled with an explicit rationale and documentation, is vital in this area of research.

Mainstream women's health research has largely neglected to include lesbians, or indeed sexual orientation, partly on the assumption that the number of lesbians in the general population is not significant. Leaving aside other reasons such as prejudice and discrimination, lesbians do constitute a small but important subgroup of women, not the least because they experience many health disparities compared to their heterosexual sisters. Over time there has been confusing evidence about the proportion of women who are lesbian. In late 1940s and early 1950s Alfred Kinsey's work suggested that homosexual men and women make up 10 per cent of the population. For many years this figure was taken as given, but in recent years new research has challenged Kinsey's estimate. In the United States the Council on Scientific Affairs estimated that 1.3 per cent of women define themselves as homosexual or bisexual, that is they have same-sex partners, or express homosexual desires. In the United Kingdom, findings from the second National Survey of Sexual Behaviour, which took place in 2000, reported that 2.6 per cent of women had sex with another woman in the preceding 5 years and 4.9 per cent had ever had a female partner (Henderson, 2002). In 2003 The Australian Study of Health and Relationships (ASHR), a national population-based survey of sexual health and behaviours, interviewed approximately nine thousand women aged between 16 and 59 from every state and territory in Australia.[6] The survey measured the three components of sexuality: current stated sexual identity (heterosexual/straight, lesbian/gay, bisexual and other), lifetime sexual attraction and lifetime sexual experience. Less than one per cent (0.8 per cent) of women surveyed identified as lesbian or gay, 1.4 per cent identified as bisexual and 0.1 per cent were undecided (i.e 2.2 per cent of women identified as other than heterosexual). However, 13.5 per cent of women reported that they were not exclusively attracted to the opposite sex and 8.6 per cent had had a same-sex sexual experience during their lifetime (Smith et al., 2003). Data from a large Australian longitudinal study of women's health by Women's Health Australia (WHA) indicates that, among a cohort of younger women aged 22–27, 6.25 per cent identified themselves as mainly heterosexual, 0.75 per cent as bisexual, 0.31 per cent as mainly lesbian and 0.62 per cent as exclusively lesbian (deVisser et al., 2003).

WHA's study provides a good example of a major women's health study that could have extended knowledge about the links between sexual orientation and women's health. When this 25-year study was first designed in 1995 no questions about sexual orientation were included, despite protests from lesbian health activists. Few years later, further approaches were made to the research team and a question was inserted in the second round of the survey for the young- and middle-aged cohorts, but excluded the older cohort. These data provide interesting comparisons between exclusively heterosexual women and those who are not exclusively heterosexual, bisexual and lesbian, but the question will not be included in future rounds. Unfortunately the situation excludes the possibility of longitudinal information about this group of women but data already collected pertaining to sexual orientation was analysed at Australian Research Centre in Sex, Health and Relationships (ARCSHS).[7]

Planning and preparation

Dominant discourse about lesbians produces them as 'invisible'. In using health services some women choose to pass as heterosexual because of exposure to discourse about, or personal experience of prejudice or discrimination. For those who want to carry out health-related research with lesbians, this can make them a hard group to reach, particularly when sampling for diversity. Until recently, few comparative, population-based studies of women's health have specifically sought information that would make it possible to compare heterosexual women and lesbians. Reviews of research with lesbian, gay and bisexual groups (e.g. Sell, 1996) have found that the results of many studies were not comparable because of different methods, sampling from diverse and convenience populations, and the use of vastly different definitions. Others have also identified problems with the use of non-probability samples (making it difficult to generalise results) and recruitment of convenience samples from sources such as lesbian bars, music festivals, or gay and lesbian organizations (Solarez, 1999). Nonetheless, in our experience community-based convenience surveys have, at times, produced some extremely useful data when arguing for lesbian inclusion within public health agendas. Philomena was involved in a collaborative project that investigated lesbians and smoking. Some basic randomisation guidelines were employed during a community survey process. When compared with existing research among women in the general population, it was clear that the results were 'robust' enough to allow the project team to confidently claim that prevalence of smoking among lesbians was higher in Victoria and urge more research (Tremellen, 1996–1997).

It is true however, that sampling bias in lesbian research is a problem that requires vigilance, reflexivity and transparency. In 2004 a survey about health and well-being was carried out among women at the Midsumma gay and lesbian festival in Melbourne. When the results were compared with the results for non-heterosexual women from the WHA longitudinal survey of women's health, there were some surprising differences. Because of the very different methodologies, the only conclusion that could be drawn from the Midsumma survey was that we could report on the health and well-being status of women attending this gay and lesbian festival and speculate that these women were more likely representative of women who were 'community connected' rather than all lesbians. When planning research that you might want to be able to compare with or even to extend the boundaries of existing research, it is important to build in methodological safeguards to ensure that this will be possible.

Recruitment/locating participants

When planning research with lesbians it is important to plan a recruitment strategy that will help you to achieve your research objectives. To overcome some of the problems identified in earlier research this may mean sampling for diversity. To do this you will need to think through whether you want to include only self-identified lesbians, or women who have lesbian relationships but identify themselves in other ways. In Sue's doctoral research she initially circulated a flyer that invited 'lesbians' to contact a 'lesbian friendly' researcher to talk about their experience with health services. Responses were received from a narrow and homogeneous sample of self-identified lesbians. Because in her research objectives she aimed to include a diverse range of lesbians, to broaden the sample ethics approval was gained for a revised recruitment flyer to be distributed. These invited 'same sex attracted, gay, lesbian or queer' women to participate in research run by a 'lesbian' researcher. This time a broad group responded including women of diverse age, educational background, socio-economic and cultural backgrounds. The difference between the two flyers was that Sue identified herself as lesbian and invited a much broader range of women to participate. The broader strategy and the use of different names brought people out that had not responded to the first simple request that appears to have been interpreted by some as exclusive. Not all women who fit into the group broadly described as lesbian are comfortable with the name for a variety of reasons and in response to a question during the interviews carried out as part of this research all indicated that they fitted broadly under the lesbian category, but of the 21 women interviewed 2 identified themselves as dykes, 5 as gay, 1 as queer and 13 as lesbian, thus the use of a wider range of terminology was successful in drawing in a diverse sample.

For many researchers the major decision will be qualitative or quantitative research. Each is a different field of scientific investigation: quantitative studies emphasise the measurement and analysis of causal relationships between variables while qualitative studies emphasise the processes and meanings and seek to understand how social experiences are created and given meaning (Denzin, 2000). Each methodology serves a different purpose and each is important; however, rigorous and ethical application of the chosen method is always essential. In United States investigation into researching lesbian health Solarez (1999) made a number of recommendations for improving research with lesbians, including addressing the pitfalls apparent in past quantitative research mentioned here, such as sampling, validity and reliability. They also call for more qualitative research to increase the depth of understanding about lesbians and more rigorous and well-designed population-based studies to create more effective non-probability studies.

Ethical and responsible research

Many countries have developed processes to ensure the ethical review and conduct of research. In Australia the National Health and Medical Research Council (NHMRC) oversees national guidelines on all research involving humans (NHMRC, 1999). While these guidelines do not specifically refer to research involving lesbians (and gay men), lesbian research would clearly meet the Council's criteria of 'research involving collectivities'.[8] In addition, issues relating to research specifically involving lesbians and gay men are addressed in the NHMRC's commentary on its own National Statement (NHMRC, 2001a) where recruitment, methodology, community involvement and confidentiality are among the concerns briefly discussed. To be ethically grounded, research involving a marginalised group or 'people'[9] such as lesbians should address some basic questions that acknowledge the greater potentials for harm for both individual participants and lesbians as a group. The main questions are as follows:

- Is the research question ethically appropriate?
- Who is involved?
- How will it be done?
- How will results be disseminated?

Is the research question ethically appropriate?

It is distinctly unpopular in these times of competitive, career-building, grant-seeking research proposals to ask the question: 'Is it appropriate to do this research at this time?' It simply means, Is there a need for this research? Will it be useful? And to whom? Yet it remains an important tenet for assessing research, particularly on populations with a history of social oppression. Much of the early research on lesbian health, pervasively conducted by heterosexuals from within the medical domain, focused on the perceived deficits, abnormalities and 'perversions' of lesbian lives and health. It has often contributed to further social discrimination and negative stereotyping. Even some recent research by lesbian organisations and researchers could be questioned, given its persistent or repetitive focus on negative health outcomes such as drug and alcohol use or depressive states. The ethical challenge for any research project involving marginalised groups is to 'do no harm' and to deliver outcomes that will ultimately improve the position of the group in society. Obviously research that is naïve or voyeuristic is not appropriate, as is research with a focus 'on' lesbians rather than for or with lesbians. Initiating discussion with lesbians/lesbian organisations about the value of the research question, or explicit reference to previous community consultations, is an obvious way to enhance the appropriateness and sensitivity of any project (see below).

Who is involved?

The ethical issues involving lesbian research will, to some extent, vary according to the identification of the researcher(s) and the consultative plan, if any.

Traditionally, there has been the view that 'objective' research demands distance: disciplines such as anthropology and sociology, for instance, have been founded on the study of 'the other'. In recent decades 'insider' researchers have responded, claiming that familiarity with, and knowledge of, one's own 'group', 'subculture' or 'tribe' brings additional value to social science research. Such a position provides researchers with 'easy access to not only the intellectual dimensions but also to the emotional and sensory dimensions [of ordinary life]' of the participant group (Ohnuki-Tierney, 1984). The topics of research, the nature of the language and questions used, the chosen research method, the recruitment approaches utilised, can all be enhanced by the researcher being 'of' or 'from' the 'lesbian community'.[10] However, as previously discussed, there are certainly tensions to be invoked by the 'insider' identity claimed by a lesbian researcher, including the negotiating and renegotiating of such positions and the challenges they produce for issues such as the methodology.[11]

In both our cases, our years of grass roots work for our community's (and our own) benefit have left us both feeling comfortably situated as a 'sister/insider'. As Motzafi-Haller (1997, p. 216) suggests, being positioned within a marginalised community 'sensitises one in conscious and/or unconscious ways to look at practices of exclusion and perhaps to write in ways that do not accept the status quo'. Yet it is also true that the role of researcher inevitably separates us, as 'sister/outsiders,'[12] from other lesbians who are participants in research projects. In addition, as Weston (1996) points out, a 'queer' identity does not necessarily translate into feelings of closeness or identification with the people we study. Recent feminist research has strongly claimed that development of a critical reflexivity is central to the challenges of such a position 'inside' the participants' world. While outsiders can miss nuances obvious to insiders they also have the capacity to identify or question subcultural 'truths' too commonplace for lesbian-insiders to remark upon. In turn lesbian researchers can neglect opportunities to challenge 'taken for granted' assumptions or 'truisms' about lesbian health and community that have shifted or were never, in fact, generalisable. For instance, in her challenge to the feminist (and lesbian) orthodoxy on domestic violence, Ristock argues that 'Critically reflexive questions can help turn our efforts in research, in service provision, and in marginalised communities from striving toward ultimate explanatory models and making simple truth claims into a quest for deeper understandings and responses' (Ristock, 2002, p. 181).

'Outsiders' researching lesbians

As lesbians have achieved greater control of our health research agendas 'outsider' or heterosexual researchers have been increasingly welcomed back into the lesbian health research field. This is particularly true for researchers who are attached to projects or organisations with a credible record in the area, or are co-researcher service providers who have promoted inclusiveness. Transparency of researcher sexual identities is highly recommended. In our experience, project 'teams' with diverse skills can significantly enhance the work irrespective of individual members' sexual identities.[13] The result of lack of transparency of the researcher's sexual identity can be seen in Sue's experience in recruiting for her PhD project, when her initial self-identification was as 'lesbian friendly' and resulted in a very limited response. Unless identities are clearly articulated, assumptions will still be made by many participants (and other researchers) that 'only lesbians would research lesbian issues', or indeed that the researcher is not a lesbian and therefore to be avoided.

Some lesbians are enthusiastic and welcoming of non-lesbian researchers who are committed to improving their health; others, however, may feel a sense of intrusiveness or distrust. Some obstacles may confront non-lesbian researchers: potential participants may be less willing and less open; gaining trust from and entry to particular groups of women may be more difficult or slower as relationships are built that may not readily exist; assumptions may be made that lead to inadvertent offence or mistakes. Support from key lesbian organisations or valued health service providers for research projects can be invaluable.

Participatory research and reference groups

The importance and value of consumer or community participation in research, whether clinical or socially-based, is recognised at the highest level in Australia (NHMRC, 2001a). The process often sounds simple but management of this aspect of any project can be complex, time-consuming and costly, dependant on the participation model chosen. It is particularly important that research areas that have traditionally stereotyped or excluded lesbians, such as clinical or epidemiological research, be transparent about their willingness to incorporate lesbians' input.

Of course, as research shows, 'consumer participation' in research means different things to different people (NHMRC, 2001b). In large-scale generic projects consumer input may simply involve some comment on the design of questionnaires to ensure lesbian inclusiveness and sensitivity. For example, reliance on a word such as 'sexual intercourse' (construed by most people as penis-vagina sex) is inappropriate when asking potential lesbian participants about sex; terms such as 'partner' are also preferable to, or should be added to 'spouse/defacto' when ascertaining relationship status.[14] Some projects have involved stand alone public meetings at particular points to gather feedback and ideas to enhance the subsequent stages. Others have recruited and trained lesbian community members to conduct surveys at relevant events (see, for example, (Tremellen, 1996–1997)).

Some projects will require a more ongoing contribution of in-depth cultural knowledge about a targeted lesbian community, for instance, young same sex attracted women, lesbian mothers, or particular service users. Such projects can be significantly enhanced by more formal partnership arrangements between researchers and lesbian representatives/groups from the outset, to ensure meaningful discussion about research questions and methods, potential ethical dilemmas, data analysis and strategies for the dissemination of results. Philomena participated in a reference group developed by a large drug and alcohol agency that wanted to examine the alcohol and drug use within gay, lesbian, bisexual and queer communities in Victoria (Murnane, 2000). The group's input led to an extension of the initial research plan, their involvement in the interpretation of the data, and partial responsibility for the dissemination of results to particular groups, such as lesbians.

Reference groups may sound great in theory, but can be extremely stressful at times due to the passions (and painful memories) certain issues evoke. They can often involve a complexity of issues: inequities of status and authority, 'ownership' of knowledge about the community, disputes when results may challenge long-held views or assumptions, and basic personality clashes. Questions of representation can also arise. No reference group can hope to represent the diversities of lesbian identities, locations or lives. It can, however, be open and realistic about its limitations while affirming the combined knowledge, experience and skills each individual brings to a project. In essence, a participatory project needs to plan an adequate amount of time for relationship and trust building; it should explicitly negotiate protocols and responsibilities of all players from the outset; it should respect the diverse skills of its members and its work needs to be transparent and appropriately accountable to the broader lesbian community.

How will it be done?

Confidentiality and privacy

As previously indicated, in the relatively short history of lesbian-owned research there has been a heavy reliance on convenience and snowball sampling techniques, or recruiting from networks suggested by a project's reference group members. From an ethical perspective such approaches create risks regarding the privacy and confidentiality of participants' names and data. In qualitative research it is more likely that women and their stories will be recognisable within their close-knit networks that are often the focus of recruitment strategies. It is also not uncommon that participants may be known to researchers, or social information about researchers be known by participants. One of Philomena's research projects involved women recruited through a lesbian cancer support group and gay community press. In such situations it is impossible, indeed unethical, to assure women of complete confidentiality. Her participant information form included the following caution:

> There is also a possibility that I may encounter you in another context to this research, for instance through social networks or community events, which may feel awkward. Additionally there is a slight possibility that some members of the lesbian community (acquaintances of yours) may recognise your story despite every effort by both of us to conceal identifying material.

Informed consent

When research projects are conducted by lesbian 'insiders' there is often an assumed level of trust between those involved. This can mean that potential participants are less attentive to the project details offered, or more willing to be involved in projects that are potentially harmful to them. Researchers can also be under pressure at times to recruit a sufficiently large participant group from an often hard-to-reach community, and within short time frames. Nevertheless, it is incumbent upon researchers to ensure that prospective participants are assessed in terms of their appropriateness and their fully informed understanding of the potential risks.

Ethics in practice

Simply *being* a lesbian does not immunise any of us against the possibility of unethical or inadequate research practices within our own communities. To paraphrase Rosaldo (1989), we can be insightful, politically correct, axe-grinding, self-interested, or just plain mistaken. We may more readily hold as 'true' or 'right' our own, often painfully lived, past beliefs and experiences, and be reluctant to take on broader professional expectations. And while being a lesbian may sensitise us more readily to the nuances of confidentiality and safety important to many lesbians, it can also render our professional/personal boundaries more permeable to the emotional and social events that arise during research activities. Most researchers utilising qualitative data can recount experiences when they have found themselves over-identifying with stories of lesbian discrimination or family rejection. They can also recall interviews when private information or views are unwittingly proffered in relation to women known to them, such as friends, ex-lovers or colleagues. Ristock and Pennell (1996) have written of situations where the temptations arise for the interviewer to take on a counsellor's role.

Any sub-community is a small world. It can be rendered oppressively so when women are disclosing stories of lesbian domestic violence or serious depression, or expecting the researcher to actively support them, especially when these occur at unanticipated moments in interviews. These 'ethically important moments' (Guillemin, 2004) will inevitably occur in research involving lesbians and lesbian researchers in particular. It is incumbent of all of us to be rigorously reflective in planning our research, to brainstorm scenarios with others, so that such events are, as much as possible, actively anticipated and continuously planned for in everyday research practices.

How will the results be disseminated?

Past decades of research on lesbians and gay men had eschewed feedback to participants and recommendations for social and political change, in accordance with positivist social science demands (Walsh-Bowers, 1992). Yet ethical research in the area of lesbian health demands a creative approach to results dissemination that extends far beyond the goal of peer-reviewed publications. There are clear responsibilities to share the results with the individuals and communities involved or affected, and to do so in ways that are timely and accessible. While funding and employment bodies may not value or reward the additional time and resources involved, it is a basic criteria for ethical research in marginalised communities such as lesbians in Australia (NHMRC, 2001b) and, one could argue, for all research.

We have both been extensively involved in activities that enable lesbians to access relevant research findings – addressing local meetings of lesbian social groups, presenting at state and national conferences, contributing articles and interviews for gay and lesbian media, producing community-focused research reports, promoting free website access to findings, adding a lesbian perspective to general publications for consumers (Horsley, 2003; Horsley, 2002; Horsley, McNair and Pitts 2001). We have also extensively utilised research results in training events for general practitioners, nurses, community health workers and teachers. Getting stories into general medical outlets to broader audiences can be more difficult but extremely important to aim for, given many lesbians will not be connected to the formal and informal information networks of the gay and lesbian community.

Finally, dissemination of results is a two-way street. In addition to formal 'talking at' research presentations, lesbians should be invited to contribute alternative theories, address limitations of the research, identify the implications for lesbian health and suggest additional research projects. This way experience and practice can inform future research, as well as research contributing knowledge to the community and to practitioners.

Conclusion

After two decades of committed effort and productivity, lesbian health has steadily gained legitimacy as an area of study, both separately and within larger projects. Yet significant tensions remain both within the field and between it and other research areas. The extended efforts by lesbian activist researchers to promote attention, and attract funding to our health issues have sometimes resulted in an inward looking, victim-focused agenda or unhelpful debates about what constitutes a 'real lesbian'. To gain attention for lesbian health, differences have often been privileged over commonalities between women; we have ignored opportunities to reposition 'sameness' as the underside of difference (Moore, 1994).

Nonetheless recent research in Australia has identified the existence of complex, active strategies among lesbians seeking optimal care and diverse constructions of personal identities that are healthy, resistant and complex. Possibilities for inclusion in large, well-funded public health initiatives are increasing, but sometimes at the expense of the more nuanced qualitative research needed to better understand issues of women's diverse, sometimes changing sexual identities, relationships and health outcomes.

In many cases, mainstream women's health researchers remain resistant, uninterested or ignorant of the importance of sexual identities and behaviours in the health status of women of all ages. As lesbian researchers we remain frustrated by current limited funding opportunities, yet we are excited by the creativity being employed by new thematic and methodological initiatives involving lesbian health research. In particular, cross-disciplinary models of research that engage differently positioned researchers have much to offer what was once regarded as a distant ghetto of unnecessary and unappealing work. The territory is shifting and it behoves us all to be flexible, engaged and responsive to new light shining upon lesbian health.

Notes

1. See (Lewin and Leap, 1996) *re gay and lesbian ethnography*; see (Rice, 1999) for example of Participatory Action Research.
2. The recent Australian Study of Health & Relationships found that less than one quarter of respondents agreed with the statement 'sex between two adult women is always wrong', and acceptance increased significantly among those under 50 years (Rissel et al., 2003).
3. See for example the Equal Opportunity Act 1995 (Vic); Anti-Discrimination Act 1977 (NSW) Part 4C; Anti-Discrimination Act 1991 (Qld) s 7(l); Equal Opportunity Act 1984 (SA) s 29(3); Discrimination Act 1991 (ACT); Anti-Discrimination Act 1992 (NT); Relationships Act 2003 (Tas).
4. From an anthropological perspective reflexivity is a complex analytical tool that involves a commitment to a multidimensional analysis of data as well as an autobiographical declaration of where you stand historically and politically (see Moore, 1994).

5. The authors would like to acknowledge Dr Gary Dowsett's and Dr Martha Macintyre's input on reflexivity.
6. The ASHR is the largest study of sexuality undertaken in Australia and the second largest of its kind in the world. It surveys a representative sample of 19,307 respondents between the ages of 16 and 50 years old.
7. See for example Hillier L., de Visser R., Kavanagh A., McNair R. P. 'The association between sexual orientation and licit and illicit drug use in young Australian women'. *MJA* September 2003, 179(6): 326–327; and Hillier L., de Visser R., Kavanagh A. and McNair R. 'The drug use patterns of heterosexual and non-heterosexual young women: data from the Women's Health Australia study'. In *Out in the Antipodes: New perspectives in Gay and Lesbian Psychology*, Walker and Ridge (eds), pp. 192–211. (Brightfire Press, Bentley, WA, 2004).
8. Section 8 of National Statement: 'Collectivities are distinct human groups with their own social structures that link with a common identity, with common customs and with designated leaders or other persons who represent collective interests in dealing with researchers. Examples may include cultural or ethnic groups, and indigenous communities' (1999: 31).
9. See Weston (1996) for a useful discussion of the historical and material processes by which gay men and lesbians have often constructed themselves as a 'people' and the implications for identity theory.
10. We use the term 'community' here in a singular and generic sense, whilst acknowledging the emerging use of the plural 'communities' to denote the many sub-communities that make up the 'lesbian community' (Horsley 2002), as well as those individuals who do not relate to such a notion. We acknowledge that 'it is correct to talk of the development of a lesbian community' in the twentieth century, but that 'the concept of one community is a distortion' (Kennedy, 1994).
11. See for example (Lewin, 1996; Platzer, 1997).
12. The title of a collection of essays and speeches by Audre Lorde (1984), an Africa American activist and lesbian who wrote on her experiences with breast cancer.
13. ARCSHS research involving lesbians has incorporated analysis, publication and presentations by researchers of diverse genders and sexualities to great effect.
14. See, as example, the Menopause Health Questionnaire offered to practitioners on the website of the Nth American Menopause Society (www.menopause.org). Under 'marital status' it lists 'committed relationship' as an option; when asking if clients are sexually active it lists as options, with 'a man (or men); with a woman (or women); with both men and women'.

3

Research with People with Intellectual Disabilities

Lynne Hillier, Kelley Johnson and
Rannveig Traustadóttir

Like many other people in our communities who have found themselves on the margins of society, people with intellectual disabilities have long been subject to research which sought to assess, categorise, predict and control their lives and behaviour (Tuhiwai Smith, 1999; Walmsley and Johnson, 2003). It is only relatively recently that they have begun to claim the right to participate in research 'about them', to have a voice in research projects and to be active as participants. It is only recently too that some researchers have begun to position differently both themselves and those with whom they are working. This relatively new paradigm of participatory or inclusive research is premised on a view that research undertaken with people with intellectual disabilities should aim to provide opportunities for them to claim a voice in research, to have their skills and experience in their own lives valued and challenge societal inequalities (Atkinson, 2004; Goodley, 1996; Ward, 1997). Such research also challenges the 'othering' which pushes people to the edges of society (Traustadóttir, 2001). Undertaking this kind of research involves a constant challenge to the researchers' own prejudices, biases and the ways in which they view their own position as experts.

This chapter explores what we have gained from undertaking inclusive research. While many of the issues involved in researching with people with intellectual disabilities are similar to those raised by other authors in this book, there are some significant differences that provide challenges for both researchers and people with intellectual disabilities. We will describe briefly two research studies in which we have been involved and then analyse their implications for undertaking research *with* people with intellectual disabilities. In the first study, carried out in Australia at Australian Research Centre in Sex, Health and Society (ARCSHS), we worked with people with intellectual disabilities to document how they saw their sexuality and relationships within the broader context of their lives. The second study was undertaken in Iceland and focused on motherhood and women with intellectual disabilities. We also explore some of the learning that has emerged for us as researchers from these experiences.

Living safer sexual lives: overview

Living Safer Sexual Lives was a three year action research project which aimed to work with people with intellectual disabilities to document their experiences of sexual expression and relationships and to then undertake action which would support them to lead safer sexual lives (Harrison et al., 2002; Johnson et al., 2001).

The study originated from concerns by a group of researchers about the lack of power that people with intellectual disabilities had in relation to their own sexual lives and previous research findings which had documented their vulnerability to sexual abuse and exploitation (Brown and Turk, 1992; Cambridge, 1997; McCarthy, 1999; McCarthy, 2000; McCarthy and Thompson, 1995), and a recognition of the need for research which placed sexuality and relationship issues in the broader context of people's lives. We also wanted to move away from a research position which saw sexual expression and relationships as problems to be managed to one which could also include the positive aspects of this experience in people's lives.

Our previous experience in working with people with intellectual disabilities had revealed that sexuality and relationships remained contested areas of autonomy for those who worked with them and for their families as well as others in the community. Most of what we knew about these issues from the research literature came from families, workers and other non-disabled adults who were the assumed experts on the lives of people with intellectual disabilities. This tended to produce research that reflected and recreated societal discourse that denied that people with intellectual disabilities are capable of, or have the right to, sexual pleasure.

However these were researcher interests. If we were to work *with* people with intellectual disabilities it was important to check if they were also concerned about these issues. Using our networks, we invited people with an intellectual disability, service providers and advocates to a meeting at ARCSHS, La Trobe University. We asked those present to tell us if there was a need for research about sexuality and relationships and if so, how we should go about it. The unanimous message from the meeting was that there was a need for research in which people with intellectual disabilities contributed their own stories of love, sex and relationships. People were also strongly of the view that these should be in people's own words. People with intellectual disabilities commented that they were never asked about decisions in relation to sexuality.

It took two years from that time to satisfy our funding body that the research could be done. Doubts were expressed about whether people with intellectual disabilities had stories to tell and whether they could tell them. It then took another three years to carry out the two phases of the research. A reference group was established at the beginning of the project which included people with intellectual disabilities, advocates, workers and researchers.

Phase One of the research involved finding and supporting 25 people (13 women and 12 men) with an intellectual disability to tell the stories of sex, love and relationships in their lives. The stories were told to qualitative researchers over an extended period of time, were taped, transcribed, and written as stories which were then taken back to the original story-tellers for checking.

In Phase Two the researchers and the reference group analysed the stories for key themes and then developed strategies from them that would assist people with intellectual disabilities to lead safer sexual lives. These included the development, implementation and evaluation of workshops for people with intellectual disabilities, service providers and families (now published as a training manual, see Frawley et al., 2003) and work with advocacy organisations and the State Government to rewrite relevant policy and efforts to reduce the isolation of people with intellectual disabilities.

Living safer sexual lives: including people with intellectual disabilities

The overview gives a deceptively simple picture of the way this research project developed. We found that there were particular challenges which needed to be met in order to undertake the work according to the principles which had been established with the reference group at the beginning of the project.

Guiding principles of the research

Researchers initially developed a number of principles to guide the research and these were then modified through consultation with service providers and people with intellectual disabilities:

- Our research should be based on respect for the participants.
- Fostering partnerships between the academic institutions and the community should be a priority.
- Participation of people with intellectual disabilities was essential to the project.
- Unwaged workers and story-tellers should be paid for their contribution to the project.
- Story-tellers should be supported psychologically and emotionally in telling their stories.
- Interviewers should be supported emotionally and structurally in work which we knew would be demanding.
- The research should be designed to minimise possible psychological, emotional or physical harm to the story-tellers.
- Sexuality should be placed in the wider context of people's lives.
- The project should be designed with an awareness of the sensitive and intimate nature of sexuality.
- The stories should be in the participants' own words.
- The project should be based on the stated needs of people with intellectual disabilities.
- Action should accompany the research and be directed at changing oppressive policies, practices and social structures and at increasing awareness of the issues facing people with intellectual disabilities.

(Johnson et al., 2001: 29)

Social challenges

Many of the challenges of this research were contextual, having little to do with intellectual disability per se, but rather with the negative ways that these men and women had been situated within our community. Essentially we found that many of the difficulties they experienced had to do with the socially disabling barriers identified by theorists who have described them in terms of the 'social model of disability' (Barnes, 1998; Barnes, Oliver and Barton, 2002).

Sexuality is often discouraged as a topic of conversation in the general population, however, this is even more the case for people who have an intellectual disability who are taught that talk about sex and sexual behaviours is unacceptable and should be confined to the private domain if at all. In our research, this was especially so for those people (about half) who had spent time in institutions and who had experienced severe punishments for the expression of sexual feelings, including the incarceration and drugging of one man after it was discovered that he had established a sexual relationship with one of the women residents. For this reason alone finding people who felt comfortable to talk about their experiences was very difficult.

We distributed a flier (put together by a member of the reference group) to the main disability groups in Victoria and included a paragraph about the research in a number of their newsletters. We also appeared on radio programmes for people with an intellectual disability, urging people to contact us if they were interested in being a part of the research. None of these strategies was successful in finding people to tell their stories and we realised we needed to take the next step of speaking to potential participants in person by attending advocacy and support groups to talk about the research. This strategy was successful because men and women at those meetings were able to make personal contact with researchers, hear about the research, have their questions answered and their fears allayed. Without this first important step, there would have been no people to tell their stories. However, this method was time consuming for the researchers.

People with an intellectual disability are rarely encouraged to express their feelings or to talk about their lives. People were sometimes anxious about our responses to their stories and sometimes found them difficult to tell, both because of the emotional content of the stories and sometimes because of the person's disability. Consequently, the process of gathering people's stories for this project was time consuming and labour and resource intensive. We met with each story-teller five times, (an introductory visit, three sessions to gather the stories and a fifth visit to take the story back to the story-teller for approval) with each session lasting between one and a half hours and half a day.

People with an intellectual disability are often very resource poor and find transport expensive and difficult. As a result we needed to negotiate suitable venues for them that were not only convenient, but also were places in which they felt safe and comfortable. In some cases this meant going to their homes, in others, to parks or other public spaces.

Gatekeepers were sometimes a problem in the process. We were keen for the interviews to be confidential and for the details about the research to be kept private as well. At times a family member or a worker at the person's residence wanted to sit in on the interview or be given more information than we felt was reasonable. In these cases we stood our ground and emphasised the importance of the privacy of the process.

Process challenges

In addition to the external challenges which resulted from attitudes and experiences unrelated to our research, we also found that we needed to rethink old ways of doing research to find new ways that suited our people with intellectual disabilities.

Reference group meetings proved at first to be a challenge for researchers and community members as each group worked towards better communication with the other. Traditionally, these meetings are often very formal and business like and run to strict timelines. We realised very early when we were challenged about language and procedures that this format would not work. We very soon made sure that there were plain language versions of all documents and we were called to account when we used unnecessary jargon (an account of the process can be found in Harrison et al., 2002). We often used working groups to explore issues in a more in-depth way and over a period of months worked in small groups to analyse the stories during reference group meetings.

At our first meeting with story-tellers we tried to ensure that their consent was informed and voluntary, by encouraging them to bring along an advocate. We prepared plain English statements about the research and made sure that everyone had a copy. People who could not give informed consent were not included in the research. This had a number of implications. It meant that the story-tellers generally had mild to moderate disabilities. We also excluded people who were currently living in institutions as we were unsure whether confidentiality could be sustained.

At times a person's disability meant that communication was slow and difficult. Moreover, in order to ensure an accurate representation and protect confidentiality, transcription of the audiotapes was done by the interviewers (not a professional transcriber). In the second interview, the transcript of the first interview was read out to the story-tellers to help them remember what they had already said and to give them context for the next session. They also had the opportunity at this point to change anything about which they were unhappy.

In order to protect the integrity of the research process and the well-being of the interviewers, each of the four interviewers was assigned a mentor from the research team. Mentors read the transcript of the first interview and helped plan the second interview. They were there for support in planning subsequent interviews and to debrief with interviewers if they needed it.

We were very conscious that many people may have had bad sexual experiences for which they may have received little support. We included within our budget money for counselling and arranged a 24 hour turn around with a sexual counselling service for any storytellers who wished to make use of it. We found that no one did, probably because most people who were willing to tell their story had managed to resolve their issues.

The research necessarily involved establishing relationships and trust and we realised quite early in the project that this could not be the traditional distanced relationship one expects in research. People were lonely, and though we were careful to keep talking about the limits of the research in terms of contact, it was often a struggle for both parties to disengage. We also undertook tasks that lay outside the research, for example, making a phone call, explaining a document for matters outside the research or providing support on a larger life issue. In some cases, a relationship has continued in some form, for example one of the researchers continues to attend the plays in which one of the story-teller performs.

Living safer sexual lives: conclusion

The stories told as part of this project were extraordinary and have challenged the preconceptions and attitudes of all who have read them. They were devastating, joyful, painful and triumphant. We also learned from this research that to include people who are marginalised in society means not that they must be subject to our research assumptions and processes but that we must learn to include them and to change the way in which we view our own research both in terms of content and process.

Mothers with intellectual disabilities: beginnings

The project about motherhood and women with intellectual disabilities was a four year project carried out between 1996 and 2000 (Sigurjónsdóttir and Traustadóttir, 2000, 2001; Traustadóttir and Sigurjónsdóttir, 2004, 2005). The project was not initiated by researchers but arose from the concerns of women with intellectual disabilities. In 1994 we interviewed a young woman leader in the Icelandic self-advocacy movement. We wanted to learn about her leadership role. She told us briefly about that aspect of her life but what she really wanted to talk about was motherhood. She was very angry and hurt because her family had recently forced her to have an abortion. They also wanted her to be sterilised which she barely managed to avoid. This young woman was grieving her lost child and trying to come to terms with what she saw as her family's betrayal and violence against her. She was in a stable relationship and considered herself capable of raising a child, she had a strong desire to become a mother.

As we talked to more women in the self-advocacy movement we learned that having children and family life were issues they wanted to put at the top of the agenda in the movement, this was especially true for the young women. None of these women were mothers and they did not necessarily want to have children themselves, but they saw it as extremely important that the movement fought for the right to motherhood and family life, and publicly discussed and protested against sterilisation.

Through our discussions with these women we learned that while growing up they had not been prepared for or given any information about motherhood; everyone assumed they would not have children. Thus, many were not sure what motherhood would entail or if they could cope with raising a child. They wanted to know if we had any knowledge about women with intellectual disabilities as mothers. We were not much help. One of us had a vague recollection of a couple of older women with intellectual disabilities who were mothers but both had their children removed and were subsequently institutionalised. There were no Icelandic studies and we only knew of a couple of studies internationally which indicated that this was a sensitive and contested issue.

After our discussions with these young women and at their urging we decided to apply for funding to conduct a research project that would focus on motherhood and women with intellectual disabilities. Two of the young women leaders from the self-advocacy movement acted as our advisors and assisted us throughout the project. Our applications to Rannís, the Icelandic Research Council, and the University of Iceland's Research Fund were successful and we were ready to begin in 1996.

Mothers with intellectual disabilities: methods and procedures

The research was conducted using qualitative methods (Taylor and Bogdan, 1998). Over a period of four years we did long-term participant observations and interviews with 30 women with intellectual disabilities. The research focused primarily on motherhood. Some of the women were mothers, others were not. We wanted to explore how a wide range of women with intellectual disabilities thought about motherhood, including those who did not have children themselves. It was important to know the meaning of motherhood for women who had children, as well as for those who did not. This chapter is primarily concerned with the mothers who participated in the study.

The mothers were a diverse group from three generations: (1) elderly mothers in their late 70s and early 80s – their children were born around the 1950s and were middle aged at the time of the study. (2) middle-aged mothers in their 40s whose children were teenagers or young adults. (3) young mothers in their 20s and early 30s who had young children of pre-school and school age. To learn about their lives in context we spent time with them, their children, partners, extended family members, and on some occasions, support workers and professionals who provided services to the mothers. Additionally, we interviewed three of the adult children of the oldest generation.

We considered it important to have long-term involvement with the mothers. This was the first research with mothers with intellectual disabilities in Iceland and we wanted to make sure we 'got it right' and gained in-depth knowledge of their lives. We wanted to understand things from their perspective. In order to do this we spent a period of a few months up to a few years with each of the mothers and took part in their everyday lives. Because we stayed in touch with the women over such a long period of time we observed many changes in their lives: children being born, children entering pre-school and school, moves to new homes, divorce, changes in support services, service workers coming and going, changes in the support from extended family and so on.

Focusing on three generations of mothers allowed us to explore how the possibility of motherhood and family life for women with intellectual disabilities had developed over a period of 50 years (from 1950 when the oldest generation was having children to the year 2000 when we finished the study). The study showed that things had changed for the better and we found that women with intellectual disabilities could, with appropriate supports, be successful as mothers (Sigurjónsdóttir and Traustadóttir, 2000, 2001; Traustadóttir and Sigurjónsdóttir, 2004). However, despite these research findings and the positive developments, we also found that mothers with intellectual disabilities continued to be faced with negative attitudes from non-disabled people, who most commonly presumed that people with intellectual disabilities lacked the competence to be good-enough parents. These findings were consistent with studies in other countries (Andron and Tymchuk, 1987; Booth and Booth, 1994, 1998; Feldman, 1994; Llewellyn, 1990; 1995).

From the outset of the study we encountered widespread notions of presumed incompetence and negative attitudes towards this group of mothers from professionals and from the general public. The mothers were aware of this and lived in constant fear of losing custody of their children, and they were suspicious and scared of strangers who might report them to child protection services. Due to this, many of them tried to be as invisible as possible in order not to draw attention to themselves and their children. At the outset this made it difficult for us to find mothers for the study. We learned that they were, indeed, an invisible group of women. No one kept records of them and no one knew how many they were.

We had two main ways to find mothers to participate in the study; through professionals who worked with them or who knew them, and through mutual friends and acquaintances. If we went through professionals it usually took a long time to gain their trust because the mothers feared we were spying on them and would report them to the system. When we approached the mothers through people they knew and trusted it took much shorter time to be accepted and trusted.

The findings of the study were published in a book (Sigurjónsdóttir and Traustadóttir, 2001). When the study was written up, everything about each mother and her family was read to her to make sure she approved of what was being said. The most important goal of the book was to challenge the prejudice and discrimination so commonly experienced by mothers with intellectual disabilities and our primary target group were the professionals who had such life defining powers over the families. We also found it important to reach people with intellectual disabilities. In order to make the book accessible to at least some of them, the findings were presented in two versions; besides writing the book in regular Icelandic, one of the chapters contained the main findings of the study written in easy-to-read language and larger print.

Mothers with intellectual disabilities: methodological challenges

Working on this project presented many methodological challenges including finding and gaining access to participants from such an invisible and marginalised group, earning the trust of the mothers, keeping confidentiality and more. The space available in this chapter only allows a brief discussion of two of these challenges; researching sensitive and contested topics, and working with inarticulate women.

Researching contested and sensitive topics

The project focused on sensitive and personal topics. Many of the mothers had gone through difficult experiences, some had had their children removed from their care, two of the mothers had also experienced the death of a child, two mothers had been institutionalised and one forcibly moved to a group home after losing custody of her two sons. All of these were painful experiences to talk about. We also discussed experiences related to the mothers' disability. Some found it difficult to discuss the stigmatizing label of 'intellectual disability' in relation to themselves as they did not view themselves in those terms, while others carried this label with pride. We also talked about issues such as sexuality, sterilisation and abortion. Some of the women found it hard to talk about these topics and cried when recalling difficult experiences. However, we also found that in some cases the mothers spoke openly and frankly about sensitive issues and it was rather we, the researchers, who found these topics difficult. We learned that we tended to project our insecurities, fears and emotions on to the women in the study and realised how important it is, when researching sensitive and emotionally charged topics, to be in touch with our own feelings and fears.

Learning from inarticulate women

Most researchers working with people with intellectual disabilities are faced with challenges related to participants who have limited ability to articulate their experiences (Biklen and Mosely, 1988, Booth and Booth, 1998). This was also the case in our research and we quickly learned that asking the classic open-ended qualitative interview questions did not work for most of the women. Instead, we had to ask clear, specific questions in plain language. We also learned to make use of family albums and other visual aids to help when talking to the women. In fact, we found that interviews were not a good way of collecting data. The method that best suited our study was participant observation. This meant that we spent much time with the women going through everyday life with them and their families. Nothing could replace this direct and personal contact which enabled us to get to know the women, build trust with them and learn about aspects of their lives and experiences that would not have been accessible in any other way. The downside was that participant observation is a very time-consuming method.

Conclusion: mothers with intellectual disabilities

Perhaps the single-most important thing learned from this project is that if we want our research to be a tool for social justice and change for marginalised groups we have to collaborate with them. We must learn the art of listening in order to hear what are important issues to explore, respect marginalised people and their experiences and include them in all stages of the research process.

Concluding remarks

People who have been labelled with an intellectual disability find it difficult to gain acceptance by community members, families or peers as sexual and/or reproductive subjects. Historically the reason behind this can be traced to the eugenics movements of the late nineteenth and early twentieth centuries, which positioned people with intellectual disabilities as immoral, antisocial and unproductive, and likely to produce offspring who also suffered from an intellectual disability (Trent, 1994).

Research practice which positions professionals as the experts on people with intellectual disabilities, and people with intellectual disabilities as having no insight about their lives tends to reflect and recreate societal discourses which deny that people with intellectual disabilities are capable of and have the right to live sexual lives and become parents. Society's exclusion of people with intellectual disabilities from the sexual arena, from marriage and parenthood is a reflection of the assumption that these are areas out of reach for disabled people and denies them common human needs and emotions. Our research projects indicate that the most significant difference between people with intellectual disabilities and other marginalised groups is perhaps the fact that what are generally seen as fundamental needs and rights for *all* are forbidden or contested when it comes to people with intellectual disabilities.

Disabled feminist Liz Crow (1996) writes that 'when personal experience no longer matches current explanations, then it is time to question afresh' (56). The two research projects described in this chapter suggest that there is the real possibility that by focusing only on the perspectives of the 'caretakers' of people with intellectual disabilities, much of past research may have produced a fanciful story which has little resemblance to the experiences of this group of people and therefore little relevance to their lives except to promote negative stereotypes, misery, exclusion and discrimination.

4

Research in a Post-colonial World: The Example of Australian Aborigines

Jon Willis and Mark Saunders

Introduction

For many of the world's Indigenous populations, a strong antipathy towards research is a common legacy of the colonial era. Colonial authorities and their experts often seemed obsessed with documenting these captive populations – either cataloguing their exoticness or recording their failures to comply with or thrive under colonial rule. Indigenous people have been poked, prodded, measured and photographed; their graves and temples have been robbed and desecrated; their urine, blood, sweat and fingerprints have been sampled; and they have been bothered, queried and harried by every foreign expert under the sun. The challenges for researchers wanting to work with these populations are clear: what research questions, what approaches and methods, what potential outcomes are going to coax these very reluctant populations into participating in research? In this chapter, we examine a range of examples from Aboriginal Australia where research has been successful in terms of both satisfactory processes and outcomes. We particularly explore the use of participatory research techniques, the value of research workers drawn from within the population, the importance of concrete and immediate outcomes, the benefits of building an information or skills exchange into the research and methods to transfer degrees of ownership of each stage of the research to the community being studied.

The most researched people in the world

Dr Paul Ryan, Acting Chief Executive Officer and Public Health Officer, Apunipima Cape York Health Council told the Senate Select Committee on the Administration of Indigenous Affairs at their Cairns meeting of 27 August 2004 that

> We do not need any more research. I think the people at Cape York feel they are the most researched people in the world, and where is the benefit in that? Yet still enormous amounts of dollars are going to universities for people to do their post doctorates et cetera. We also do not need any more delays, because we cannot afford them. Just like more research and policies, delays are luxuries being bought at the expense of the physical and emotional wellbeing of the people who are our first peoples and who represent, I might add, the heritage of all Australians. They add a richness to our national life which is being impaired and is in danger of being lost.
>
> (Official Committee Hansard, 2004: 28)

This feeling of being the most researched people in the world is not unique to the people at Cape York, but is a trope that is often heard from Indigenous peoples around Australia (Coleman, 2000: 1; Blanchard et al., 2000; Smallacombe, 1999; VicHealth Koori Health and Community Development Unit, 2000: 24) and around the world (for the San see Nilles et al., 2001: 4; for the Pima see Tribal Contract Support Cost Technical Amendments of 2000, 2000: 46):

> Maori consider themselves to be one of the most researched people in the world. Often the research has been conducted by non-Maori using scientific and positivistic methods, identifying 'problems' which they consider exist and then providing solutions based on their own worldviews. The outcome of this research has contributed to the marginalisation and disenfranchisement of Maori across all sectors of modern society.
>
> (Wihongi, 2002)

Along with the idea of overrepresentation as the subjects of research, a range of other complex issues are raised in these two quotes, including the idea that the 'answers' to the 'problems' of Indigenous people are already known without the necessity for research, that research is inherently colonialist in that it contributes to the further marginalisation and disenfranchisement of Indigenous people, and that the only way to avoid inflicting further iniquitous enquiry on already disadvantaged people is to hand the research enterprise over to Indigenous people themselves so that they can conduct it according to styles that frame the research questions, methods and results in terms that do not perpetuate further disadvantage. In this chapter, we argue that these views are both right and wrong. Ryan's cynical view of the dubious benefits of research, although comprehensible, is nevertheless incorrect: the people of Cape York are not the most researched in the world – that privilege probably belongs to white, middle-class North Americans – and the nature of their unique and significant social and health problems is not well understood, nor are the solutions to problems obvious. His frustration, and by extension that of many Indigenous people, reflects an experience of poorly designed, overly intrusive or inferior research that fails to lead to improvement, and research that stands in place of action. The first lesson to learn from this experience is that research with Indigenous people should be *necessary*. It should be conducted with methods that have strong surface validity, and it should aim to bring both immediate and long-term benefits to participants.

A second part of this idea is that the necessity, the validity and the benefits need to be framed in terms that are relevant to the Indigenous people who are being studied. Knowing that a research project that intrudes on their lives may benefit mankind in the long run, or that advances human knowledge, or that simply allows their story to be told is insufficient. Such benefits are far less palatable to the average person, Indigenous or not, than a project whose benefits are immediate or foreseeable to them or people like them. This does not mean that the researcher should imaginatively dream up possible immediate benefits – a mistake often made on ethics approval applications. If there is no benefit to participants, this should be stated upfront and clearly and the researchers should prepare themselves for their project to be rejected; usually it means that the project needs to go back to the drawing board and be redesigned in a way that does provides some locally relevant benefit. We are not saying that research that does not benefit participants should not be done. Often a lack of immediate benefit can be traded off against benefits from the way research is done: somebody from the community might get training, participants might be recompensed in some way for the annoyance or inconvenience of participating (for example, a community barbeque, a CD voucher, a T-shirt or other payment to participants), or a community feedback session or report might be built in to the writing-up component of the project. However, such compensation should not be used to 'sell' research that has no point, and the point of research should be clear in terms that are comprehensible in local economies of knowledge as well as in academic circles. There is a lesson to be learned from the experience of Worth and

Adair who relate the experience of approaching a senior Navajo man, Sam Yazzie, with the view of enlisting his support for the film project that they discuss in their book, *Through Navajo Eyes* (Worth and Adair, 1972):

> Adair explained that we wanted to teach some Navajo to make movies .... When Adair finished, Sam thought for a while, and then turned to Worth and asked a lengthy question which was interpreted as, 'Will making movies do the sheep any harm?' Worth was happy to explain that as far as he knew, there was no chance that making movies would harm the sheep. Sam thought this over and then asked, 'Will making movies do the sheep good?' Worth was forced to reply that as far as he knew making movies wouldn't do the sheep any good. Sam thought this over, then, looking around at us he said, 'Then why make movies?' Sam Yazzie's question keeps haunting us.
>
> (Worth and Adair, 1972: 4–5)

A second notion embedded in the Ryan and Wihongi quotes above is that research is inherently colonialist in that it contributes to the further marginalisation and disenfranchisement of Indigenous people. This reflects not only the experience of Indigenous communities with bad research, but also post-colonialist theory. Following Spivak (1988) among others, the idea is that research cannot help but frame the investigator as the authoritative representative of subaltern experience to the detriment of those whose experience is colonised via representation within 'persistent colonial hierarchies of knowledge and value' (Gandhi, 1998: 7). Mick Dodson, the Aboriginal Social Justice Commissioner and academic, suggests that the gaze of the coloniser and that of the researcher are inextricably linked when he writes: 'Since their first intrusive gaze, colonising cultures have had a preoccupation with observing, analysing, studying, classifying and labelling Aborigines and Aboriginality. Under that gaze, Aboriginality changed from being a daily practice to being "a problem to be solved"' (Dodson, 2003: 27). Colonisation, in this view, invents both the problematic Other and from this invention derives an investigative and classifying apparatus that can only respond to the unknown in terms that further compound both difference and difficulty. Further, Marcia Langton argues that there is a range of possible racisms in the way that Indigenous people are represented on film, but which could also stand for the way that they appear in research: 'The easiest and most "natural" form of racism in representation is the act of making the other invisible. Indeed, racism can provide a complete and satisfying comprehension of black identity (which is why it persists) and one that is linked to the viewer's ideological framework' (Langton, 1993: 25). Aboriginal philosopher Aileen Moreton-Robinson argues that differences in representations are fundamental and relate to the different subject positions that Indigenous and non-Indigenous people occupy in historical context, and reflect different positions in 'the historicity of interconnected relationships of domination and contestation' (Moreton-Robinson, 2000: xxii). Her view emphasises recognizing the importance of these differences because such representations are not just symbols, but pattern the way that Indigenous and non-Indigenous people understand and perform embodied reality. Representations – and by extension misrepresentations – can drive material change. Researchers see this in action when their work feeds into public policy and practice.

Michaels (1990: 18) has argued that the possibilities for misunderstanding and misrepresentation occur in communication with Indigenous people because such communication belongs to a class of what sociolinguists call 'asymmetrical speech events in which interpretations are not efficiently shared. These are communications across class boundaries or between persons of unequal status' (see also Bernstein, 1971; Labov, 1972). Michaels suggests that in such communications, participants' interpretations of a speech event (say, an interview) and of the meaning of what is said during it are different for participants from divergent social situations. So all manner of social stratifications, not only race and historical positioning in a colonial setting can affect the capacity for discourse during research processes. As Michaels puts it

> Social structures (class, gender, ideology, associational divisions) are not just abstract matrices; they imply conditions for who is likely to speak to whom (when, under what circumstances, via what channels, etc.). It is my thesis here that the general limits to shared meaning ... conform with associational grouping, consequences perhaps of the relations of production (and consumption?) in society which may be described, with varying accuracy, as social or class structures. Thus, an Aboriginal extended family, or a group of auto mechanics, an office of executives or a congregation of Pentecostal Christians, or an ethnic community, who work together, socialize together, etc., will tend to evolve similar interpretations of, for example, a TV program. But between groups who do not meet in symmetrical social discourse, interpretations may continue to vary.
>
> (Michaels, 1990: 18)

Does this mean that the only choices that are open to the non-Indigenous researcher are to misrepresent the experience of Indigenous people by classifying it in colonialist terms that diminish its intrinsic nature and importance, to render all Indigenous experience problematic because of its distinctive features; or to render all difference invisible by reframing it as a variety of non-Indigenous experience? Many Indigenous thinkers would argue that this is the case: non-Indigenous accounts of Indigenous lives and experience by definition cannot help but misrepresent:

> Representational and aesthetic statements of Aboriginal people by non-Aboriginal people transform the Aboriginal reality. They are *accounts*. It is these representations that Aboriginal as subject becomes, under the white gaze imagining the Aboriginal, the object. The audience, however, might be entirely unaware that they are observing an *account*, usually by the authorial We of the Other. The creative efforts ... to represent some particular Aboriginal 'reality', even if there is an attempt at involving the Aboriginal subject in the production, is always a fictionalisation, an act of creative authority.
>
> (Langton, 1993: 40)

Even where the representation is by an Indigenous person, the ways in which research is produced for public consumption through publication can take control of the final form of the publication out of Indigenous hands so that it becomes a misrepresentation. Historian Jackie Huggins has critiqued the presentation of Sally Morgan's *My Place* in just these terms:

> And for Pete's sake, why are all the good bits, that is, the oral histories, in the back of the book instead of the front? The family's testimonies are the book's only strength. Not placing them in the significant first position reads like power, control and subjugation over incredibly beautiful narratives. And that jumbled bit in the middle appeared as if white editorial intervention had reared its ugly head yet again. It just didn't fit. As a Black writer I could not understand nor find a path through this maze of Anglified hyperbole. Overall there is little which indicates the writing and story of an Aboriginal. I would swear white editorial intervention has desecrated the text.
>
> (Huggins, 2003: 63)

In the rest of this chapter, we look at ways of reducing the possibility for misrepresentation of Indigenous people and their experience in research, drawing particularly from the practical experience of the authors in this field. Many of these methods rely on developing teams of researchers that include both Indigenous and non-Indigenous researchers, or with the use of Indigenous reference groups in the development of data-collection methods, styles and techniques of analysis and for suggesting and checking the appropriateness of the interpretation of results. These methods are suggested not only by the social justice value of including Indigenous people in research as a way of diminishing the colonising impact of research. They are also suggested by the value of integrated Indigenous input into research methodologies as a technique for reducing the possibilities for misunderstanding and misrepresentation. As Moreton-Robinson puts it, in relation to feminist analysis:

> An Indigenous woman's standpoint is informed by social worlds imbued with meaning grounded in knowledges of different realities from those of white women. ... All indigenous women share the common experience of living in a society that deprecates us. An Indigenous woman's standpoint is shaped by the following themes. They include sharing an inalienable connection to land; a legacy of dispossession, racism and sexism; resisting and replacing disparaging images of ourselves with self-defined images; continuing our activism as mothers, sisters, aunts, daughters, grandmothers and community leaders, as well as negotiating sexual politics across and within culture. Such a standpoint does not deny the diversity of Indigenous women's experiences. Indigenous women will have different concrete experiences that shape our relations to core themes.
>
> (Moreton-Robinson, 2000: xvi)

Successful methods for working with Indigenous people

In his book, *Collaborative Research Stories*, Russell Bishop argues that good collaborative research between Maori and Pakeha (and by extension between all Indigenous and non-Indigenous people) has a basis in Indigenous self-determination. Good collaborative research, in Bishop's terms, occurs within *whakawhanaungatanga* – a Maori word meaning literal and metaphorical *whanau* (i.e extended family) and their processes (Bishop, 1996: 216). That is, the research team is composed of outside researchers and members of the community who form a *whanau* or family-like group

members of a cognatic descent group of limited depth who participate in an ongoing and occasional basis in activities of a corporate nature;

land, marae, knowledge. They will usually identify themselves as members of a *whanau* bearing the name of the founding ancestor. Membership is flexible and the collectivity can survive membership change.

The term can cover a 'kin cluster', a group of kin who regularly co-operate for common ends and accept a variety of kin or quasi-kin limits as the basis for recruitment for the purposes of carrying out the research, with each member assigned a kin-like place within the group. Using *whanau* in a metaphoric way to identify a research group means that a series of rights and responsibilities, commitments and obligations and supports that are fundamental to the collectivity are identified. These are the

> *tikanga* of the *whanau*; warm interpersonal interactions, group solidarity, shared responsibility for one another, cheerful co-operation for group ends, corporate responsibility for group property, material or non-material (e.g. knowledge) items and issues. These attributes can be summed up in the words *aroha* (love in the broadest sense), *awhi* (helpfulness), *manaaki* (hospitality), *tiaki* (guidance).
>
> (Bishop, 1996: 218)

These acknowledged processes and practices then govern the conduct of the research, as well as formalised hierarchies that are drawn from equivalent positions within literal *whanau*. Management of the research comes to be in the hands of those who by tradition and through descent are oriented towards the collaborative concerns, interests and benefits of the *whanau* as a group, rather than those of just one or two individuals.

Entering into structures such as *whakawhanaungatanga* with a community for the purposes of research can guarantee that research will proceed in different ways and at a different pace than in situations where the researcher, or worse, their institution or funding body, is in charge of how the research is done. In Australia, some similar approaches have been taken in the conduct of research with Aboriginal communities, though perhaps without the degree of formal structuring of the Maori example. Willis (1997) conducted his PhD research on blood-borne disease transmission risk within Pitjantjatjara men's secret ceremonies while becoming an initiate of the ceremonies himself, and his research was conducted according to the strictures of Pitjantjatjara ceremonial law and bound by his junior position within that law. His work was guided by the Pitjantjatjara philosophy of cross-cultural joint work used in the management of Uluru-Kata Tjuta National Park: *tjunguringkula* waakaripai, or 'always working together' (Tjamiwa and Willis, 1992). These strictures affected the way he was able to record data, limited the detail which he could include in his thesis, determined the way that the University of Queensland had to deal with the examination of the thesis and governed the disposition of the thesis once examined. Willis, his thesis supervisors, the University's Dean of Postgraduate Studies, the three male thesis examiners and the librarians at the University's Fryer Library all entered into formal agreements that made concessions to Willis' responsibilities as an initiate for how Pitjantjatjara ceremonial knowledge was to be managed through the PhD process. As with many collaborative research efforts, the collaboration did not end when the thesis was completed. His Pitjantjatjara collaborators have continued to make use of Willis' expert knowledge developed through the doctoral research, calling on him at various times to provide recommendations to their health services on the management of ceremonial injuries and the promotion of condoms, and asking him to give evidence about what he learned in a number of Native Title court cases. The research process, like the kinship relationship, remains open-ended.

Not all researchers are able or willing to develop kin-like relationships with communities in order to conduct research; not all communities want to adopt every researcher they work with; nor do all projects warrant such a fundamental reframing of researcher's personal and professional identity or community membership. Other methods have been successfully used to provide a solid and reliable basis for collaborative work to proceed. Partnership with a community-based organisation is one excellent method for proceeding. The Victorian Aboriginal Community-Controlled Health Organisation (VACCHO), for example, has developed memoranda of understanding with mainstream groups that acknowledge mutual goals and processes that guide collaborative work processes, as well as deal with potentially thorny issues such as acknowledgement and control of Indigenous intellectual property, and an equal distribution of power with the relationship (Waples-Crow and Pyett, 2005). Elements of the relationship that Waples-Crow and Pyett identify as key to a successful partnership include a long time-frame, building trust, valuing each other, getting educated about Aboriginal culture, good planning that involves all stakeholders, a useful project; a community-initiated project, identifying the partners and formalising the relationships, supportive work environments and cultural awareness and sensitivity (Waples-Crow and Pyett, 2005: 14–15). Many of these elements are interrelated – building trust can only happen when relationships develop over a long time-frame, and with mutual cultural awareness and sensitivity.

If there is no obvious community-based organisation to collaborate with, inviting community leaders to form a reference group for a project can also provide a solid base for working with Indigenous communities, provided the researchers have sufficient expertise to convince potential reference group members that the project is viable. An easy way to do this is to employ an Indigenous researcher as a leader within the research team. Both the Queensland AIDS Council (QuAC) and the Australian Research Centre in Sex, Health and Society (ARCSHS) have used this approach to pursue collaborative work with larger groups of Indigenous people than are encompassed within discrete communities. Both organisations employed an experienced Indigenous community development worker, Mark Saunders, as a key member of their research teams to guide the development of their reference groups as well as providing advice and insights throughout the research process. At QuAC, Saunders was asked to develop a strategy that would engage Indigenous communities in South-east Queensland in the effort to reduce HIV transmission among Indigenous gay men. Saunder's approach focused on winning approval and support from opinion and moral leaders within the broader Indigenous community by encouraging elders from Southern Queensland to attend the Minjerriba Elders' forum to discuss Indigenous sexuality and sexual health. The aim of the project was community-initiated in the broadest sense, in that it derived from the National Indigenous Australians' Sexual Health Strategy and the National Indigenous Gay and Transgender Health Strategy, both of which grew out of extensive community consultation. The intention of the workshop was to develop and test a collaborative method that would allow Indigenous people to openly discuss sexual health issues as a foundation for sustained behaviour change assisting in the reduction of HIV and sexually transmitted infections (STI) transmission. During the three-day forum, information was provided to Elders on HIV/AIDS and the immune system, testing for HIV and confidentiality associated with testing and treating STIs. Presentations were given on treatments, gay youth, suicide and drug use (Gallagher 1999). The forum provided a sound base on which Indigenous programmes at QuAC were based for some years, and ensured community support for future QuAC initiatives.

At ARCSHS, Saunders and his colleagues, Willis and Anderson, have used a similar method to research the impact of high rates of mortality in their community on Indigenous men's ideas of health and health care, and gay Indigenous men's experience of racist, homophobic and sexual violence. In the men's health project, a group of male leaders were invited to join a reference group. Each discussed the research topic in an open-ended way with Saunders to identify main issues, and quotes from these interview-discussions (or Yarns to use the local term) were then used as points for discussion in a group discussion with the whole reference group. The transcript of the group discussion provided further quotes to form a list of discussion points for open-ended discussions with other individual men outside the reference group. Each 'yarn' was recorded and transcribed. The iterative nature of the methodological development meant that men were never interrogated by an interviewer, but drawn into a discussion of issues that had been raised by a member of their community. Also, the interpretation of the issues was carried out through group processes by members of the community. A similar process was used to explore issues of violence with gay men: each member of a reference group yarned with Saunders about how they saw the issues; then quotes from the individual discussions were used as discussion points during a group workshop conducted over a weekend away at a country retreat. Again, this was recorded and transcribed, and further quotes drawn from the transcript which were used as discussion points for a second weekend retreat with a group of gay Indigenous men.

The initiation of research projects with Indigenous people is often the most difficult step, and how research is initiated and by whom can be the critical determinants in whether a project is successful. A key point to remember is that research questions should reflect community needs and priorities rather than simply researcher curiosity, always acknowledging that research is rarely a priority for communities, and that setting research priorities may be a task that communities need assistance with. If the research questions are already set, as with some government-initiated research, then development of proposals should be done collaboratively with the community, a task made much easier if there is an existing relationship to work on. Such existing relationships can be established by researchers doing pro-bono tasks for the community, for example by working on programme evaluations, drafting community reports, or performing needs analyses. Raelene Fennell, the Health Promotion Coordinator at Dja Dja Wrung Aboriginal Co-operative in Bendigo has described a process used to research health needs prior to negotiating a Health Outcomes Agreement with the Victorian Department of Human Services:

Some research that was done in Bendigo resulted in a report called the Health Needs Analysis. Marc Williams [a Koori researcher] put that report together and he was employed at Dja Dja Wrung and worked in conjunction with the Department of Human Services. He did a survey of our local Community in Bendigo, and that covered Castlemaine, Heathcote and Maryborough. Marc put out a survey of questions in December 1997 and people were asked to fill out that survey. The answers highlighted what our health needs were.

So we approached five agencies: GP Divisions, Bendigo Health Care Group, Council, Loddon Mallee Women's Health Service, and Community Health Bendigo. At first we were unsure of how we were going to approach these agencies, but we thought we'd send them a letter and try and get representatives from each of those organisations. So we got them to a meeting in December 1998. At this meeting we were asked to show evidence for why we wanted the things we were asking for. What they instantly wanted was data. At that time we did not have a copy of the Health Needs Analysis. So we set up another meeting and this time we made sure we had the report of the Health Needs Analysis with us, because they didn't want to discuss anything until we had information and data to prove what we were asking for. So we handed them the report and they read through that. I was the head of the negotiating group with these five agencies. Every time we met we talked about what we could achieve from working together. Each of the other organisations wanted to get something out of working with us and we wanted something from each of them. What we talked about needing for our Community came out of the Health Needs Analysis. That report backed up what we were asking for. If it was approached the right way, people from the other organisations would come back and make suggestions. It was a lot of hard work while we were doing it. We signed off on the Health Outcomes Agreement on the 30th of August 1999.

(VicHealth Koori Health and Community
Development Unit, 2000: 13–14)

Where there is no predetermined agenda, research questions should ideally be framed collaboratively. Paul Stewart, a Research Officer at the Victorian Aboriginal Health Service in Melbourne has described the

genesis of the Young People's Project, a longitudinal study of the health
of young urban Aboriginal people:

> The Young People's Project came out of an evaluation of the Child
> Health Promotion Project that was done in about 1994/95. A part of
> the Child Health Promotion Project evaluation was to go back to the
> Community and ask them what was the next thing we should be
> looking at in relation to health. And the Community came up with:
> young people and drug use in the Community. So we started in 1996
> with collecting information from focus group discussions with a
> number of people, especially young Kooris who were homeless,
> employed, unemployed, and at school. We also interviewed key
> people.
>
> (VicHealth Koori Health and Community
> Development Unit, 2000: 15)

Both of these projects were carried out by community-controlled health
organisations, and Salina Bernard, Chair of the Victorian Aboriginal
Health Service Health Research Ethics Committee in Melbourne has
described the value of locating research within such organisations:

> I found that Aboriginal Community controlled research is the most
> beneficial research that can be done because it has the involvement,
> commitment and the participation of the local people which can
> open up the doors for the researchers. Without those people and
> those networks and that commitment, the research is going to go
> nowhere and you are going to have poor research findings. You are
> going to have research that provides you with information that is
> wrong, that is usually documented in a way that is biased and does-
> n't represent the views and needs of the people being researched.
> Generally this is pretty poor research and just shouldn't be done.
> Negotiating with Aboriginal people to undertake the research is
> essential, getting them involved and employing them as Research
> Assistants, so they are involved in the whole process of research: they
> are involved in the planning, they are involved from the very begin-
> ning, from that you get an easier path to research.
>
> (VicHealth Koori Health and Community
> Development Unit, 2000: 20)

There are a range of other issues to consider before committing to
research with Indigenous people. Indigenous research may require

extended timelines, and the processes involved in developing relationships needs to be built into these timelines. Researchers may have to do the bulk of the process work in the early stages of any relationship, because, again, research is rarely a priority, and setting research priorities may be even less of a priority for communities and their organisations. There needs to be a mutual acknowledgement from the outset of all and competing interests, and some resolution of these interests in a formal way if necessary. This avoids arguments and bad feelings down the track. By a formal way, we mean memoranda of understanding, or at least an exchange of letters setting out expectations and responsibilities. For example, it is usually good practice to deal up front with matters relating to storage of the data and issues of publication. As Esme Saunders puts it in relation to health research with Victoria's Koori communities:

All Koori research projects should begin from the assumption that: research material and data will remain the property of the Koori Community concerned; projects may only be conducted according to principles negotiated and agreed with Koori Communities at the outset; prior to the publication of research data or reports, the approval of the publication texts by the relevant designated consultative Koori organisation is required; publication of the research data will include details of the joint university/community context of the research and the role of the Koori Community in formulating the direction and work of the project.

(VicHealth Koori Health and Community
Development Unit, 2001: 11)

In relation to publication it is also important to think about whose worldviews or voices are represented in the text of the research. This is a process issue that can be affected by such things as: the questions asked; the methods used to collect data; the methods and processes of analysis; stylistic issues of 'voice'; and the fora and format for reporting on the findings of the research. Voice in research texts is also constrained by the nature of the publication, as well as the conditions of its production. We do well to remember Muecke's methodological warning that where tangible benefits of involvement in research do not flow back to the people being researched, the voices of Indigenous people reflected in the research may be significantly muted or even intentionally distorted:

For how long have Aboriginal peoples been cornered in their camps by missionaries, anthropologists and others whose demand has been a constant one for a discourse that would become familiar to Aboriginal people even if it was strange at first: the confession? 'Tell us what you are like', the white institutions seem to be saying, 'sing us your songs once more and tell your stories'. As if the production of discourse can only be aligned with truth or liberation, or at least be a good thing generally. But in the face of this powerful demand, could it be the case that Aboriginal peoples have learnt to retain a judicious silence, only giving out a certain amount of carefully constructed discourse, making sure we are aware that in their economy of discourses the first separation is between the 'public' and the 'secret' and that a great wealth of culture lies below the surface.

(Muecke, 1988: 410–411)

Conclusion

Whether research with Indigenous communities is conducted within relationships forged over a lifetime of mutual respect, or within time-limited associations drawn together for the purposes of a single collaboration, issues of accountability arise for both the members of the research team, particularly the Indigenous members, and for participants in the research enterprise. It is therefore important to determine from the beginning the multiple people and organisations to whom the research is accountable, and have a plan in place for who will disseminate the findings to these people and organisations, and how it will be done. Accountability plans should also include getting permissions right (for example, seeking the approval of relevant community elders, leaders and organisations), as well as acknowledging the need for formal and perhaps multiple ethics processes. There needs to be some thought put into how to deal with a range of cultural sensitivities:

Non-Koori researchers will be required to respect Koori cultural practices which include: 'family' as a centring concept and the various obligations associated with particular kin relationships; personal as distinct from professional relationships in establishing conditions for further interactions; the significance of Elders and Community-based organisations in Community life; the need for extended time-frames in which decisions are made and the collective nature of those decisions; the status of individual autonomy within a cultural system of collective responsibility for social action; the first languages of Kooris as the languages of authentic communication amongst Community members; the concept of 'women's business' and 'men's business'; and the publication of only appropriate pictorial material and texts.

(VicHealth Koori Health and Community
Development Unit, 2001: 10–11)

Some of these potential problem areas can be avoided through a process of 'coming together' to do research – through whakawhanaungatanga, or the Pitjantjatjara equivalent of *tjungurungkula waakaripai* – in a joint effort, for example, between research institution and community organisation, formalised by a memorandum of understanding that defines: who 'owns' or controls the research grant and who controls the workers; issues including publication, copyright and cultural copyright, authorship or other acknowledgement; and appropriate and equitable payment for a variety of expertises including cultural and community expertise. Such processes of coming together should use a framework like that described by Bishop, where five key areas of initiation, benefits, representation, legitimisation and accountability ensure a degree of self-determination for Aboriginal people in collaborative research (Bishop, 1996; cited in Wihongi, 2002: 1).

It is also important that within these research associations, care is taken not to burden Aboriginal team members with providing all the project's legitimation, either to the Aboriginal communities being researched or to the wider world of research consumers. What Marcia Langton has said of film-making is equally true of any research enterprise:

There is a naïve belief that Aboriginal people will make 'better' representations of us, simply because being Aboriginal gives 'greater' understanding. This belief is based on an ancient and universal feature of racism: the assumption of the undifferentiated *Other*. More specifically, the assumption is that all Aborigines are alike and equally understand each other, without regard to cultural variation, history, gender, sexual preference and so on. It is a demand for censorship: there is a 'right' way to be Aboriginal, and any Aboriginal film or video producer will necessarily make a 'true' representation of 'Aboriginality'.

(Langton, 1993: 27)

Research with Aboriginal people needs to be conducted with the highest technical standards, not least because Aboriginal communities' experiences of research in the past has often been bad, and because there are many poor representations of Aboriginal experience evident in the research record. Getting the structure for an Indigenous research project is very important, but ensuring that the structure produces the best possible data is equally important or the efforts of all involved are wasted, and this requires a continuous critical and reflexive examination of the mechanisms that are being used to produce knowledge about Aboriginal experience. Stephen Muecke has noted that Aboriginal experience tends to be defined in advance because of a complex series of apparatuses of exclusion and co-option.

It is defined differently in legal, anthropological, medical and just about every other social sphere. While these (white) constructions of Aboriginality are necessarily artificial, it is also a problem for Aborigines to 'express' a true Aboriginality independently of them. Shrinking from these definitions would tend to vacate a space in which the wheels of 'expression' would spin idly, if that is the theory of representation employed. In practice, however, Aboriginal writers *do* engage with specific issues of representation and control and bring up issues based on their specific knowledges. These unconscious or culturally-subsumed Aboriginal readings should perhaps be articulated in an alternative to the expressive theory of literature. The alternative would combine both attention to texts and to their social conditions of production and circulation as a necessary part of the aesthetic. Rather than seeing the text as a place where the desire to speak is liberated, it could be seen as a site of multiple constraints pertaining both to form and contextual relations. These constraints are not negative, they tend to make sure that a text will have a specific application in renegotiating meanings. That is, if the text is not made to refer back to a self-identical transcendental subject, but to a range of subject positions which can be dynamically entered into. And is there is an awareness of distinctive repertoires of knowledges, different readerships and the ideological pressures which privilege different ways of reading. This is not just a question of adding a 'sociological' dimension to an already adequate literary aesthetic. It is a way of saying that the renegotiation of subject positions, the definition of context and reading and ways of rethinking the idea of 'the book' are all part of a contemporary literary aesthetic in which Aboriginal writing plays a leading part.

(Muecke, 1988: 417–418)

We believe that ideally these continuous critical and reflexive processes are made much easier by structuring research within a collaboration between researchers and the community being researched, and by building possibilities for joint critical reflection into every phase of the research enterprise, from the framing of the initial questions through to the publication of the results of the research.

5

Duty of Care: Researching with Vulnerable Young People

Lynne Hillier, Anne Mitchell and Shelley Mallett

Young people are one of the most regularly researched populations, particularly in the area of health and well-being. Much of this research on young people has, in recent years, focused on identifying those individual and group-based behaviours and practices that place them at risk of harm. Many researchers, reflecting the needs of policymakers and service providers, also seek to identify health promoting behaviours and practices among young people. Research with young people, especially research focused on so-called risky practices, is, however, rarely the simple matter that it might at first appear. When conducting research with young people, researchers must address a range of complex practical and ethical issues, as well as the theory and content that underpins the research design and analysis. For example how will young people be located, accessed and recruited to the study? Will researchers offer participant payments to reimburse young people for their time? Are young people able and/or capable of giving informed consent? Can researchers guarantee confidentiality and anonymity to the young people? What is the duty of care to young people in the study? These issues are particularly challenging for projects which seek to work with marginalised, often invisible, populations of young people who may or may not be legal minors.

Drawing on the experience of teams of researchers at Australian Research Centre in Sex, Health and Society (ARCSHS) this chapter explores some of the practical, ethical issues associated with conducting research focused on young people. First, we consider the challenges and difficulties presented by conducting the research in a particular site – in this case, sexual health research in schools. Second, we examine the particular practical and ethical dilemmas arising in research with two marginalised populations – homeless and same-sex-attracted young people. The challenges of these three situations and how these challenges were met will be explored, as will the common themes which can inform any work with young people.

Researching with young people in schools

Schools are the most common site for research about the broader community of young people. In this site large numbers of young people can be accessed and research outcomes can be readily disseminated. Despite this, work in schools is never unproblematic. Duty of care, issues of consent, fear of doing more harm than good are the key issues which assert themselves in school.

Working in schools

Twice in the past five years a team at ARCSHS has conducted a large sexual health survey of 16 and 18-year-olds in secondary schools in all states and territories of Australia. The sample of eligible schools is carefully drawn to reflect the complex demographics of the Australian school-based population. The geographic distances involved means that no researcher can visit every site to discuss participation and carry out the work. Schools have to be 'cold called' and persuaded to participate. For each school there is a substitute school if all efforts fail, and sometimes a third school if possible. Nevertheless, the task is to create willingness and commitment in schools where none was before. This process is essentially a strategic challenge.

Gatekeepers

Young people are the most strenuously protected population when it comes to any research and when the issue is sexual health then the barriers are really raised. We know that the age of first intercourse for young people has fallen over the past 40 years in Australia from 19 years for women and 18 for men to 16 years of age for both in 2002 (Smith et al., 2003). Approximately 30 per cent of 16-years-olds have had sexual intercourse and 50 per cent of 18-year-olds and large numbers engage in other sexual practices such as deep kissing, genital touching and oral sex (Lindsay et al., 1997; Smith et al., 2003). This makes the need for realistic information on the sexual knowledge attitudes and behaviours of young people even more paramount. Nevertheless, twin and contradictory assumptions play into any request to conduct research with young people in schools. On the one hand, young people are completely innocent and should not hear of any sexual matters, and on the other hand, once they do hear there will be no middle ground but they will immediately put all knowledge into vigorous practice. These are difficult concepts to work with for researchers because they are seldom articulated, let alone opened to debate. The challenge therefore is not to counteract such thinking but to work within it. With all projects involving young people researchers first come up against necessary gatekeepers in the form of institutional ethics committees who rightly insist that the research is sensitive, age appropriate and unlikely to be unduly distressing. In the sexual health area this is arguably more fraught than in other areas. Time spent negotiating content and means of support for participants is well rewarded (for this survey, each student gets a card with national 'help lines' for follow-up questions). Apart from University committees, most schools systems (independent, or State) have their own ethics committees which will inevitably defer final responsibility for student participation and informed consent to parents. Nevertheless, the approval to proceed at a systems level is a necessary precursor to approaching schools and, more importantly, provides the schools themselves with protection from 'wearing' any consequences of the research. The letter of approval from centralised education authorities is critical to opening doors.

The key to obtaining such a letter and to working with gatekeepers generally is not to engage in the debate about whether or not the research will harm young people but to focus clearly on the benefits which can be expected to come from the outcomes. A track record in feeding research outcomes back at the schools level is a huge help in such a debate, but being able to make a commitment to this process is vital. Such a commitment must go beyond publishing results in academic journals. It must offer constructive and realistic means to see that the research gets back into practice at a schools level. Our commitment to this process for our schools surveys has been

- a plain language report of the outcomes distributed to all participating schools and other interested practitioners;
- a four-page summary of this report to enable the teacher to digest the key points quickly;
- a set of power point slides and overheads available online for committed teachers to present the data back to their own schools; and
- a willingness to work with curriculum developers to integrate the findings into sexual health classroom materials.

Issues of consent

In all cases with young people in schools a letter must go home to parents. Asking adolescents, some of them as old as 18, to seek signed permission from their parents is a more difficult undertaking and something which many find embarrassing or demeaning. Nevertheless, there is no way of working with young people in schools without getting parental consent. Negative consent which requires parents to actively withdraw their children is highly desirable in solving these problems but seldom permitted in the sexual health arena. Many letters and consent forms never go home and even fewer return to school. Prizes for participation may have some impact on this process but a far more important factor is the actual commitment of the classroom teacher who is conducting the survey. Encouragement at the school level has proven to be the single greatest inducement to getting young people to follow through the consent process and participate.

These issues are relatively easily resolved compared to the larger number of dilemmas presented by groups of marginalised young people where issues of consent take on greater proportions along with challenges of recruitment and duty of care.

Young people who experience homelessness

Homelessness among Australian young people (12–25 years) is a significant social issue with major public health implications and social costs for individuals, families and communities (Chamberlain and Mackenzie, 1998). Public health research reveals that this diverse population of young people – whose homeless experience may be temporary, intermittent or ongoing – are highly vulnerable to a range of health issues (Ensign, 1998; Rossiter et al., 2003) including mental illness (Booth and Zhang, 1997; Sleegers et al., 1998), suicidal acts (Greene and Ringwalt, 1996), substance abuse (Mallett et al., 2003; Baron, 1999; Bailey et al., 1998; Kipke et al., 1997; Kipke, Montgomery and MacKenzie,1993), sexually transmitted infections (STIs) (Hillier, Matthews and Dempsey, 1997), Hepatitis C (Rosenthal et al., 2003; Roy et al., 2001) and unplanned pregnancies (Gwandz, 1998). These marginalised young people are also more likely than home based-peers to leave school prematurely, spend time in juvenile justice centres or gaol, and have difficulty accessing and maintaining employment (Inciardi and Surratt, 1998; Kral et al., 1997).

Researching this population is therefore important but poses particular challenges for researchers. Here we report on a range of research implementation issues encountered during a five year (2000–2004) programme of longitudinal research with homeless young people undertaken in Melbourne. Known as *Project i*, this research included surveys with 700 young people aged between 12 and 20 years who were experiencing homelessness, a two-year longitudinal study of 165 young people who were newly homeless (i.e. out of home for at least two nights but less than six months) and surveys and interviews with service providers.

Ethics: pro-active engagement with institutional ethics committees

Many researchers choose not to undertake research with vulnerable or marginalised young people due to perceived difficulties in negotiating ethical approval, including legalities of obtaining informed consent. Researchers often consider institutional ethics applications onerous, particularly when they have to do deal with multiple committees. As we dealt with at least eight ethics committees during the course of the project we quickly learnt that it is important to be patient with committees and to see them as an ally and not as an annoyance or enemy in the research process. We fostered strong relationships with our institutional committees to help ensure that we maintained ethical relationships with our research participants, many of whom were highly vulnerable minors. One way of doing this was to establish a system of quarterly reporting with the University committees. In addition, we also developed a critical/adverse incident protocol with the committees. For example, if, in the course of an interview a young person reported current or past sexual abuse for the first time or they indicated that they were currently suicidal or homicidal, our interviewers followed our emergency procedures protocol. Within 24 hours of the interview, interviewers completed an incident report that was then passed on to the ethics committee within four days. We had many such incidents in the course of the research and felt that we received strong support from the committees around these issues.

Recruitment

Recruitment was a highly challenging, time-consuming and costly aspect of our research. We needed to recruit service providers, newly homeless young people and those who had been homeless for over six months. Given the highly mobile and at times invisible nature of this marginalised population we knew that it would be impossible to recruit a representative sample of homeless young people. Nevertheless we aimed to recruit young people from a range of settings, including youth-focused services, schools and street sites. As such it was necessary for us to develop a multi-faceted recruitment strategy which hinged on the employment of a full-time Community Liaison Officer (CLO) to oversee all aspects of recruitment for the project. Together with the Research Director, it was the role of the CLO to engage the service sector, identify relevant services to assist with recruitment of young people for the project and negotiate ethical approval and permission to recruit from services and some community sites. The CLO needed to directly address service providers' collective suspicion about the value of research and persuade them of the potential benefits of the study, including the need for and value of an evidence base about these young people's practices. Without their support it would have been extremely difficult to locate participants.

Successfully engaging and recruiting the youth service sector

A number of strategies were used including the provision of clear accessible written information in a brief form and the opportunity to attend research information forums. Two smaller reference committees of critical experts in the field were used to advise on recruitment, analysis and dissemination strategies on this project. This was more productive than working with one large committee. At the level of the individual service, letters were sent with follow-up phone calls and the offer of a research information session. Interviewers were assigned to specific services and developed a working relationship with them which was constantly reviewed. The service sector was kept engaged and informed by the use of a website and a monthly research report.

Successfully recruiting homeless young people

Engaging the interest of the service provider was the most effective means of recruiting young people. Posters and recruitment fliers were placed in all of the identified youth services. In addition, active recruitment took place in street and community sites such as parks, train stations and shopping centres where homeless young people congregate. Young people were paid $20 for the first interview, increasing by $5 for each subsequent interview up to a maximum of $40. A free call telephone number was established for young people to contact the project and travel vouchers were provided for young people to travel to and from interviews.

Informed consent

Informed consent is a difficult issue to negotiate when conducting research with minors, especially vulnerable minors. Within Victorian State government legislation there is no precedent or law that enables minors under the age of 14 to give legally recognised consent. They may give informed *assent* but not informed *consent*. Between the ages of 14 and 18 they are deemed capable of giving consent in some contexts and circumstances. *Project i* negotiated these informed consent issues with university and state ethics committees, who determined that we could seek informed assent/consent with young people aged 12–18 years if we recruited them from street sites and not homelessness or other services. If in the course of the research these young people returned home or into the care of their legal guardians then we were compelled to obtain informed consent from young people's legal guardians. If young people aged 15 years and under were in services when we recruited them, then we obtained informed consent from their legal guardian at the time they were recruited. Only one parent refused permission for their child to continue participating in the research. If young people were 18 years and over and we recruited them from homelessness and other non-statutory youth services then we were not ethically or legally compelled to obtain informed consent from their legal guardians. At present young people 16 and over are generally considered independent minors by statutory authorities. Protection services rarely work with young people in this age range. When they do it is because they have had a continuing, longstanding involvement with them.

While technical, legal informed consent issues seem straightforward in theory, in practice they are often difficult issues to negotiate with minors and vulnerable young people. Interviewers had to determine that potential participants, whatever their age, were not substance affected or otherwise mentally/cognitively incapable of making an informed decision to consent to participate in the research. They also had to ensure that young people understood the consequences of their actions and their rights as participants to withdraw from, and/or seek clarification and further information about the research. This was not always easy, straightforward or immediately evident. Often young people were keen to participate in the research because they knew that they would receive remuneration. If an interviewer was sure that a young person was unable to give informed consent for any reason then she/he was instructed to respectfully decline to recruit the young person into the research. In circumstances where it was unclear whether or not young people were substance affected or mentally incapable of participating, interviewers conducted the brief screening survey to determine their eligibility and their capacity to understand and respond to questions. If during this process it became evident that young people could not respond to questions then they would receive partial remuneration and the interviewer would discontinue the interview. If an interviewer remained doubtful about a young person's capacity to give informed consent then she/he was instructed to go through the research information and informed consent form step by step with the young person to determine if she/he understood each bit of information on these forms. A young person would be asked to restate each salient point in their own words and to indicate if they understood what this would mean for them as research participants. Interviewers were instructed to read the forms to participants because we anticipated that some participants would have literacy issues.

Together with the ethics committees we deemed that the project had an ethical, if not legal obligation to report and take further action if young people revealed an intention to commit suicide or homicide or reported current sexual abuse, during the course of the interview. This obligation was outlined to the young people on the informed consent form and emphasised by interviewers during the informed consent process. Participants aged 18 years and under were also clearly informed of our ethical responsibility to seek their parent or guardian's consent.

In order to maintain high standards of practice, particularly in relation to informed consent, we instituted specific quality-control measures. Interviewers taped all of their interviews and the research director and/or the CLO listened to new interviewers' early tapes to check that they were undertaking the informed consent process and survey questions correctly.

Duty of care

Young people who experience homelessness are often highly vulnerable and marginalised. Some report mental health problems, self harm and suicidal intent, a history of sexual assault, and/or drug and alcohol abuse. Many feel vulnerable because of their unstable housing, poverty and/or disconnection from family and friends. In conducting research with this population we had to balance research priorities with ethical considerations about privacy, confidentiality and the safety of the young people. We developed a range of measures to prevent harm associated with the research and demonstrate a duty of care to the young people involved. These measures included the development of a training and emergency protocol for dealing with revelations of past and current sexual assault, or intention to commit suicide and/or homicide, an extensive referral guide to other services and a follow-up protocol for young people who became distressed during the interview.

We were also mindful of our duty of care to protect casual interviewing staff and research officers and so developed extensive protocols for this purpose, such as the provision of mobile phones, on-call support, thorough debriefing and clearly articulated protocols.

Tracking

One of the greatest challenges in conducting longitudinal research with homeless young people is to keep track of them over time. In the course of the project it became clear that there is an art to successful tracking. Interviewers need to have appropriate expectations and attitudes as well as refined tracking processes and protocols. They need to be imaginative, persistent, maintain a sense of humour and consider themselves akin to detectives. The project was successful in part because of the following processes:

- A standardised locator log was developed and filled out for each young person at the outset of the study. Detailed information about the young person's current address, mobile phone, email and home address was collected as well as the address, phone numbers and emails of at least three other people (family, friends and/or service providers) who had contact with the young person. Interviewers recorded and updated how each young person wanted interviewers to identify themselves when making contact with the nominated people on the form. Information on the form was updated each time the young person was interviewed.
- Participants signed a permission letter to enable us to track the young person through government agencies (e.g. Juvenile Justice (JJ) and Child protection facilities and welfare agencies) and permission was sought from senior bureaucrats for this to happen.
- The project allowed a sufficient window period for research interviews to be conducted to factor in the time it takes to track young people.

- A free call number was established to enable young people to make contact with the project to update their contact details and schedule interviews.

- Tracking was conducted during the day and night using multiple methods such as phone calls, sms messages, letters, postcards, messages left with people or services and physically searching known locations.

- Contact was maintained with participants in between their interviews by sending postcards, birthday, Christmas and reminder cards.

- Where possible interviewers were flexible about when and where they conducted interviews and sometimes telephone interviewing was necessary.

Tracking is expensive and time-consuming. Research budgets need to reflect this if research is to be effective. Tracking is also tedious and often frustrating. Interviewers' efforts to locate young people need to be recognised, valued and celebrated, especially when they are successful. *Project i* maintained 80–85 per cent follow-up rates with participants at six data points across two years.

Research with same-sex-attracted young people

Over the past decade we have witnessed a great deal of social change in the area of sexuality in Australia. The two national surveys carried out at ARCSHS with same-sex-attracted youth (SSAY) over the past 10 years (Hillier et al., 1998; Hillier, Turner and Mitchell, 2005) have been both an influence in, and a witness to, this change. Despite improvements, there is still a way to go. Today many young people who are sexually attracted to their own sex still suffer the double indignities of abuse and discrimination in their communities on the one hand and invisibility and neglect on the other. Being non-heterosexual places these young people in a particularly vulnerable position in their families because heterosexuality is likely to be regarded by them as the only acceptable form of sexual expression. Sexual attraction, particularly to the same sex, is different from other demographics because it is largely invisible and many young people choose to keep it this way at least for a while, sharing the secret with no one, although research tells us that this is changing (Hillier, Turner and Mitchell, 2005). As a result, a representative group of same-sex-attracted young people is difficult to access for research because their invisibility means that they cannot be identified and contacted through the usual channels. In this section we describe the challenges we faced in conducting research with same-sex-attracted young people and how we overcame them.

In 1995 research with 1200 rural students in Australia showed that 11 per cent of the young people were not unequivocally heterosexual. Focus groups and interviews with teachers revealed high levels of homophobia in these towns leading to concerns about the well-being of this stigmatised group (Hillier, Warr and Haste, 1996). In research with homeless young people, 14 per cent of whom had had sex with someone of the same sex, sexuality was often the reason given for leaving home (Hillier, Matthews and Dempsey, 1997). In a 1997 national survey of the sexual health and well-being of 3,500 Australian students (Lindsay, Smith and Rosenthal, 1997) eight to nine per cent were not unequivocally heterosexual and in a repeat of that study the figure was seven per cent (Smith et al., 2003). The 1997 study revealed negative health outcomes for these young people including higher levels of drug use and higher reported rates of STIs than the heterosexual students.

In 1997 it was clear that our research focus should move to same-sex-attracted young people; however, there were many challenges inherent in carrying out this research and we were unsure how successful we would be in meeting them. Two decisions smoothed the path of the research project; the first about terminology and the second was the setting up of a Reference Group.

We chose to use the term 'same sex attracted' for a number of reasons. First, young people tend to experience sexual attractions long before they assign themselves with a sexual identity and so by using attractions as our criterion we were maximising our potential research population. Second, unlike the terms 'gay' and 'lesbian', 'same sex attracted' is more user-friendly for organisations and young people. We were, for example, given permission to distribute the rural survey through education departments using a question about attraction where we may not have been able to use the terms 'gay' or 'lesbian'. Third, by using the term 'same sex attracted' we do not foreclose on young people's sexual futures. Young people who are same-sex-attracted today may or may not become the gay or lesbian adults of the future. Our second decision, given the overwhelming challenges to the research, was to arm the project with a Reference Group of experts who could help guide the project along the way. This proved to be a pivotal decision in the success of each project.

For the remainder of this section on research with same-sex-attracted young people, we present the challenges of conducting the first (Hillier et al., 1998) and second (Hillier, Turner and Mitchell, 2005) national surveys with same-sex-attracted youth and the various strategies we used to overcome them.

Stigmatised research – from the moral arena to the safety and rights arena

Research about stigmatised populations can itself become stigmatised. In 1997, it was almost impossible (outside research funding for HIV/AIDS) to obtain funding for projects about sexual diversity, in part, because Governments were concerned about community backlash. Fortunately this research fell into a block of funding about the sexual health and well-being of marginalised youth, with decisions about populations left to the researchers, and so funding became available for the project. In order to address the stigmatisation of these young people, the research when completed was taken back to community and to government and the realities of these young people's lives could no longer be ignored. The research helped reframe youth sexual diversity from a moral issue to one concerned with the safety and rights of same-sex-attracted young people. The research data were then used as a pressure point to free up further funding.

Researchers working with stigmatised groups can also become stigmatised and marginalised in the academy. In this case, the research was one of many projects at ARCSHS on similar issues and researchers carried out their work in a supportive collegiate environment.

Do no harm

Same-sex-attracted young people are a vulnerable group. There are a number of ethical considerations in planning research with young people who keep their sexual preference invisible for reasons of their own physical and social well-being. We know from past research that disclosure of sexual preference is likely to result in social rejection, discrimination and abuse (Hillier, Harrison and Dempsey, 1999) and coming out needs to happen when a young person is ready. The challenge for this research was to gather the data without exposing young people's sexual preference through direct targeting or by research in which young people could be identified.

Moreover, in order to make the process as safe as possible for the young people, participation needed to be as much as possible within their control. The way we did this was to provide a number of different participation options (the Internet, the post and the telephone) and young people could choose the one that was the most convenient and/or safest for them.

Another potential for harm to young people participating in this research was the inner turmoil that it could cause. Many of these young people worked hard at suppressing their sexuality and involvement in the research, particularly the telling of their own stories, could potentially prompt them to face their issues before they were ready. One way to address this problem was to provide telephone numbers for referral in the advertising and on the surveys. As well, the website contained links to a variety of organisations that are SSAY friendly and provide information and support. In retrospect, we found that the telling of the stories was therapeutic for many of the participants and we were often thanked for 'listening'.

Parental consent

In normal circumstances, when minors (children and young people under 18 years) are involved in research, ethics committees dictate that parental consent must be obtained. Given that same-sex-attracted young people tell no one at all about their sexuality at first when they are sorting through the issues (this may take several years), and given that they almost never disclose to their parents first, parental consent meant either that there would be no one in the research or that young people would be forced to tell their parents before they were ready. Neither of these outcomes was acceptable to the researchers and so an argument was mounted against needing parental consent. The human ethics committee accepted that the arguments were reasonable and young people 14 years and over were recruited without parental consent.

Informed consent and anonymity

Because parental consent was not required, it was important that young people be given enough information about the project to make their own decisions about participating. This was included in the advertisements as well as on the hard copy and web-based questionnaire. Again, with the vulnerability of the group in mind and the risks of disclosure through sending a signed consent, we argued against signed consent and for implied consent in our ethics application believing that by filling out the questionnaire, young people were clearly agreeing to participate. One important criterion attached to this was that young people were assured complete anonymity in the reporting of the research. This meant that names, locations and in some cases other details that may have led to them being recognised were changed in publications.

Difficulties of recruitment

Recruitment was one of the most complex and challenging aspects of the project. We wanted to gather data from a marginalised population which could not be recognised and which remained anonymous for reasons of its own safety. In our previous research, rural youth were accessible because they were located in rural schools and homeless young people were accessible through services. Schools were not an acceptable option because it would put young people at risk of exposure and it was unlikely that education departments would give their approval for the research. Homosexuality was still regarded as a moral issue in the late 1990s. Though at this time it was possible to locate some same-sex-attracted young people attached to the gay community, they were more likely to be 'out' and to have known about their sexuality for a long time. We wanted a range of young people in the research, including those who had spoken to no one about their sexuality and/or were unsure about their feelings. In previous work we had used focus groups and interviews to gather qualitative data but for reasons of anonymity, face-to-face techniques were clearly not an option for this group. We canvassed telephone interviews but decided they would be difficult to set up and dangerous for young people. We needed to find a method which did not single these young people out but which allowed them to participate in the research safely and discreetly. Our solution was to advertise the research to all young people around Australia in the hope that same-sex attracted-young people would come to us in their own time and place. We advertised the research in national youth magazines, youth organisations and networks, newspapers and radio asking young people to go the website and fill out the questionnaire, leave their contact details on an answer phone or post a coupon to the researchers with their address on it for the questionnaire to be posted out to them. In order to ensure depth to the data, we asked young people to send us their stories about when they first knew, the good times and the bad and their hopes for the future. In the first survey, 200 hundred of the 750 participants wrote their stories for the project and in the second survey 600 of 1749 contributed their stories. We were mindful of the trust young people showed in us by sharing their stories with us and felt keenly the responsibility to ensure that the research outcomes were used to make a difference in their lives.

Research into policy and practice

The marketing of this research was consciously directed towards creating and supporting processes of social change. The data was initially released in the form of a community report. Decisions about what would be emphasised in the report had already been made with the current difficulties for SSAY in mind. The report concluded with eleven recommendations for change in the areas of school policy and curriculum, appreciation of the diverse nature of SSAY, particularly in relation to culturally and linguistically diverse young people and those from rural and remote areas, and in expanded options for counselling and supporting them. These recommendations had no official status but represented an explicit 'call to action' to practitioners and policymakers responding to the research.

The press release was constructed around these same recommendations with the key focus placed on the lack of safety for same-sex-attracted young people in schools. The headlines reflected a change in emphasis from morality to concern about the well-being of same-sex-attracted young people in schools. 'Schools unsafe places for gay youth' and 'Schools with an attitude problem' are indicative of the headlines which featured in newspapers in all states and territories that day and which led to 31 radio broadcast news items as well. On the first week also the website on which the report was available recorded many thousands of hits. There was clearly a climate of public interest which exceeded that which we had experienced with other research projects and a readiness to look at the issue in the safety framework. Even more important, the second report built on the momentum of the first and we were asked to provide pre-release briefings to a number of government departments who distributed the research reports to their staff and made recommendations for the implementation of policy change in line with the findings of the research.

Conclusion

Young people inhabit many worlds and have multiple identities. The daily negotiation of these different identities can result in them being exposed to a range of risks to their health and well-being. It is important that the difficulties encountered in working with young people do not deter researchers from gathering vital data that can make a difference to their young lives.

In this chapter we have described our experiences of successfully carrying out research with three groups of more or less vulnerable young people. These projects have all been challenging and at times frustrating but we have also been able to see the rewards that come from changes in policy and practice informed by the data we have been able to collect.

It is important that the hard lessons learned from these projects are not lost to researchers in the future and that the developmental work on their projects can begin with the hindsight that our learning offers.

6
Methodological and Ethical Issues in Conducting Research with Older People

Susan Quine and Colette Browning

In Australia, 13 per cent of the population were aged 65 and over in 2002, and this proportion is expected to rise to 25 per cent by the year 2050. Over the next 50 years people aged 80 years and over will constitute the most rapidly growing population group, and these patterns of population ageing are reflected worldwide. In order to design effective programmes and policies for our ageing populations, we need to provide a sound evidence base. Through participation in research older people can help provide this evidence base. Not only can older people provide data about their levels of health and functioning to assist health and social planners, but they also can provide us with their perspectives on the lived experience of ageing, thus contributing to society's understanding of the ageing process and old age. As noted by Browning, Minichiello and Kendig (1992, p. 164), 'The better we understand the underlying processes of ageing, the better the chance that preventative action will be taken to preserve health and vitality in old age.'

The research community often reflects the broader negative social perceptions about ageing and older people. As such older people are often excluded from research. Many large-scale epidemiological studies choose 60 years or lower as a selection criterion for participation. Researchers may exclude older people from their sampling frames on the basis of stereotyped views of older peoples' sensitivities to certain topics (for example sexuality), or assumed irrelevance of the research topic to older people. For example, older people are often not included in studies of physical activity (Ory et al., 2002). Research ethics committees may assume that older people are less able to give informed consent owing to diminished cognitive functioning or frailty. While these stereotypes may hold some truth for some older individuals, the majority of older people approached in community settings are willing and able to contribute to research. The marginalisation of older people in contributing to research is largely driven by the attitudes and practices of researchers and institutions. In order to address the ethical and methodological issues involved in research with older people, we also need to define what we mean by 'older people'. Definitions of old age are largely socially constructed. For planning purposes the onset of old age has been defined as the age at which people are eligible for retirement pension support. In most Western cultures the age of retirement is 65 years. However, in response to population ageing, there has been a call by governments for a later retirement age. Will this approach change our definition of 'old'?

In the research literature the age focus for gerontological research is defined primarily as 65 years and over. However, it is noteworthy that individual differences in functioning are large across the older age range. Knowing a person's chronological age does not always allow us to predict their levels of biological, psychological and social functioning. Despite large individual differences in functioning in older people, at the population level there is evidence that the capacity to age well may reach a threshold by the early 80s. Baltes and Smith (2003) argued that while people in their 70s may have the reserve capacity to improve their physical and cognitive functioning through appropriate interventions, by their 80s older people are more likely to have multiple illnesses and disabilities that overload the capacity for improvement in functioning. While endeavouring to maximise older people's contribution to research, we need to ensure that we use methodological approaches that are sensitive to the individual needs, capabilities and wishes of older people themselves.

This chapter focuses on methodological and ethical considerations in the area of research with older people.

Sampling and recruitment

To illustrate these issues we will draw on case studies from our own research that include both quantitative and qualitative approaches. We focus primarily on research with people in community settings.

Defining the target population and sampling frame

When conducting research with older groups it is important to carefully define the target population, which raises a number of questions: Who are the target groups? Are they defined in terms of age? Will men and women be included? Will people from culturally and linguistically diverse backgrounds be included? Are we targeting older people with particular problems (for example, those at risk of falling) or those with particular strengths (for example, older people who are active in the community)? Given increasing longevity, a definition of older adults as those 65 years and over is too crude to be useful, and interpretations of data from people over 65 can be misconstrued if based on the assumption of homogeneity of health and experiences. Sixty-five-year olds are likely to differ from 90-year olds both physically and mentally, and in their needs and expectations. People born in different cohort may share some common features, but differences are likely to occur when separated by a 20 or more year period. When conducting and writing up research it is therefore important to justify the age categories used and to describe carefully the sample and population from which it is drawn (Dura and Kiecolt-Glaser, 1990).

In large community-based-studies existing databases such as electoral roles can be used to construct the sampling frame. The Health Status of Older People (HSOP) project used such an approach (Kendig et al., 1996). The sampling frame was defined as all residents of private dwellings in metropolitan Melbourne, aged 65 years and over. The electoral roll was used to develop a clustered sample of potentially eligible older people from 40 inner Melbourne postcodes. Clustering was used to minimise the travel costs of interviewers and older age groups were over-sampled to ensure representation of the full age range. Eligibility was determined through home visits or phone contact. Out-of-scope individuals were defined as those living in non-private accommodation, those who could not speak English and people who could not be interviewed for health reasons. Comparisons with Australian Census data showed that the sample was representative of older people in the Melbourne community, apart from those too ill to be interviewed and non-English speaking people. As the main aim of this study was to obtain information about the health and health-related experiences of well older people living independently in the community, the exclusion of very ill or frail individuals was appropriate. However, exclusion of people who could not speak English was primarily the result of the large costs associated with employing interpreters and translation of data collection instruments. Older people from culturally and linguistically diverse backgrounds did participate in the study, but only if they could communicate in English. Under-representation of key groups has been raised as a major issue in the literature.

Sampling issues: Under-representation of key groups and exclusion criteria

In quantitative research we sample because it would be too expensive to study an entire population, and also because it is unnecessary if appropriate probability sampling is used which enables inferences to be made, with confidence, to the population. However, with older people specific sampling problems have been noted (Bowsher et al., 1993). One is the under-representation of older women in community samples, partly due to the unavailability of a sampling frame from which to draw participants, and also because their physical disabilities may mean they are less likely to frequent community social centres where participants are often recruited. Probably the most extreme example of under-representation is the frail older people living in remote areas who are unlikely to be sampled. While the older frail people in the community are likely to be under-represented, those residing in hospitals and nursing homes are often over-represented in clinical studies. The consequence of this imbalance in sampling is proliferation of the negative image of old age.

Further under-representation in sampling is evident in the exclusion of older people from different cultural backgrounds – often on the grounds of poor English proficiency – yet our research findings emphasise the importance of detecting cultural variation to facilitate the provision of culturally appropriate health services. Australia is a multicultural society in which the most rapidly ageing groups are migrants, many of whom do not speak English well, and whose use of health services is lower than that for Anglo older Australians. In 2001 the proportion of people aged 65 and over who came from culturally and linguistically diverse backgrounds was 20 per cent and is projected to increase to 23 per cent by 2011 (Australian Institute for Health and Welfare: AIHW 2002). Minimal research has been conducted to identify ethnic variation in health concerns and expectations of older Australians from non-English speaking backgrounds.

Qualitative research by one of the authors (Quine 1999a) using focus groups and interviews facilitated by bilingual health workers has helped identify similarities between migrant groups and the Anglo mainstream, such as the common concern about inadequate medication labelling and directions for use. It has also revealed some basic differences between Anglo and migrant groups – for example, in the use of herbal remedies, relationship with doctor and pharmacist and awareness of health rights. In addition, concerns and expectations specific to a particular ethnic group, such as the preference for medication administered through injection rather than orally have also been identified in Italian older people. Findings such as these can be used to raise health professionals' awareness of the similarities and differences which exist between patients and clients from different ethnic backgrounds, and thereby avoid the use of a blanket approach when communicating with or planning policies for ethnic older Australians.

Older Australians provide considerable informal care to family members and others (Plunkett and Quine 1996; Quine and Chan 1998). However, our research suggests that in the area of volunteerism there are ethnic differences in the provision of such care (Quine 1999b). While Anglo older Australians were willing to provide informal care and peer support to older people outside their immediate families, local community or ethnic group, this concept was less readily accepted by older people in the ethnic groups surveyed (Italian, Arabic, Greek). Although some of this reluctance may be attributable to lack of confidence in speaking English, this tendency was also evident in migrants who were proficient in English. Clearly, such cultural variation needs to be identified through research to avoid misunderstandings and maximise volunteer input.

Another example of under-representation in sampling is evident in the case of older people with mild cognitive impairment, or those with sensory impairment such as hearing or vision loss. Often a cognitive screening instrument is used to exclude from studies older people with cognitive impairment. Questions arise as to where to set the cut-off score for exclusion. How do cut-off scores relate to the older person's ability to respond to an interview, or fill in a questionnaire? Given that, from a population perspective, cognitive impairment increases with age, a rigorous application of cognitive screening in community studies may result in large numbers of older people (particularly those over 80 years) being excluded from studies. Older people with sensory impairments may not be able to participate as a result of the data collection methods used. For example, a telephone interview may be problematic for a person with a hearing impairment. Rather than excluding people with impairments the approach that should be considered is designing research protocols and instruments that are responsive to the needs of older people with cognitive or sensory impairments. Even in studies concerned directly with illness or disability, exclusion criteria are often problematic. Cohen-Mansfield (2002) noted that in dementia drug trials strict exclusion criteria rendered many trial outcomes invalid.

Older people may also be excluded from studies based on concerns regarding their ability to give informed consent. Decision criteria used by ethics committees tend to favour the protection of people who, because of physical, cognitive or mental illness, are assumed to be unable to give informed consent. However, while protecting people who are unable to give informed consent is a worthy goal, paternalistic views of older people may result in their exclusion from research becoming a form of discrimination. Proxy or surrogate consent is a method used in research where potential participants are unable to give informed consent owing to severe cognitive, psychiatric or physical disorders. Recently a US National Institute of Mental Health workshop addressed the issue of consent in geriatric neuropsychiatric research (Kim, Applebaum, Jeste et al., 2004). Kim et al. (2004, p. 803) concluded that current risk management approaches might force the '... halting of all research with incapable subjects or relying only on guardians or other court-appointed decision makers'. They argue that in the case, for example, of clinical trials of new drug treatments for Alzheimer's disease desperate patients and family members may feel an urgency to find ways to retain participation in the hope that the treatment will have a positive outcome for the patient. Yet, potential participants with severe impairments need to be protected particularly in trials where direct benefits may not be obvious. The balancing of this protection with the imperative to find effective treatments for severe neurodegenerative diseases in older people is a challenging ethical dilemma that needs further input from the various stakeholders, including researchers, patients and their advocates and policymakers.

Recruitment issues

Locating potential participants is not a problem with a population accessible through an institution (e.g. hospital, nursing home) (Quine and Cameron, 1995) or geographic location (retirement village) where patients and residents provide a captive audience, but locating target groups composed of people dispersed throughout the community can be problematic. For example, older people who have recently retired cannot easily be accessed through their workplace because of confidentiality of names and addresses. Consequently, recruitment of retirees may involve contacting senior citizens clubs and retiree organisations; church groups; returned service men's clubs; sporting clubs, such as bowls and golf; and recreational organisations such as traditional jazz clubs. Recruiting through advertisements in newspapers can be costly and not always productive (Wells et al., 2003; Thompson, Somers and Wilson, 1997).

Recruitment difficulties arise when the sampling frame cannot be easily defined. Wells et al. (2003) point out that the absence of a sampling frame for a late-life transition like retirement is especially problematic in prospective designs where participants need to be recruited before they retire. They argue for a range of sampling points and strategies. In their Healthy Retirement Study the sampling occurred in three stages. The first stage involved identifying the organisations that would be approached for participation. Next, a sample of employees was identified from each organisation. Finally a sample of intending retirees was identified. However, as described by Wells et al. (2003), this strategy failed to yield the required sample size of intending retirees. It was decided to approach unions and superannuation funds to assist with the recruitment of participants. The required sample size was still not achieved with this method, and finally a media campaign including newspaper advertising and articles was implemented to achieve the required sample size. The authors concluded that using organisations is not an efficient way of recruiting participants for this type of study because of the difficulty in accessing lists of employees and lack of interest by the organisation in retiring employees.

To facilitate recruitment, consideration should be given to the venue in which the research will be conducted. It should be wheelchair accessible, close to public transport and have parking facilities. Apart from the physical aspects it should provide an appropriate and nonthreatening setting so that participants are put at ease. Often this means recruiting (and conducting) research in a familiar setting. In the HSOP project participants were interviewed in their homes, which reduced the inconvenience of participants needing to travel. However, interviewing people in their own home raises issues of encroaching on privacy and may raise concerns by the participants about their personal safety. In that study the interviewers underwent extensive training, and protocols were developed to address these issues. In a focus group study of retirees conducted in Melbourne, we found that older people who had retired from blue-collar jobs were not willing to attend the focus group sessions held on the university campus, whilst this was not an issue for white-collar retirees. Blue-collar retirees were wary of entering unfamiliar territory and travelling to a venue outside their locality. We solved this problem by holding focus group sessions in local veterans' clubs which they frequented. While in general we do not use monetary incentives to recruit study participants, this may be necessary for hard-to-access populations, such as blue-collar retirees or homeless older people. For the blue-collar retirees we offered a small incentive – a $20 voucher to spend in the veterans' club where the focus groups were held – which increased recruitment and was appreciated. No such incentive was required to recruit the white-collar retirees.

In the studies we conduct, there is usually no, or minimal, monetary incentive, but any costs incurred by participants are reimbursed. Many older people who are no longer in the workforce exist on low incomes, with many being on or around the poverty line, and women being most at risk of living in poverty (Gibson, 1998). Consequently, a deterrent to participation in a research project is the costs incurred. While these may only be small, such as bus fare or petrol and parking fees, this may be sufficient to discourage involvement. When research with older people (especially the frail aged or disabled) is conducted away from their home, it is customary to either collect participants from their homes by car, cab or health service (hospital, clinic) vehicle (see, for example, Smith et al., 2002).

The importance of personal contact to recruit and retain participants has been noted repeatedly in the literature (see, for example, Park and Cherry, 1989) for community and clinical studies, and has been evident in our own research. Personal contact appears more effective in recruiting older people than newspaper print advertisements or posters, or pamphlets in doctors' offices and in pharmacies. While older people can be selected through a formal sampling procedure and then contacted through a letter, recruitment is higher and retention greater when a personal contact is part of the procedure. Bowsher et al. (1993, p. 875) note that 'The most effective recruitment tactic is personal contact by the researcher in person's place of residence or frequently visited centre. This strategy is enhanced even more if the researcher is introduced to the potential subject by a familiar and trusted person'. The importance of a personal approach has been reported for all modes of interview/questionnaire administration: face to face, self-administered and telephone. For example, Worth and Tierney (1993) found that the main factor ensuring success in recruitment and completion for a telephone interview was a personal contact prior to the conduct of the telephone interview. Again, we have found this to be the case with our own research studies. Resnick et al. (2003) asked research nurses from the Baltimore Hip Studies how they recruited older women to exercise intervention studies following hip fracture. The nature of the personal contact was found to be important. The factors that facilitated recruitment were the perceived expertise of the nurses, having a caring attitude towards the participants, emphasising the benefits of participating in the study and using role models to show how older women are capable of engaging in physical activity.

An interesting aspect of recruiting older people is the tendency to deny impairment or vulnerability, which impacts negatively on recruitment. For certain studies, such as those researching falls, fractures and implementation of home safety, potential participants may not volunteer or refuse to be involved, because they do not see (or wish to see) themselves at risk. For example, a home safety programme found that there was a major problem convincing older people that they were at high risk of falls (Thompson, Somers and Wilson, 1997). Most older people did not believe they were old enough or in need of help to volunteer to be part of the study. A similar finding was observed in one of our studies of older women (mean age 83) recovering from hip fracture who did not consider a protective device 'hip protectors' relevant for them, despite being at high risk of a subsequent fracture (Quine and Cameron, 1995). Such reluctance to acknowledge vulnerability can be overcome by offering speaker presentation sessions in community venues on the topic, wherein the characteristics of those who are at risk are described and the issue of vulnerability is raised, which can then be openly discussed and reappraised. If older people cannot accept that they are personally at risk, another strategy reported by Thompson, Somers and Wilson (1997, p. 440) was to use the wording 'if this (programme) is not for you, please do consider it for the safety of your older friends and relatives'.

Success with recruitment is also dependent on factors including the type of study, extent of demands on participants and study duration. Recruiting older people into a clinical trial that may be physically invasive and cause discomfort or inconvenience is very different from recruiting into a qualitative study based on interviews. Study design is also important in terms of burden on participants. Older people may be willing to volunteer for a cross-sectional study requiring a one-off interview or assessment, but not willing to participate in a longitudinal study requiring frequent visits or procedures over an extended period. There are clearly many factors to consider when developing a recruitment strategy, and as Cameron (1997) has pointed out, it may be necessary to develop specific strategies for each clinical trial, health promotion programme or qualitative study.

Data collection methods

Quantitative approaches in gerontological research have a long history with early studies focusing on age differences in cognitive functioning and studies of health problems and illnesses in old age (Woodruff-Pak, 1988). Quantitative approaches have typically used surveys including mail-out questionnaires, structured face-to-face interviews and telephone interviews as well as laboratory-based approaches where participants are tested in terms of their cognitive and physical functioning. Over the past 20 years there has been an increase in studies focusing on qualitative approaches (Rowles and Schoenberg, 2002; Poole and Feldman, 1999; Gubrium and Sankar, 1994). Qualitative approaches uncover the meanings and values associated with older people's lives with few *a priori* assumptions on the part of the researcher (Reinharz and Rowles, 1988). Methods include in-depth interviewing, ethnography, biographical approaches, content analysis and focus group discussions.

Researchers and Ethics Committees are concerned to avoid imposing a burden on potential research participants when proposing and conducting research with older people. One aspect of burden is the requirement to travel in order to participate in the research project, and is one reason for using telephone interviews so that the participants can remain in their own home. While this mode of administration is clearly not suitable for the hearing impaired, it has been found to be acceptable to older participants and an efficient method of collecting detailed information for a number of older person surveys in which we have been involved. The New South Wales Older Person's Health Survey (NSW OPHS) (OPHS: Baker et al., 1999; NSW Health, 2000) and the Melbourne Longitudinal Studies on Healthy Ageing Programme (MELSHA) have both used Computer Assisted Telephone Interviewing (CATI) to collect data from older people. Interview periods of 30–45 minutes have been sustained. Telephone surveys also enable a large number of respondents to be interviewed. The NSW OPHS (NSW Health, 2000) conducted in 1999/2000 completed 9,000 useable interviews of people 65 years and over living in the community.

The personal contact afforded by face-to-face interviews is appreciated by many older people, particularly if this occurs in their own home. However, the study costs are greater given the travelling time of the interviewer. Interviews at home also provide the opportunity to assess the environment for aspects such as safety and security, the use of mobility aids and the ability of the participant to function in that setting (Smith et al., 2002). Medication inventories and food supplies can also be checked. For example, in the HSOP project we were able to inspect (with permission of the participant) the full range of medications used by the older person. Interviews that allow the participant to tell their story may be more acceptable than structured questionnaires, but are limited to small-scale studies. Our experience conducting large-scale surveys has been that structured questionnaires are tolerated by older people, especially if there is opportunity within the interview to give verbatim responses to open-ended questions (Kendig et al., 1996). In-depth interviews often result in the disclosure of intimate information about the informant. Ensuring confidentiality of this information is paramount. Ethical withdrawal is also an issue to consider where a close rapport has been established with the informant perhaps over a number of visits. The researcher should clearly state at the outset the frequency of the interviews so that the informant is aware of when the interaction will come to an end (Rowles and Schoenberg, 2002).

Self-completion questionnaires can also be used effectively with older people, but layout must be particularly clear and typeface larger than usual to facilitate legibility. Eyesight difficulties and certain conditions, such as arthritis, can make it difficult to write lengthy responses to open-ended questions, and therefore in general should be used infrequently and included only when considered essential.

Focus groups rely on the ability of participants to interact verbally on a topic in a group setting, and have rarely been used to collect data from people over 65 years. This could be attributable to a belief that, even after the exclusion of the cognitively impaired, the limitations of mobility and visual and hearing impairment associated with ageing would render the method infeasible and pose a burden on participants. It may also reflect uncertainty that such people would be able to interact effectively as members of a focus group. In 1993, one of the authors found that it was feasible to use focus groups with older women (median age: 83 years) recovering from hip fracture (Quine and Cameron, 1995) which provided insightful information on their views about hip fracture and the use of hip protectors (Cameron and Quine, 1994).

It was however necessary to modify some of the guidelines (Quine, 1998a). Group sizes should be smaller than the usual 6–9 participants, with only 4–5 participants recommended for disabled older people, or those over 70 years. The smaller number enables all participants to have the opportunity to contribute and encourages greater interaction. Given the problems of hearing and sight, and in some instances the space needed to accommodate wheelchairs, the number of participants is physically constrained. Older frail participants do speak less and make greater use of non-verbal indications of their agreement or disagreement than younger able-bodied participants. Consequently, recording of focus group sessions relies more on note-taking of non-verbal responses than is customary, to supplement the verbal tape recording of the session. It is therefore particularly important to have a scribe, in addition to a group facilitator when conducting focus groups with older and/or frail people (Quine, 1998b). The length of a focus group session is generally around 90 minutes, but for the frail aged the session should be shorter to avoid fatigue and burden. In our hip protector study (Quine and Cameron, 1995) this was around 30 minutes.

Sensitivity in form of address and question wording

While researchers should always be sensitive to the needs of their study participants, there are some pointers that are specific to older people, born in a earlier era, and the 'form of address' is one of these. In focus group methodology, only first names are usually used between participants to maintain confidentiality and encourage informal interaction. However, with older generations, especially those over 70 years, this may be interpreted as lack of respect. It is therefore advisable to ask each participant how they would prefer to be addressed, for example Miss Smith, Mrs Brown, Mr Jones, rather than assume the use of first names. The site of the recruitment may also be relevant in that study participants recruited through an institution, such as a hospital or nursing home, are more likely to expect the formal use of title (Quine and Cameron, 1995) than those participants recruited from the community. With the research we have conducted in Australia the use of title is also related to the age of the interviewer (Quine, 1998a). Other things being equal, a mature aged interviewer is more readily accepted on first name terms by older people than are younger interviewers. In addition, this guideline may be culture-specific. For example, Wood and Ryan (1991) conpare North American culture, where a difference of 15 or more years is necessary before age status becomes unequal, with Korea, where this can occur when the age difference is as little as one year.

Sensitivity in the wording of questions is also important. Marital status is a good example. While younger generations may be prepared to respond to a structured question which combines the responses 'married' with '*de facto*', older people may be offended by this and prefer separate response categories.

Conclusion

Conducting research with older people is a rewarding activity that has the potential to contribute to our understanding of older people's lives and the ageing process. Rowles and Schoenberg (2002, p. 13) note that '... there is an increasing recognition of the critical role that qualitative gerontology can and should play in changing societal images, exposing prejudice, providing practical insight, and making contributions to policy'. Similarly, when using quantitative methodologies we need to pursue research questions, the answer to which will make a difference in the lives of older people. In this chapter we have highlighted some of the methodological and ethical issues that need to be addressed in conducting research with older people. The key message is to be sensitive to the variability in capabilities and wishes of the older people with whom you will conduct research and tailor your methods and research questions accordingly.

7
Social Research with HIV Positive Populations: A Conversation

Jeffrey Grierson and Peter Canavan

The history of the HIV pandemic has had the voices of those living with the virus at its centre, even before the virus was known and even before the syndrome was named. These voices have not spoken with unity, though neither in cacophony. At times, and in places, the voices of those living with HIV have been silenced, dismissed, undermined or deified, but they have always been there. It has been through the respectful and honest consideration of the experiences of living with HIV that the best of responses have been formulated, in government, in communities, in clinical professions and, occasionally, in media. Conversely, the greatest damage, both for those with HIV and the rest of the community, has come through the denial of these voices.

Research, and social research in particular, has had a part to play in creating a space for these experiences to be heard, examined critically and to play a role in informing policy, practice and process throughout the HIV response. This research effort has also been close to the centre of the AIDS response since the very beginning. In the fog of uncertainty and fear that characterised the early years of the pandemic, the need to know, and, importantly, document what was happening was met with numerous instances of the collection and analysis of information. Some of this happened within established academic institutions, but just as often it was within newly emerging community organisations, clinics and support groups that this knowledge was constructed and debated. The uncertainty also helped engender a climate of critical debate, and not just about the behavioural and experiential aspects of HIV, but the medical and clinical understandings as well. While this level of community engagement with scientific 'knowledge' may have come as a shock to some academics, scientists and clinicians, it is important to remember that many of these came from within affected communities, and so in many ways the multiple subjectivities that are now so familiar in this field were also there from the beginning.

To an extent there has been an artificial distinction that has been drawn between social research that addresses prevention issues and that which has been concerned with the lived experience of those with HIV. In part this has reflected the funding streams for research, but it has also mirrored the structural organisation of the community and clinical sectors in HIV/AIDS. In Australia there has been considerable dialogue between these two broad areas of social research and many projects have been co-located within them. As we start to see at a global level a belated acknowledgement of the importance of people living with HIV/AIDS (PLWHA) in prevention efforts, admittedly often framed in terms of clinical technologies, there is a greater concordance between international policy and our own research effort.

Sadly, in many parts of the world there has been little serious research attempting to understand the complexity of the lived experience of HIV beyond the purely clinical. Often those with HIV have been positioned as failures of prevention where research has focused on illness, treatment, care and palliation. To some extent this has changed as antiretroviral treatments have been rolled out in the developing world, but the research response is still less than ideal. In Australia we have been privileged to have had a dedicated programme of social research addressing the lived experience of those with HIV/AIDS funded by the federal government. While originally conceived as a research programme focused on care and support needs, the vital dialogue with HIV positive communities and organisations has ensured that it long since evolved beyond such a narrow definition. The relationship between HIV positive communities and social research is one of enmeshment, rather that a system that processes data from people with HIV and feeds it to service providers. This enmeshment is evidenced by the multiple positions that individuals occupy, as both researchers and people living with HIV or from affected communities, in the dialogues that occur around the development of research priorities and protocols, and in the co-construction of interpretation of research findings. This conversation between research and community is not always an easy one. To function effectively it needs to operate across multiple disciplines, multiple constituencies, multiple forms of governance and multiple applications. But when it works, it is a mighty fine thing.

The following is an edited conversation between Peter Canavan and Jeffrey Grierson

Peter is the HIV Living Programme Coordinator for the National Association of People Living With HIV/AIDS (NAPWA) and Convenor of the AIDS Treatment Project Australia (ATPA). He has been an advocate for HIV positive people since 1988 and has played a major role in advancing HIV treatments access, research, clinical trials and information and education issues. Peter has served on committees including the Clinical Trials and Research Committee (CTARC) and the HIV Committee of the Australian National Council on HIV/AIDS, Hepatitis and Related Diseases (ANCAHRD) and was President of NAPWA from 2000–2002. Jeffrey is a senior research fellow with the Australian Research Centre in Sex, Health and Society (ARCSHS), a psychologist by training he has worked in the community sector, government and academia in the HIV sector for 18 years. The HIV Futures surveys are national cross-sectional omnibus surveys conducted every two years since 1997 and they have occupied much of both authors' time.

The conversation between Peter and Jeffrey ranges across a number of areas of importance when working with positive people. In many ways these issues are not particular to positive people or confined specifically to HIV. However, some are. The conversation begins with a consideration of the kinds of research that are carried out with communities of positive people and how the perspective and voices of positive people can begin to influence the development of that programme of research. Peter and Jeffrey examine how agendas are set, research is funded, and particular research projects are established. While the conversation is strongly rooted in the Australian experience, the general principles for the involvement of the researched in setting the agenda are universal.

PC: I guess there are different types of research with HIV positive communities. There's the epidemiological research which tells us who we are, in essence, and where we are. It's more focused on statistical pictures, if you like, of our population. There's the clinical and medical research and that focuses on our health and to some degree our well-being, but it's very much focused on clinical trials, measurements in terms of clinical markers, experiences with side effects and toxicities. And then there's the social research which tries to capture a sense of what risks are being taken by the community, the context those risks are happening in and the behaviours that are in place to support or otherwise the risk behaviours. And then there's research which looks at not only who we are and what motivates what happens, but how we live and the social dimensions of our lives, studies which answer the questions about, not just living with HIV, but having a life in which HIV is contextualised. So, I guess the last part is the particular part that we find hardest to get done and of most interest to us as positive people.

JG: So what's the way in which positive perspectives actually get played out across those broad categories of research?

PC: Well, I guess the way that it gets played out is defined by the nature of our involvement in setting that research agenda, in participating in that research and the processes that support that involvement and participation. We participate with representatives who sit on the scientific advisory committees of the epidemiology and the social research centres. Plus there is the HIV Living Reference Group that ARCSHS (The Australian Research Centre in Sex, Health and Society) has, the Research Link Project that the National Centre in HIV Social Research has and then there are the various specific areas that are covered under the National Centre in HIV Epidemiology in Clinical Research (NCHECR) such as toxicology and pharmacology, immune based therapies, oncology. Those are really important ways for us to engage with the researchers themselves and as a group of people who are deciding what questions are to be asked and the sorts of issues that need to be taken into consideration and that's a really useful place for us to be. We can not only just be in the meeting where we are a positive person who reminds people of what they're there doing, researching our lives, but it also allows us input into the design so that those studies reflect not only what they're after, but some of the issues that we feel need to be taken into consideration, whether they're ethical issues or other dimensions of living with HIV or quality of life issues. We also do other things such as skill up our representatives with specific training and we've done that for all of the representatives of the working groups of the NCHECR, where we've involved the researchers from NCHECR in training around ethics and how to understand a protocol and case studies. Not to make them experts, but to actually make sure that they have a good baseline knowledge of ethical issues, research design, how protocols should be, what things should be considered and some examples to look at that. We also enter into discussions on a one-to-one basis with directors and we sit on the committees that are responsible for funding strategic research in the country such as the MACASHH (Ministerial Advisory Committee on AIDS, Sexual Health and Hepatitis) subcommittees.

JG: What I think is really important is the extent to which positive people and positive communities through systems of representation can actually be involved in agenda setting, rather than at the end of, or when a research project is up and running and having something put in at that point. I think that's actually really unique about HIV, the extent to which that happens rather than just a token involvement at the end and I think that differs across different types of research.

PC: That's right. I mean, if you look at some of the early clinical trials, access to AZT for example, positive people and ACTUP demonstrating about early access and with experimental treatments and stressing the need to broaden the base to create access and balance that against research needs at a time in the epidemic where people clearly needed access to a new and emerging therapy, and that changed I think the whole access arrangement and it then became part of the research agenda. There's been other research where we've actually done quality of life measures and economic impact with Monash University to look at getting Calix, a particular oncology drug for the treatment of Kaposi's Sarcoma. Now, I mean, I know there are all different spin-offs and different aspects, but for us they're all part of the research and its interface with access at that level.

JG: For me as a researcher, one of the structural things that actually makes that possible is the funding arrangement where the bulk of the PLWHA research we do is block funded, so we are able to develop a research agenda within that funding when we've already got the funding and that makes it a lot easier for us to actually work with communities to look at what the issues are that need researching rather than one-off funding where you've got to do that whole process of deciding on a research design, writing the application, waiting for it to be assessed, getting the funding and that can take two years, and then you start research – all within set parameters about what will be funded in that research round. It's much harder to get community input on that sort of process which says, for example, the funding now might be around mental health, but when you do the community consultation they say, we know that's not the issue, it's something else.

PC: It really does stress the importance of the centrality of positive people again in being at the tables where decision making occurs. There's a real danger if we ignore those tables in an environment where you've got competing health interests and HIV is positioned more and more as a chronic manageable illness with a lot of the hidden realities associated with the illness disappearing from people's immediate vision and HIV becoming less visible in the wider communities, even in some of our own communities. You run the real risk that those agendas are quite narrow in terms of what is seen as strategic. But it matters how you see those issues and what prevention of transmission really means and how broadly we can understand that. Does it include a context which embraces a broad social model which looks at our sexual lives and the way that we feel valued and supported in our communities, or does it just look at what our clinical markers are, the impact that treatment has and its relationship to epidemiology? Treatment and care are an important part of prevention and therefore issues related to things that make us feel good about ourselves, support us and make us feel valued. Will those things feed into an understanding of what the government considers is important to be researched?

JG: I think the whole history of the HIV epidemic in this country has made some of those routes of influence possible, and I guess you take the whole history of community involvement in reacting to the epidemic or directing the response that wasn't to do with research initially. It was about treatment care, support, prevention, but that flavour of involvement has been picked up by the research. I mean, it was there at the time of the establishment of the national centres and so there's an expectation in some ways that that should be part of it. It's almost self-evident.

Now the conversation moves on to examine more closely the nature of partnership between researchers and the positive communities and to consider the burden of that partnership and the nature of representation. Peter and Jeffrey discuss the costs and benefits of working in partnership – cost and benefits that accrue to both parties. Peter is particularly concerned that the burden falls disproportionately on certain community representatives.

PC: I think that has been a hallmark of Australia's success, really, the true nature of partnership, the true nature of participation, collaboration and cooperation. You know, those things happen then we truly do have a response which does welcome our input, which doesn't see it as being pitted against that of institutional researchers' needs, but has been complementary to and supportive of communities' needs. I think that's what makes a real difference and if we have that operating and working well through all sectors: government, through the community, through our relations with clinicians and the clinical side of things, then we're likely to get a better response because it's informed by all of the dynamics that are influencing HIV. Good leadership is embracing those principles and putting them into practice through representation, which is not about tokenism. It's about, 'we want to know, we want to hear, we think what you have to say is important and we want to help you develop the capacity to express yourselves in a way that is of use to yourselves and means something to the work that you want to do in sharing our desire to reduce transmission or prevent it, and to minimise the social and personal impacts of HIV on positive people'. So that's true partnership, I think, that's what has made a big difference.

JG: One of the things that's always concerned me working in HIV around the issue of representation has been that we can say all that stuff's really important and it's really valuable and it makes the response better, but what's the burden on the positive community and particularly people like yourself who are in some ways spokespeople for all, or working almost professionally as a positive person? There aren't a lot of positive people who are willing to do that sort of work and the need to be heard in all those settings, and I'm thinking about the clinical research particularly, you need to get people to build the capacity to engage with that research. One of my concerns has always been: what's that actually cost the positive community, that sort of representation? I mean, it's great but what's the cost?

PC: It's a hard one to know exactly what the cost is.

JG: I see it played out particularly amongst positive women, because there are so few positive women who are going to be the person sitting on the committee to represent positive women.

PC: Well, clearly the cost really is that if we're not resourced, if money doesn't go into or value doesn't get attached to skilling people providing capacity for the organisations and individuals, then the real cost is that fewer and fewer people will want to do the sort of thing that myself and others do. And as the complexity of it increases the fewer people there are that are able to do the job, and the less appealing it is for new people. So you're talking about both maintaining corporate memory and workforce development within the positive community.

In turn, Jeffrey is concerned about representation in a different sense. He is concerned with achieving a balance between documenting what is common to most or all positive people while reflecting the diversity of the individual experience of living with HIV.

JG: One thing that interests me when you say that, because I'm quite interested in the whole idea of representation, is, as you gain expertise and capacity in research, how do you maintain the sense of what that means for punters who don't have expertise and capacity in research? It's almost like being co-opted in some way into the research way of thinking about things. How do you say, well, before I actually knew why you were doing this, I would have found that really problematic?

PC: Well, from personal experience I did science through school, so I have a natural interest in some of those aspects. When I started to get involved and found myself going to a lot of conferences I was finding that I had a great interest in a lot of the science that was in presentations on clinical and even molecular biology, and I found myself exploring it, but I really had to stand back and think, what do I need to know? What is really useful here? Is it useful that I know the particular pathways, the particular reaction of a molecule and how that impacts on lipodystrophy? It may be interesting to me personally and it may be of interest scientifically, but for our constituency it's really not what people desperately need to know. So it's important that we have ways of understanding what our positive constituency want to hear and that's where I think the real link, if you like, is between what we do as advocates and what our communities want. So we do that importantly through surveys, through people writing about their experiences, by putting out a question to our membership and getting people's experiences which help to inform a particular issue we might want to understand more about, whether it's welfare, discrimination or disclosure, whether it's sex, whatever it is. So that's the way that it informs us about the lived experiences of people and what's important to pick up from that, to bring into an advocacy setting around helping shape the research. It's not about what I want the research to be. It's about what is coming from people and that changes as our experiences change. If we don't have ways of keeping abreast of that change, then we do become moribund and redundant and we do start to stray from what we should be doing, which is to be reflexive and which is to be absolutely addressing what needs to be addressed at that moment in time, not five years ago. We used to not have the sort of formal mechanisms in place to do this in the early days. We used to inform ourselves by anecdotal experience which would often be borne out through the research. But now that we have the institutions, the mechanisms for input and all of that in place, we still learn from each other but we have proper processes where we can get the evidence to support what we feel. So it's not just always reacting out of a situation of crisis, but it's having a sort of a vision about what qualities or what sort of things make a good life or what you don't want it to be like.

JG: Yes, that's the same, when we talk about the sort of priorities that you have to set in your work, I mean, it's the same for us. When I've got my research hat on I think there has to be that level of personal engagement with the work that you do. You actually have to bring in those things that you personally think are important and you sit them against the information that you get from formal mechanisms of constituency, or strategy or politics. But, yes, you have to bring that personal engagement with it otherwise you get mechanistic.

PC: And we have to find ways too, don't we, to do what we're trying to do to broaden the base of people who can add to that experience and come to the tables and to start to articulate that we're not just one community of positive people, but we're many different communities working in alliance. That means that the issues that positive women have on some things are quite different to Indigenous people or to gay men or to people from culturally diverse backgrounds. So it's very hard to talk across all those perspectives but it's really important to foster people who can bring those unique perspectives to the table.

JG: That, for us, is another aspect of capacity development. You don't learn this stuff at university when you're doing a psychology degree and it's one of the things that is hard for people when they become involved in HIV research, being able to, at least be sensitive, across that whole range of groups and diversity, but you know, to do it well it's more than just being sensitive to those issues. It's actually being able to engage with them and that takes time. Maybe that's why so many researchers in HIV have been in the middle of the epidemic for years and years and years, but you can't come out of a university degree with a way of doing that.

PC: No, you can't and you can't come out of a diagnosis of HIV with a whole range of skills. It might make it more meaningful in some ways, but it does speak for the importance, I think, of having people from the affected communities actively involved because I think we bring unique perspectives in arriving at our solutions, whatever they might be, not only ours, but our communities' solutions to the issues, because how I feel about my day living with HIV will be very different to somebody else who observes my day living with HIV, and mine will be different to a mother who has a child to look after and has to try and deal with treatments issues related to that child, or an Indigenous person in a remote community who's got issues with keeping their medications.

JG: And you may have a completely different experience to a gay man who lives next door to you.

PC: Absolutely.

JG: I think that's really at the core, at least for social research of the balance we have to get between looking at what are the common experiences without actually replicating everyone's life, individually being able to say things at a usefully broad level, but not too broad so that it's meaningless and that's a real struggle sometimes.

PC: It needs to embrace the sort of complexities that one person has in dealing with HIV, whether it's around adherence or psycho-social issues or depression or whatever it might be. I think we really want to know more, and not that you want to, as you said, replicate everyone's individual lives, but to move beyond the sort of statistical presentations that are so important to inform in a general sense. But there's an equally important scientific side which is based on qualitative understandings that come from those in-depth interviews with people that really do help to flesh out some detailed work around an individual that can highlight what we have in common as people with HIV. I've often wondered what it is that unites us and connects us. Why it is that I enjoy sitting in a room with other positive people? What keeps us all going, what makes us survive, what makes us happy, what makes us feel valued and supportive? How are other people doing this? How are other people sharing their experiences? What themes can we pick up from them that resonate with me that help me to move on in my own life and help others that are in the same process?

JG: For me, one of the things I had to learn very early on my research career was to shift away from just identifying differences. When you take health psychology or health research generally it's often about identifying problems and the differences between groups. What working with PLWHA research has done is made me realise that it's just as important to find a way to identify commonalities and resilience and the positive sort of things that make living with HIV possible. It's a real shift in how you think about the science of what you do, it's why you actually need a multi-disciplinary environment or network, because you can go and ask a sociologist or an anthropologist or health economist how they do this in their work and then you bring it in bit by bit to find a way to do good scientific research that actually ethically and personally does the things that you think this research should be doing.

PC: Well, that's absolutely right. Our national response is based on a broad base model and it doesn't make sense to me to limit our understandings through research by just picking up on biological understandings, linking it always back to epidemiology without that understanding of how things play out within communities and how culture and sexuality and religion and power and gender imbalances and ethnic differences and people who are challenged intellectually or linguistically, how all of those things impact on, all those vulnerabilities, if you like, impact and make a community more or less resilient and how you can over time capitalise on those things which can help in the response holistically.

JG: It's a big ask, isn't it?

PC: Huge ask, but it's not really because we've been doing it really effectively. It's a huge ask to say let's wind it back and go back to the biomedical approaches because I think what you risk there is actually deconstructing relationships that people have. It's a big ask to keep investing dollars, energy, people, commitment, resources, all of those things into a broad base social model, but I think it's really the only way that we're going to achieve the sort of answers to really complex questions which are totally imbedded in not just the answer to how is a virus transmitted but in the complexities of that question.

A tension in representing a positive perspective is the need to increase the skills of positive people in research and of bridging the knowledge gap of social researchers who find themselves working in a highly medicalised arena. One way in which this is achieved is through a reference group that brings together a range of expertise and that acts as an advise mechanism and/or sounding board.

JG: I guess the other side of that issue is the pressure to have a 'good-enough' understanding across a whole range of disciplines. When I started on the HIV Futures project, one of the really daunting things about that was that I felt that I had to understand the clinical stuff really, really well. That I had to understand immunology and I had to understand pharmacology. It took a while to get over that and actually realise that I had to have the capacity to engage with it but I didn't have to be a pharmacologist in order to conduct the survey.

PC: No. You either need someone who's going to help you understand what's useful and translate it for you or you need to be able to have the ability to be informed about the things that your community thinks are important. That naturally has to involve an element of trust. Trust between me and my communities, if I'm doing the advocacy, or helping set the agendas or participating in the research design, and trust between me and you as a researcher that you're not going to do the wrong thing by me, that you're hearing what I'm saying clearly and that you're honouring the relationship and the partnership that we have.

JG: It's also working in a space that you can say, Jeffrey, you're talking crap.

PC: Yes, yes.

JG: And that's part of the trust in terms of where researchers sit in this epidemic. Being able to be told, no, you're being a complete idiot.

PC: Being able to have hard talks, being able to say all of those things, and as you said earlier, being able to work with the differences that we have and to reach common understandings and I think that's a key thing, rather than pitting one against the other and saying your agenda is this, my agenda is that and never the two shall meet. Well, I think we've proved time and time again that we can successfully, if we look at HIV Futures for example, we can successfully pull together a reference group of positive people selected from the organisations as representatives to come to the table to talk to you about the sorts of things that we would like included and things that we want to know and for you to say, that's fair, this is not, this is reasonable, let's do that a different way.

JG: And that's great, and that's one of the reasons I actually love Futures and the whole process of that is because I'm not there going, oh, no, you can't ask that because it's not scientifically valid. It's actually about a really vigorous discussion about – if I do that, this is what you're going to end up with and that's going to be really useless. It's also great having a reference group that doesn't have *a* positive person on it, but a reference group of positive people, that's extraordinary. I'm comfortable enough in that situation to say, no, I don't want to ask that question that way; this is going to be a real problem politically or ethically if we do this. That is actually a discussion, it's a really genuine discussion that – as a researcher you don't get to do that very often. HIV is pretty extraordinary in that regard. You get to live with your research in a very, very different way.

PC: There's a whole completely different culture operating that requires that we demonstrate a capacity that earns trust through the ways that we participate in working towards solving problems and in the ways that we form true partnerships. We can see that your reference group is a way where you haven't got tokenism, you've got a whole positive group coming from around the country drawing their experiences from their various constituencies and jurisdictions coming to the table where we talk to each other and there's mutual respect because you've set it up so that we're really centrally involved, not tokenistic and able to inform you in the best way that we can, as completely and as comprehensively as we can about the things that are important for you to take on and you respect that trust and you respect that relationship and that partnership by giving us that space, that time and honouring that through taking that on and interpreting that in a way that only you can do with the skills you've got as a researcher. We need to know in a way that is going to satisfy your concerns as a researcher too, and the concerns of your institution and the broader concerns of public health and learning to trust is a big part of that.

JG: Part of what's made the reference group work is that people actually understanding where we're coming from, from a career point of view or from a professional point of view as well as where we're coming from as a member of the communities that we're working with. So, when we want to put something in the survey, I can either say that's really critical, we need that for policy reasons or I can say if we ask this in this way, we're more likely to get it published. And people will actually respect why that's actually a part of the equation as well.

PC: Yes, and you know, we see this operating so often. It's the dynamic and the tension between process and product. There's a certain number of products that researchers traditionally get scored against or funded for and yes, that's important that you have that peer acceptance and that you see that as part of your responsibility, that you meet some of those obligations. But equally important for us is that process is paid due attention to. Valuing those processes means that you value our input, our voices, our participation and the diversity of our views right from the word go, not as an afterthought when a product is released. And part of the process is about informing and communicating results.

JG: And letting go of results too.

PC: And letting go, yes.

The discussion now moves to the outcomes of research, to the stage in the process when the engagement is with the findings and issues of ownership of the findings may arise. Whose research is this anyway?

JG: That's another thing that's really hard for a lot of people to get used to when they come into this field. Resisting the urge to control how the findings are interpreted once you've reported them. Working in this area is that you have to really get over that pretty quickly. I mean, take the mental health questions in Futures, the first time we did that it was really interesting to watch the data on antidepressants and the depression scale being used both to say people with HIV are under this enormous mental health burden, and to say, people with HIV are actually managing very well in mental health terms. The findings were being used to argue both of those and I could come in and take my position but it would be part of a discussion and a debate. No one was going to take me seriously if I stood up and said, no, no, no, what the data mean is this and you should not interpret them any other way.

PC: And that's so important, isn't it? The processes that are involving people mean that there's more of a sense of a likelihood of wanting to have some degree of ownership over the results, and ownership over working with the results and learning from and passing that on back to communities. And that then plays out in terms of practice; research into practice. If people feel engaged with something then they're more than likely to pick it up and read it, more than likely to think well, this is important because we've been involved right from the word go, this is what we think has been important enough to get involved in, so let's find out about it. And then there's the question of how that translates into good public policy. If the research is done in that way, you've got a better chance that your policy is going to be a broad based policy because it's inclusive. I think there's a very strong relationship between the processes of involvement and participation that maybe costs more and is more time consuming but will lead to better practice in the community, in clinics, amongst researchers working with communities and with public health policymakers.

JG: One of the really notable things, particularly with positive people, but with gay community as well in this country, is the level of engagement with research. I look at something like the Futures questionnaire and I ask 'would I complete that if that came through the mail box?' And then I get 1000 of them back and I look at it and I say 1000 people sat down with this 40 page questionnaire and filled it in with this level of detail. That's extraordinary.

PC: That's right, and it's not an easy do, is it?

JG: No, because we don't accept simplistic research questions. None of our projects are ever terribly easy to be involved in because we don't ask you to just fill out a standardised one page questionnaire. Because of that whole process and the sort of research that creates, the projects are often quite complex.

PC: Yes, and I mean that's enhanced, isn't it, I think by the buy-in that our organisations have and the way that that's able to be communicated to the constituencies as an important piece of research for you to participate in, that we've had a say in it right from the word go, that addresses and answers some questions that we want to know and answers some more important public health issues as well. But there's something for everyone in it.

Finally, ethics of researching with positive communities are addressed. Peter talks of honouring the researched and Jeffrey acknowledges the burden that places on the shoulders of the researchers. Together they acknowledge that sometimes the researchers are also the researched and that presents special challenges as individuals move between roles or occupy multiple roles simultaneously.

JG: I think that the combination of the relationship between research and community, and the fact that researchers actually live and socialise in that community creates a very particular flavour in the research. It makes us actually think about the research questions in a different way, so that we would never consider putting transmission as the core concern of something like Futures. I like to call it an ethic, it gives us a way in which to do research that's part of the way we live.

PC: Yes, it's about the interests of the people that you're serving through this research, that are participating, and it's a way of honouring them saying, we're not going to do you over in this process, we respect your rights as human beings, we're doing it within an ethical framework, a human rights framework and that's really important to the way that we value, we consider our research should be constructed.

JG: When we talk about the capacity in, say, the positive community to engage with research it's not just through the representatives, but it's actually in the community. With something like Futures, it's an enormous responsibility as a project and that can be quite daunting as well. You know that what you write in the report, for example can do enormous service, or enormous damage. And if you get it wrong, if you ask the question the wrong way or you ask the wrong question you could have really quite devastating consequences. The good thing about the capacity in the sector is that in some ways it ameliorates that responsibility because people will engage with it and will say, is that right, or that is wrong? That actually makes it easier because you know that people are going to read your work or listen to you in a really active and engaged way and take some of the responsibility for how the work is used.

PC: That's saying we value your input, we are not going to be reductionist in our approach. I think where that relationship that we've developed as the researcher and the researched and with the model that we're talking about with the little reference group are wonderful models because they do embody that trust and they do embody that social responsibility and they encourage participation and all those things that we've said about them. But they also open the way to look at even different ways of working as well. There's the potential for us to think about researchers working within communities within organisations to pick up on in a more focused way the organisational needs or questions, to complement the other ways of working that we currently do.

JG: We are now where we can have this spectrum of social research, from fairly independent and investigator driven research projects through to research projects that are very driven by community and particularly I work on some projects that are very investigator driven, very theoretically driven, very paradigm driven through to stuff I'm doing with the Victorian AIDS Council that are very much organisationally driven. I think we have got to a stage where we can say this whole range of things is actually really important and it's not a choice.

PC: I think it is important in the way that you see social research working with people, creating opportunities. It's about having your community liaison people, seeing if it's possible to draw from the affected communities to fill those positions, having people who are conducting interviews from affected communities. It creates an up-skilling of those people, it creates financial reward it creates potential pathways for them to participate further, it creates trust between the interviewer and the researched and it really does further the whole issues of working together.

JG: Is it something we consciously think about or not? I guess sometimes it is and sometimes it isn't, because you know, when you talk about who crosses over to the dark side of research. Well, of course it's going to be people we know and people we've worked with and that generally means affected and infected, but the conscious bit is that creating those opportunities fits inevitably into that research ethic. That's another odd thing; you have to occasionally look outside HIV to see how odd some of this is. I quite enjoy going to mainstream health or disciplinary conferences and meetings, and just looking at what people are doing and realising that what we're actually doing is so different.

PC: It is so different and if you look at the way immunology works in this country now in HIV it's quite different to the way hepatologists work with their patients around Hepatitis issues or any of the other consumer health groups. I think they have very different relationships to research than the ones that we've helped foster and create over the last 20 years and I think our responses and the outcomes have pro-gressed really instead of staying static in those relationships of research and researched.

Maybe what this conversation demonstrates best is that our knowledge about the lived experience of people with HIV is co-constructed, not just by researchers and representative organisations but complex networks of experience, expertise and history. If the research response has played some part in carving out a space where HIV positive voices are heard and taken seriously, the enmeshment of those with HIV in the research response has given it a richness, texture and emotional honesty that has fulfilled, in practice, the calls of many in academia for a truly trans-disciplinary social science.

8
Who's on Whose Margins?

Michael Hurley

I really love the sense that I have lived through history too. That we have in my lifetime, and in the years that I have been politically active and out, gone from being a vilified, marginalised, criminalised minority to being a people that have come out, forced the world to change and built a community.

(Australian gay historian Graham Willett, 2005: 4)

What is socially peripheral is so frequently symbolically central.

(Stallybrass and White in Shields, 1991: 5)

Minority discourse is thus not simply an oppositional or counter-discourse: it also undoes the power of dominant discourses to represent themselves as universal.

(Gunew, 1994[1])

They've turned their suffering into a resource.

(Genet in Dollimore 1991: 352)

This chapter discusses how marginality is conceptualised in various places and how these conceptualisations are used. It does so in relation to social theory, empirical data and selected research practices. The discussion raises the possibility that, in some social research contexts, practices which assume marginality can reproduce social deficit accounts of the groups being researched, and in the process reinforce social marginalisation of those groups.

Part of the power of 'marginality' is its affective force. It resonates with many people's experience of everyday life, particularly those aspects which feel unfair or which hurt. In that sense marginality enables both political and emotional performativity. One key problem, however, is whether accounts of marginality framed primarily in terms of invisibility, silence, 'hurt' or social neglect actually enable a sufficiently wide-ranging, systematic voicing of the social capacities that are also part of experiences of marginality. Another is, how are we to assess changes in relations between margin and centre? Part of the focus needs to be on what is new or emerging: what are the dynamics of the relations between historical legacy, the present and social change?

When marginality is configured as not much more than either a description of social difference or as a politico-moral flourish, it prevents analysis from understanding social realities as dynamic processes. It offers no way to assess the nature of change. Without this recognition of change,[2] especially where it involves shifts in power relations, 'contestation' risks being – in Gunew's terms – 'simply' oppositional. Indeed, within this way of understanding marginality, to leave the (political) margins is to join the centre.

From these preliminary remarks, we can begin to see a twofold risk in installing 'marginality' uncritically. First, if we theorise marginality without relating it to empirical investigations of social and cultural practice then instances where the relations between centre and margin are displaced or change are likely to be overlooked. Amongst other things, this minimises the ways those instances generate new social resources, new cultural pedagogies and new social possibilities. Second, it's also the case that marginalised groups can have a vested interest in their own marginality, and sometimes produce non-strategic, social deficit accounts of themselves. Sometimes this is a cultural default, a form of inertia. It is produced by quite material pressures. How can marginal groups get funding for their work if the funding itself is tied to being able to prove a social lack or a health threat? The difficulty is that though the lack or threat is real, and needs to be addressed, the process of doing so often engenders practices of self or group representation that sideline the existing strengths of social capacity and power.

My overall concern is whether the concept of marginality is sufficiently robust by itself for analytic purposes (Dennis, 2005). What needs to be in play to make it adequate for theorising, understanding and researching social differences? That question should not be understood as meaning I am querying whether there are any structured inequalities between different groups of people. Rather, I am querying the effects of using attenuated versions of the concept.

Research and the researched

Social research, particularly applied social research, is often spoken of formally and casually as though it is primarily or only an instrumental activity that produces innocent knowledge without ethical or political dimensions or implications outside of a research ethics approval process. In this commonsense discourse, considerations of ethics become a matter of legality and disciplinary sanctioned activities (confidentiality, legality, methodological soundness) and any political or social implications are seen as a question of how the research is used by others. The instrumental is related to making the project operational: formulating research questions, devising the best methods for getting the questions answered, seeking ethics approval, gathering the data and presenting and discussing the results.

As will become obvious, a myriad of issues arise in relation to these seemingly simple descriptions of aspects of research practice. Some qualitative researchers would say that I have already built in a focus on a particular kind of empirical data collection. They would see the problem as epistemological: the methodological reduction of 'empirical data' to facts generated as though they pre-exist social relations and simply await discovery.

I do have a certain sympathy for criticisms such as these, and need to acknowledge that, from my point of view, there are no theory-independent languages for observational purposes. Even so, that does not mean the problem of evidence has been solved. However, I do not intend yet again rehearsing long-standing epistemological arguments about the relations between theory, facts and the real world (Adorno, 1978; Chalmers, 1999; Haraway, 1991; Lakatos and Musgrave, 1970). I propose instead to look at some of these issues with reference to particular kinds of social research practice and their contexts.

The contributors amongst whom I include myself, work on the assumption that, for whatever reasons, some groups of people are more disadvantaged than others. Those people are seen as marginal in their relation to social goods: health, education, income, security, social respect and participation and, again for diverse reasons, as being more socially vulnerable: to ill health and disease, unemployment, poverty and political and social violence. 'Vulnerability' should be understood here as a potentiality or a likelihood, rather than as an a priori imposition of a structural necessity.

'Marginality' is not simply a category for either *describing* or *expressing* aspects of particular peoples' lives. It is an analytic category that has its own history. Aspects of that history underpin the work of the researchers in this book. They use aspects of the history of marginality to explore and query how power operates to structure social experience, and how it operates within the ways people make sense of what is going on in their lives. Though the researchers to a degree share this perspective, they also have quite different ways of conducting their research and different conceptual frameworks. There is nothing unified about their methodologies or methods. Nor is the research positioned as 'servicing' the margins from the outside. The research tries to recognise what it is that structures everyday life, what people do that works, as well as what they do that does not work, and then asks how what works might be further harnessed. These involve issues of structure, agency, social capacity, performativity and care of the self.

The contributors are researchers who have a variety of collaborative relations with the people and groups researched. Their respondents are sometimes connected to, serviced by, or members of organisations with which the researchers have collaborated for the purposes of doing the research.

These organisations often have systematic inputs into research agendas, particularly where the same or similar projects occur over time with the same groups of people or populations. The organizations are involved in scientific advisory structures, steering committees and reference groups which have diverse roles, including: suggesting matters requiring research; building ownership of research projects; the formulation of research questions and their expression in the relevant research instruments; the recruitment of respondents; types of recruiters; the working out of suitable samples and analytic themes. It is not that the researched set the overall research questions, though they may well influence them and the wording used in instruments. Rather, they raise matters that are considered and turned into research questions. In other words, the research is informed by the margins through a series of reflexive interactions between the researchers, the researched and organisations that negotiate on their behalf. It is also the case that these organizations have relations with their members, the groups they service, funders, national strategies and other organizations. The matters they raise are informed by these relations, by other research and by what is learned in service delivery and advocacy. Collaborative activity of necessity brings with it critical reflection and absolutely requires the methodological formalising of reflexivity.

A key aspect of this kind of social research is recognition of the dialogical nature of the social relations that structure it. These are generative of research processes as much as of formal links. Reflexivity partly consists of enabling the differential positioning of collaborators within the research design, and of intellectual 'distance' in analysis.[3] This, in turn, can allow for strategic intellectual and social engagement without collapsing them into each other. Positioning this kind of reflexivity within social research brings with it social, political and instrumental challenges. It can make the research much more analytically acute and useful, as well as slow it down.

In order for organisations, groups and individuals to broker, negotiate or inform relations with others they have to have ways of 'representing' themselves. Representation is relational: 'a practice of selection, combination and articulation' (Julien and Mercer, 1988: 4). Amongst other things, 'marginality' is a representational strategy for articulating contextually how it is that the group or organization wants to be seen or understood. It establishes a public speaking position. One of the problems for community-based or non-government organizations is that they are seen by media and government agencies as speaking for *the many*: their members; or the people on whose behalf they claim to speak; or those who, for practical purposes, are excluded from participating; or those who do not want to participate, in the negotiating process. In that sense, whatever the best intentions of the organisation, *the many* often become secondary in the politics of representation. For both the organization and for the spoken to (government, funders, researchers, the media), this is expedient because it is a practical way to do things. However, this practice of representation means that organisational spokespeople and associated individuals ('Parma is a woman with HIV/breast cancer/a disability') become the 'voice' for everyone. They are forced into a position of tokenism by being made 'representative' of the whole, in order to take the opportunity to speak the issues of the many.

Marginal groups are unavoidably caught up in restricted economies of enunciation, that is, where and how they can speak publicly. (So is everyone, but the power relations shift according to who is speaking, where and to whom.) As Julien and Mercer argued in relation to the emergence of new forms of black filmmaking in Britain in the 1980s:

> First, individual subjectivity is denied because the black subject is positioned as a mouthpiece, a ventriloquist for an entire social category which is seen to be 'typified' by its representative. Acknowledgement of the *diversity* of black experiences and subject-positions is thereby

foreclosed. Thus, secondly, where minority subjects are framed and contained by the monologic terms of 'majority discourse', the fixity of boundary relations between centre and margin, universal and particular, returns the speaking subject to the ideologically appointed place of the stereotype – that 'all black people are the same'.

(Julien and Mercer, 1988: 5)

This seeming refusal of 'spokespeople', whether understood in terms of a representative or a character in a film, is not being put as an argument against people speaking for or about group interests at all. It is, however, a recognition that the doing of this is inevitably partial and requires constant negotiation because it is as much a process of being *seen to* represent all, rather than one of claiming to. What Julien and Mercer acknowledge is the relativities and limits involved. They initiate a discussion of how to include these within understandings of representation as a constant process of negotiation. Julien and Mercer see all this as enabling, because 'it brings a range of critical issues into an explanatory structure' (5). I might point out that this was a discussion between members of a marginal group, black gay men, occurring within a special issue of a prestigious academic journal within a minority academic discipline: film studies. Who gets to speak where?

The lessons here for researchers are several:

- They need to understand and be sensitive to the representational context in which they are recruiting for, or brokering ownership of, the research project.
- They need to make sure the representational process does not unintentionally skew their sampling or recruitment by only including those that the brokering organization approves.
- They need to be aware of what it means to ask individuals or projects to bear the burden of representation of the many.

What the work included in this book indicates is that the research reported on rarely involves a sense of the researched as being 'over there', as somehow 'foreign'. They are subjects rather than objects ('populations') of research. This matters when one sees national and international social research, both quantitative and qualitative, that misses the point. One of the main problems usually is in the questions asked. Social researchers often have an inappropriate relation with whom or what is being researched. The inappropriateness has multiple sources. They can be reductively characterised as having a primarily instrumental relation with the researched. Such a relation often distorts the process of research question formation because the researchers in effect *assume* two things in advance:

- that the potential research groups can be approached *only* when needed for research purposes (i.e. there is no need for ongoing, collaborative relations) and do not have to be included in any process after data collection;
- that the researchers understand in general how the lives of the researched are socially constituted.

These assumptions in turn sometimes affect how the wider research questions are operationalised in favour of ease of implementation (cost, sampling, recruitment, data analysis). They can very clearly affect discussion of results when the data are discussed in ways that unintentionally misrepresent or show no awareness of, or sensitivity to, political realities or policy environments.

Further, in contexts where research questions are primarily devised in relation to what has been done in other narrowly focused, disciplinary-based research (literature searches) a closed feedback loop emerges. The result is an over reliance on scholarly literatures that bear little relation to either the relevant social theory or what the researched groups, or the practitioners who have attempted to use it, have said about the research (design, results, analysis). What we see is a relaying of scholarly self-referentiality, rather than reflexivity. The limits to the 'scientificity' of peer-review processes here often have to do primarily with checks on the adequacy of method: the relations between method and instrument of data collection and between method, data results and discussion.

In research practices that have only an abstract and/or highly contingent relation to the researched, the 'grey' literatures produced by researchers, the researched and practitioners have little status (evaluations, discussion papers, minutes of meetings). The same occurs with the ongoing feedback and discussion amongst researchers and between researchers and practitioners. These discussions, whether formal or informal, that inform the devising of research questions and instruments, methodological refinement and analysis, disappear in some genres of research description and reporting. They are granted no epistemological status in discussions of method or project rationale. Rather they are represented and positioned as subjective elements with no formal or evidentiary value, and are believed to threaten the integrity of the research design (Latour and Woolger, 1979). Whereas in the Humanities some of the 'grey' documents would count, under certain circumstances, as primary sources for research purposes, and then be subjected to protocols of verifiability and analysis, in some versions of the 'harder' social sciences they often disappear from view. That is, unless the same information can be collected by other means: surveys, interviews, case notes, literature searches.

The problem remains even when what are thought to be the same kinds of information are collected by these other means. The process of research questions being primarily determined by a scholarly literature that has itself begged the question of where do research questions come from is further compounded by practices of discussion and analysis where the social categories involved are taken for granted. In other words, the social nature of language is ignored so that 'interpretation' is restricted to the validity of the relations posited between units of data. Any evidentiary issues to do with the role of language, genre and writing in description and discussion are minimised or ignored. As Chandler, Davidson and Harootunian (1994: 1) put it for work in the Humanities: "questions and evidence are therefore 'correlative' in the strong sense that facts can only become evidence in response to some particular question."

When such narrowly formulating research then becomes the evidence base on which practitioners are required to justify programme design and implement interventions, the result can be ill-conceived health promotion priorities, policies and practices and the researchers say, 'Not my problem, I do research not health promotion.'

In contexts where much of the research funding is strategic, either through specific national strategies or policy that sets funding priorities, claims that researchers and their research are not implicated in wider processes often seem disingenuous. However, one might more generously see these claims as an acknowledgement that more and more social research is 'applied research' and that there are challenges and difficulties in doing it. There are necessary demarcations that require constant negotiation. The shifts in research policy context, however, are not helpfully understood by positioning notions of curiosity-driven research only outside of applied contexts. To do so is to devalue the kinds of curiosity and disinterestedness evident in much of the best applied social research and to make mistaken claims about the relations between disinterestedness and the critical distance necessary for good research. Researchers situated in proximity to the researched are as capable of producing research results unpalatable to or challenging for the researched, as those who have no articulated relation with them.

Though social research, especially HIV social research, may have its own specificities, these are not problems particular to it. Much international social research is funded by institutions which have very clear senses of the relations between the research and what they want it to do and frame their project selection processes accordingly. This is not, in principle, an issue of compromised methods, though expectations may have to be monitored and negotiated. The funders and the researchers want the authority of 'scientificity': certificated researchers who engage in peer-reviewed research design and publication. The funders and the researchers also want the relations between the research and the researched to be ethical. Increasingly, consent has to be brokered not simply between an interviewer and an interviewee, but between research aims, the associated instruments and the researched. In these cases the researcher is seeking consent from a population (Kaldor and Millwood, 2005). This spills over into negotiations between both researchers and organizations connected to the researched and between different organizations involved in brokering relations with the groups affected both by the research and the issues under investigation. This poses particular challenges for international research (Lo and Bayer, 2003) in which several countries may be involved simultaneously with a likelihood of intricately linked, cross-country and intra-country co-ordination involving layers of committees, and training of multiple teams of recruiters and instrument administrators. Challenges multiply when there are multiple organizations claiming close ties with the people being researched.

An example of how these matters can play out occurred in 2004 in quite spectacular ways. A consortium of Cambodian, Australian and US clinical researchers initiated negotiations for a clinical trial of the HIV drug tenofovir as prophylaxis against HIV infection among sex workers. That is, the trial was exploring pre-exposure prophylaxis (PREP) as an HIV prevention strategy. This occurred in a situation of limited access to HIV treatments for people living with HIV and where new HIV infections were ongoing. On the available evidence the researchers negotiated consent with a sex worker organization, but another sex worker organization with more official status later claimed not to have been consulted. I am not aware of any public evidence documenting whether the first organization talked to the second or whether there was any brokering process that occurred between them. The Cambodian government effectively prevented the proposed research, 'slamming the studies as unethical experimentation on Cambodian guinea pigs'. This followed protests from the second local sex worker organisation, and from international HIV activists who mobilised around the issue at the International AIDS conference in Bangkok (Machon, 2005). There were legitimate concerns expressed by local sex workers about compensation for any side effects from the drug, but also what Machon refers to as 'scaremongering' around the drug itself.

One critic of Machon's account has since argued in relation to issues of informed consent that 'Gilead made false and misleading comments about tenofovir as a single therapy' (Bourdier, 2005: 25). As well, US policies prevented funding the distribution of injecting equipment as part of risk reduction strategies needed in a clinical trial for HIV prevention purposes. From Machon's point of view, what happened 'could seriously hamper the HIV research effort in resource-poor countries at a time when it is needed more than ever' (Machon, 2005: 6).

Proximity, situatedness and formulating good research questions are all matters of articulation. The problem is one of the relations between ideas, researchers, research practices, and the researched. In that sense I am engaging in a series of reflections on the challenges of articulating those relations in relation to the concept of marginality. There are no guarantees in the manoeuvres required; however there are ethical and political principles involved. Articulation involves an endless shuffle, a constant reverberation, between researcher and researched, just as it does between centre and margin.

Marginality and measurement

While Willett in the quote that introduced this chapter would be the last to argue that gay men and lesbians are no longer vilified or discriminated against at all, he is arguing that the situation in Australia *as a whole* has changed dramatically for gay men. He sees marginalisation as typifying the past. The key words are, perhaps, 'in my lifetime'. He is marking out political change as characteristic of the past 25 years. I begin the chapter with Willett's statement because it constructs marginality in relation to change and politics. In other words, the experience of marginality from his perspective is not a straightforward synonym for permanently being in a minority. Indeed he refers to 'being a people' as a state of having moved on from being a 'minority'.[4]

Obviously Willett is not referring to population statistics. Whether we use social identities such as gay and lesbian, or refer to various same sex practices with research categories such as 'men who have sex with men' or 'same sex attracted young people', either way the people being referred to are statistical minorities (Ca'ceres et al., 2006; Couch and Pitts, 2006). Rather, Willett configures being in a minority as a social and political effect of marginalisation.[5] One question we might ask here is what are the social effects of being a very small number of people and how that might affect social position over time? Willett's other work indicates that he is well aware of place in this process, of the social differences between cities, states and the metropolitan and the regional.

Willett includes being 'marginalised' in a list of past horrors, positioned between being 'vilified' and 'criminalised'.[6] From his historical perspective, marginalisation largely disappears from the present, because of changes in social attitudes ('vilification') and to criminal legislation. In the lifetime he refers to, male homosexual practices have been legalised in every Australian state. There have been various, if uneven, changes to state and national discrimination legislation, and, again over time, a general equalisation of age of consent. Similarly, after examining legal records and judicial practices between 1980 and 2000, one sociologist of criminality has argued that the status of Australian male homosexuals has shifted from being 'criminals to legal subjects whose sexual identity accords rights of citizenship and includes a legitimate claim on protection from violence' (Tomsen, 2002: 95).

Marginality, from these perspectives, is a matter that includes legalisation, equity in legal access and changes in social status. Increased legal status and a lower frequency of negative events are criteria for assessing degrees of marginality and for concluding that marginality has decreased. We could on this basis begin to construct criteria by which marginality and degrees of social marginality could be measured or assessed. Note, however, how marginality sometimes emerges as a static state when configured this way for measurement purposes which require the data to be collected at a particular point in time. For this not to be the case, we require both quantitative longitudinal studies of changes over time and qualitative studies of processes of change.

What then are the indicators against which we can assess claims of marginality? At what point is a group no longer marginalised? Notice that sometimes marginality is used behaviourally to speak about practices such as injecting drug use or sex work, but at other times it works around much bigger categories such as 'gender' (women), race and ethnicity, and at still other times around disability.

Arguably, each of these uses requires quite different analysis, even where 'marginality' is the common term. What does it mean, for example, to call women a 'marginal' group when statistically, in Australia at least, they are a majority (just) of the population? Clearly the claim is about something more than numbers. It suggests that to understand how marginality is being used we have to consider social relations. The suggestion is not that numbers are irrelevant, rather that they have social assumptions built into them. However, you cannot collect data without framing assumptions. They underpin the kinds of questions asked. The issue is one of which assumptions – how are the questions best asked? What social relations are presumed and how are the categories used to ask questions and analyse answers? That question is no different epistemologically to that asked by statisticians who outline their assumptions.

We might consider here developing distinctions between temporary tactical disadvantage, ongoing tactical disadvantage (political marginalisation) and trends towards social incorporation over time, whether driven by justice, politics or economic commodification (de Certeau, 1988: xvii–xx). However, these too are not straightforward matters. For example, the Melbourne *Age* newspaper recently reported on an international survey of 17,000 people in 16 countries which asked about their attitudes to the United States of America (Coultan, 2005: 9). The pollsters concluded: 'the United States remains broadly disliked in most countries surveyed ... The magnitude of America's image problem is such that even popular US policies have done little to repair it' (http://pewglobal.org).

When is 'an image problem' indicative of marginality? The answer is specific to who and what is being discussed. If, for example, gay men and lesbians use media representations as an index of homophobia (www.glaad.org) then we could say 'image problems' are a measure of marginalizing processes (Hurley, 2005). We might also distinguish between 'image' and attitude as markers of marginality or marginalisation. Are attitudes sufficient as indicators of marginality? At a general level, the answer would need to be no. However, we could ask, in what contexts, or in combination with what other factors, might negative social attitudes be markers of marginal status? Does racial abuse during an assault based on the racial characteristics of the assaulted confirm marginality? It confirms racism, certainly, but what if the assaulted person is a member of a ruling elite as well as a different racial group? Who is currently marginal in Zimbabwe?

Perhaps I am labouring too hard. Marginality refers to

- sets of social relations that are indicative of structures of social, political and/or economic inequality and/or disadvantage; and,
- the cultures of the people who are affected by these structures.

We might note that neither one of these criteria includes what it means for individuals to feel marginalised. Yet that sense of personal threat to safety is common in the research into marginal groups and for some is associated with self-harm, mental illness or impaired capacity to access social support. How can these matters be factored into frameworks used to assess marginality?

Elsewhere I have suggested that the marginality of urban gay men cannot be only understood or assessed by degrees of equality in legal rights (Hurley, 2005). I suggested that any assessment needed to occur across at least three domains: consumer citizenship, social citizenship and legal citizenship. It is the multiplicity of domains that matters here for research purposes, rather than the theoretical adequacy of the concept of citizenship. Domain multiplicity ensures that plenitude is incorporated into the analysis, as well as social and political deficiency. This plenitude involves including both the capacities and strengths present in marginalised cultures and the relations between those capacities and their commodification and representation in wider media cultures and social formations. Now I would add two other domains to do with legacies and innovation. The first would include the affective legacies associated with being a small population emerging out of histories of social siege (homophobia, the AIDS epidemic). That would enable analysis of shifts in socialities of resilience (Russell, 2005) and *ressentiment* (Owen, 2002; Tapper, 1993). The second domain would address the dynamics of social and cultural innovation: what has been learned, the mechanisms of cultural reproduction and the identification of socio-cultural potentialities.

On the basis of the above discussions, we can begin to think of analysing marginalisation on at least two axes: historical and contemporary. The historical would be a measure of change *over time* using sets of agreed upon social indices particular to the group in question. Each index would then have a scale of relevant items. For example, in the case of gay men or lesbians we might use legalisation of homosexual acts; degrees of equality under the law (the relevant scale might include: age of consent; access to superannuation, reproductive technologies, benefits accruing to 'domestic' partnerships; right to military service etc), changes in rates of physical assault and murder, changes in social attitudes, frequency and nature of representation in the media. The contemporary would be a scale of current comparative equality measures. The scale could include items such as equality of access (to income, education, employment, health, medical and welfare services), social discrimination, media reporting of relevant issues etcetra.

Any study of legal change and some social and cultural shifts in relation to homosexuality in Australia over the past 35 years makes it hard to claim gay men as gay are now marginalised in anything like the ways they were before. Having said that, a major complication occurs when we take into consideration that in the past 20 years over 90 per cent of HIV infection, AIDS diagnoses and AIDS deaths in Australia were amongst gay men and that in the first ten years this unleashed significant degrees of homophobia. The differential effects of this on gay communities over time are very hard to assess; however, based on a range of research data there seems little question that those effects are lessening amongst HIV-negative gay men. Even within this context, and as difficult as it was to see what was happening during the period of rising death rates (1983–1995) I think the assessment of major social shifts holds. Major shifts, however, are not reducible to the establishment of social equality.

Agreement on historical and contemporary scales would allow us to identify marginality at the level of the group, but of course that tends to assume all members of the group are socially homogenous. It not only constructs the group through notions of social identity (sexualities, 'ethnicities', genders), which may or may not be useful, it also asks us to consider the claims of multiple identities and the relations between them. It is fairly clear, for example, that while one can make a strong case for saying gay men as a group in Australia are no longer marginal in ways anything like they were 30 years ago, there are subgroups of whom this cannot so easily be said: young gay men or lesbians, and gay men living with HIV. Gay men and lesbians from culturally and linguistically diverse backgrounds and those living in regional areas may also be exceptions. Is it the gayness that creates marginality or a combination of it and any of age or ethnicity or health status or Indigeneity or disability? Are the criteria to be quantitative indicators or those developed from qualitative research into life experiences or a combination?

For example, a national survey of same-sex-attracted young Australians in 2004 (n = 1749) indicated that 76 per cent felt 'great' or 'good' about their sexuality (Hillier, Turner and Mitchell, 2005: vii). More had disclosed their sexuality to someone else in 2004 than in 1998

(95 per cent versus 82 per cent) (2005: ix). However, the research also found high levels of discrimination and physical and verbal abuse that had 'a profound impact on young people's health and well-being.' Same-sex-attracted young people who had been abused 'fared worse on almost every indicator on health and well-being than those who had not … [and] were more likely to self-harm, to report an STI and to use a range of legal and illegal drugs' (Hillier, Turner and Mitchell, 2005: viii). Other research indicated over-representation of same-sex-attracted young people amongst homeless young people (Hillier, Matthews and Dempsey, 1997; Rossiter et al., 2003).

In the case of people living with HIV in Australia, the HIV Futures 4 survey (n = 1059) reports 26.9 per cent as living below the poverty line and 33.5 per cent experiencing less favourable treatment from health services because of HIV (Grierson et al., 2004: xv–xvi). On both of these indicators the percentage for gay men was lower than for others who completed the survey.[7] We can conclude from this that gay men living with HIV are less likely than others to live under the poverty line, but there are no comparable data for HIV-negative gay men. How do we then take this into account if what we are trying to do is factor in experiences of living with HIV into assessments of the marginal status of gay men?

As Willis et al. noted in relation to HIV-positive Aboriginal and Torres Strait Islander (ATSI) respondents in the HIV Futures 2 survey: 'we recognise that although surveys are good instruments for understanding broad social and cultural patterns in relatively homogenous populations, they may not adequately represent qualitative differences where there is considerable diversity in lived experience' (Willis et al., 2002: 2). Lawrence et al., (2006) began to address social heterogeneity amongst Indigenous men who have sex with men by carrying out a state-based survey and qualitative interviews with a specific sample of those men, as distinct from analysing Indigenous responses in broader population samples.

In this discussion I have been using available data on Australian gay men and begun to indicate some of the analytic challenges in distinguishing between their overall 'marginality' as a group while taking into account the heterogeneity of their composition. Assessing whether they are a marginal group would require establishing a calculus of indicators. I say a calculus because amongst the challenges is identifying at what point the difficulties in the negotiation of everyday life in a subgroup or a series of subgroups outweighed general positive indicators for the group as a whole. This leaves aside, so far, questions of productive experiences of marginality, irrespective of negative social indicators, and how, if at all, members of a particular marginal group want to be part of the centre.

Any investigation of the field of 'marginality' quickly shows up multiple and conflicting discursive practices and disciplinary differences. It also exposes major time lags in when and where 'marginality' appears, as either or both an organising category in social theory (the metaphor of centre and the margin), and as a way of operationalising empirical social research. Further, in social and political theory 'marginality' is often a relatively politicised category closely linked with issues of race, sexuality and particular formulations of power. It has antecedents in earlier discussions of colonialism and class.

In social research into health, 'marginality' is often configured 'naturally' as an unproblematic given, with a mostly unspoken link to what are configured as pre-existing social categories: 'women', 'black women', 'Third world women', 'intravenous drug users', 'sex workers', 'people with disabilities' and 'gays and lesbians'. The social, political and theoretical constitution of these categories *inside and outside of the research* disappears in the process of making them operational. Indeed what sometimes emerges is a conceptual slide between 'marginal groups' and 'hard to reach populations'. They often become synonyms. This slide then 'reappears' on the field of service delivery. 'Hard to reach' populations are often intrinsically linked to notions of risk practices and collapsed into 'at risk groups'. This is one of the ways empirical social research is compromised by disciplinary practices that produce social deficit accounts of their research respondents.

One way of understanding this is through examples of how aspects of the research process are linked to wider social issues and to how research itself is configured.

In 1998, the Australian Bureau of Statistics (ABS) wrote to many major research institutes recommending that they reconsider the wording of questions used to collect data on Indigenous Australians. The suggestion was that instead of asking a general question about cultural background, they specifically ask 'Are you of Aboriginal or Torres Strait islander descent?' The letter from the ABS was prompted by a letter to them from the Office for Aboriginal and Torres Strait Islander Health (OATSIH). As a consequence of this letter the national HIV centres involved in the Gay Periodic surveys which collect data on gay male sexual practices in state capital cities changed their research instrument. Previously the question had been 'What is your ethnic background?' and respondents were then asked to tick a box indicating that they were Anglo-Australian or to answer 'other' by specifying Indigeneity or ethnicity. After the question was changed to meet the request from the ABS, the number of Indigenous respondents to the Sydney Gay Men's periodic survey almost doubled and the number of Indigenous respondents to the South east Queensland survey tripled. The larger increase in South east Queensland can be further explained by the use of a key Indigenous HIV Educator in recruitment for the survey at the same time as the question was changed. This was consistent with recommendations on data collection made in the National Indigenous Australians' Sexual Health Strategy in 1997 (ANCARD, 1997: 99–101; Lawrence et al, 2006: 6–7).

We could amplify the meanings attached to this example. Historically and politically, there is reason to do so. They involve issues to do with including Indigenous peoples in research, establishing statistical visibility and statistical validity, cultural sensitivity, the category of 'hard to reach' populations and the configuring of marginality. In other words, they provide a matrix for introducing a discussion of how marginality plays out in social research. However, I am using this example to make a simple point. In this instance, asking the right question and using appropriate recruiters moved the respondents out of the category of 'hard to reach'. The example indicates that the category was not usefully applied to any of the population (gay-community-attached indigenous men), the samples (Sydney, Brisbane), or recruitment techniques. Their status as 'hard to reach' had been an artefact of research practices rather than a characteristic of them as a population.

The problem of how to recruit a sufficient sample was resolved because the Indigenous organisation OATSIH existed as a unit inside the Commonwealth Department of Health and Ageing and was funded at a level which allowed it to develop the social capacity to influence the main official statistical counter in the country. There was, however fleeting, a relationship between the two organisations. In addition, the example shows that simple actions are sometimes very effective. (How it had come about that Indigenous people had been asked to include themselves in many kinds of research as one of many ethnic groups[8] is of course no small matter. That too had been a form of marginalisation.)

What is a simple example, however, has other dimensions. These issues play out in many contexts. As Hanif Kureishi (1986) put it graphically: 'It is the British, the white British, who have to learn that being British isn't what it was.' These contexts include how the researched see themselves, as was the case with the Indigenous Australian respondents discussed above. Johnson-Eilola discusses how this applies in relation to both statistics and what is seen as 'information'. He focuses on how 'white' is used as a descriptor of race in census data and the associated complications in New Mexico, USA. In order to make an ethical point he notes that respondents and researchers recontextualise information in different ways to the same end, identifying as, or being identified as, 'White rather than Hispanic' and how this acts to minimise differences in quantitative income data. In other words, a proportion of respondents from Hispanic background identified as White and their incomes were distributed accordingly. He then points to how researchers sensitive to these issues,

> recontextualise the representation of income among citizens, coming up with the category that is now commonly referred to as 'White, non-Hispanic'. The categories are not 'clean', in a technical sense, because White*, White, and Hispanic do not neatly add up-but rather than cooking the information or somehow making it invisible, [they] show the conflicts ... This is messy and not very satisfying, but at the same time it prevents readers from easily absorbing information – the recontextualisation asks questions it cannot answer, and that is its strength.
>
> (Johnson-Eilola, 1997)

So one issue here is how data are represented. The asterix in 'White*' flags an issue with how the figures are derived, 'the conflicts'. The general issue is whether the method and discussion sections of research reporting encourage readers to see the ways in which the mechanisms of data collection and presentation – the use of the social categories 'White' and 'Hispanic' to organise the data – affect the nature of the data and how they might be understood. In the specific New Mexico case referred to, Johnson-Eilola believes that the income disparities become clearer.

Margin as metaphor: being structured as powerless

Some readers may be disconcerted by the reference to the centre/margin distinction as a 'metaphor', as though that means it is simply a figure of speech with at best rhetorical effects that have no bearing on empirical research or social realities. Bear with me. From my perspective, metaphor is a primary constitutive element in both conceptual discussion and social practice. Concepts are what we use to make sense of the real and affect how we do so. Metaphor has clear consequences for the kinds of research questions asked, the devising of data-collection instruments, the representation of data and the discussion of results. It is a central component in the doing of research. The metaphor of the centre and the margins is not only an intellectual ordering mechanism, it also plays particular roles in different discourses.

Adjectival use of 'margin' in 'marginalised' populations seems innocuous enough, however what is involved in conceptualising and grouping people as marginal? At its best the concept considers the structuring of social differences between groups of people, but it is not a marker of just any form of difference. Rather it marks out forms of social, economic, cultural and political difference and then organises these differences in relation to the unequal distribution of power: a powerful centre and a less powerful margin. While to be marginal is sometimes conceptualised only as being at the edges, this ignores or neglects the ways that marginality involves relationality: differential power relations. In that sense marginality is also about proximity.

Once we get to here, however, the utility of the metaphor loses quite a lot of intellectual as distinct from political force. This is most evident when we take a quick look at the binaries at work in the production of the metaphor of centre and margin.

Is this a spatial metaphor? Are we dealing here with a page (the margins) or a circle (the centre)? Is the metaphor geographical (city as rich centre, regions as poor thus peripheral)? Is the metaphor more abstractly conceived as a power relation (powerful/powerless) and then applied economically or socially (centre/periphery)? If so, how do we deal with changes over time? For example, when a developing country becomes a developed country (South Korea, Japan, Singapore) it is no longer marginal in economic terms or peripheral in a global economy or politically marginal regionally. The success of these countries has a profound impact on how regional relations might be thought in Asia. In fact referring to 'Asian' countries individually quickly begins to undo associated developmental metaphors such as North/South. Are Laos, Cambodia and Burma, for example, in this sense in the South?

A key problem is that the metaphor instantly assumes a particular concept of power. It speaks of power as centralised, as primarily political then economic, then social, and as primarily repressive (Foucault, 1978). Further, it does this in relation to notions of human rights, and makes these notions in the form of legal equality the first port of call. In the arena of health and welfare politics, as in many other arenas, this question of legal equality is further distributed socially; equality of access, equality of service provision, equality of opportunity, equality of quality. In each of these the 'centre' is required to act inclusively. The centre becomes 'the government' or government agencies rather than the structure of social relations as mediated by the state. Small surprise then that the centre might think as a consequence that those to whom it distributes its largesse have to be held accountable ('mutually responsible') or assimilate into culturally preferred forms or take on political forms acceptable to formal political process.

Smith, for example, showed in her research that those disability groups in Australia which relied primarily on direct action to demand their rights were both positioned as 'aberrant' by government funders and positioned themselves as politically marginal: 'what defines them is what ultimately excludes them from influencing politics' (Smith, 2003: 353). At the same time she acknowledged that 'this marginality is a source of power and allows them to challenge governments without concern for any threat of losing funding or legitimacy' (Smith, 2003: 353). Clearly what is at stake here is how the relevant groups want to function, their aims. Their strategies might be seen as having a broad agenda setting force politically rather than state funded advocacy or service provision. Political marginality in this context is mobile and potentially dynamic over time. In Sydney, Women's Refuges were established initially by squatting long before they were provided by government. The originating impulse was political. The price was financial instability. Government funding lessened financial instability, and increased policy purchase but removed, to various degrees, organisational autonomy (Weeks and Gilmore, 1996).

What is important here is how marginality is configured in relation to social identity in different political and policy environments. As Johnson put it, 'The politics of identity is just as much about the construction of powerful, majority and "mainstream" identities as it is about marginalized and less powerful ones' (Johnson, 1997). In Johnson's analysis, marginality is sometimes an indirect effect of how 'mainstream' is being established, rather than produced by a direct policy or practice of marginalisation.

Marginality, however, is not only relational, and power is not only differentially distributed as an effect of (centralised) social structures. Marginality and power are *productive* and often require thinking in specific contexts rather than just generally. The marginal are not always powerless. At this point I am giving the concepts of marginality and power a Foucauldian inflection (Foucault, 1978; 1976).

Marginality takes its political force from its roots in political struggles against the uneven distribution of power.[9] It is, in that sense, a concept that emerged in resistance to specific forms of dominance, and this is still perhaps its primary focus. If we explore the origins of 'marginality' it is not hard to find it in struggles against colonialism, racism, as well as in discussions of disability and youth cultures. Variants of it have been part of the understanding of class differences. It is often analogous to notions of oppression. Feminists and gay and lesbian activists developed and critiqued the notion of marginality over the past 20 years. It was formed in relation to activism and social capacity building, not simply theorised and then enacted. Nor was it simply about resistance to dominance. It involved recognising and relating to the social capacities and forms of everyday life within marginalised cultures.

Marginal people often have cultures of their own, formed in relation to the wider social and political contexts in which they live, *but not determined by them*. The overthrow of apartheid, for example, involved forming links within and between the cultures of the townships, political organisations and internationally. Nor is opposition to marginalisation in the name of a redistribution of power the same as saying we want to be you.

But already we are in trouble. The rhetorical force of the category 'marginal people', its capacity to describe and explain, is progressively weakened and made shrill the further the category is generalised and homogenised.

So one question we might ask is how useful is the metaphor for describing, understanding and explaining these differences in power? A second question is what happens when the marginalised are made the subjects and objects of research? According to Dollimore (1991: 229), 'To be against (opposed to) is also to be against (close up, in proximity to) or, in other words, up against'.

The problem that I see in many uses of the metaphor of 'margin' and 'centre' is that the links between them are dissolved. The margin is represented as always and everywhere marginal. In some versions, the margin is either reduced to being wholly 'other' (and lesser) or only valourised as difference. In the first, marginality is understood as an (unjust) deficit experience. In the second, marginality is romanticised or made exotic or ideologically privileged. The first is commonly seen in health and welfare research, in human rights politics and in forms of 'minority' politics primarily formulated in relation to legal equality. The second is seen in analyses driven primarily by notions of resistance formulated in relation to a homogenous centre. This centre may be highly mobile and at its best not just identified with government ('heteronormativity', the 'White gay, middle-class establishment'), but the outcome is always the same; the speaker is oppositional, morally superior and unfairly deprived of social power or equality.

These metaphors play out in quite complex ways in social research, but to what extent do metaphors of marginality provide useful analytic purchase? I explore this issue in relation to how metaphors of marginality are used, and I argue that particularly when linked to simplistic versions of identity politics and notions of risk they are of limited use in empirical description, data analysis or social theory.

Margins and 'the mainstream' I

Variations on the margin and the centre as a metaphor in social theory and analysis are found in many academic disciplines. Notions of the centre and the periphery have histories in geography and politics. These histories are often formulated spatially (the North and the South), hierarchically (First world, Third world; developed/underdeveloped), descriptively (the rich and the poor). They are often attached to questions of cultural and economic value (the metropolitan and the provincial). The history of the metaphors is a history of what it means to be socially 'inside' and 'outside'.

However innocuous the metaphors seem at first sight, they implicitly distribute a combination of power and 'insight'. Insight becomes a matter of 'positional superiority' (Said in Shields, 1991: 5). That is, the analyst, whether researcher or politician, speaks about 'the other' as on some margin, as someone separate, different to and in a position to be commented on. Speech such as this often goes on to distribute tasks. The South is said to require development while the North has to find its political will (rather than engage in re-development). (The North is never 'over developed'.) These tasks frequently involve questions of global economics and social relations. They develop the authority of commonsense. Statistical frequencies become coincident with social values (the normal, the average). They become hegemonic, seemingly unquestionable.

And yet there is also a history of questioning. It is a history often linked to questions of both race and colonial domination. Franz Fanon wrote in his 1956 essay 'Racism and Culture':

> The unilaterally decreed normative value of certain cultures deserves our careful attention. One of the paradoxes immediately encountered is the rebound of egocentric, sociocentric definitions ... There is first affirmed the existence of human groups having no culture; then of a hierarchy of cultures; and finally, the concept of cultural relativity ... We have here the whole range from overall negation to singular and specific recognition. It is precisely this fragmented and bloody history that we must sketch on the level of cultural anthropology. There are, we may say, certain constellations of institutions, 'established' by

particular men, in the framework of precise geographical areas, which at a given moment have undergone a direct and sudden assault of different cultural patterns. The technical, generally advanced development of the social group that has thus appeared enables it to set up an organized domination. The enterprise of deculturation turns out to be the negative of a more gigantic work of economic, and even biological, enslavement.

These metaphors have both intellectual and socio-political histories. The histories are simultaneously part of Fanon's reference to 'the framework of precise geographical areas'. It is a history that includes those who speak from the margins and those who reflect on what it means to do so.

When Spivak asked 'Can the subaltern speak?' she was posing the question of what happens to the voice of the marginalised in representations of them as subordinate, especially women (1988; 1989). For Spivak, the term subaltern is not a synonym for the oppressed. Rather, it refers to how people are discursively silenced or made invisible by being structurally positioned outside of hegemonic discourse. For her, the margins are the point where hegemony begins to break down and social and political agency can emerge. Spivak develops an analysis in which the margins are not so much positioned at the edge, but are constituted by a silence at the centre. Silence is understood discursively. It refers to the social conditions governing who can speak, how and where, and, just as importantly, who listens and how. It does not mean there are no utterances.

The issue becomes one of hearing that silence, representing it and acting on it (de Kock, 1992). Spivak's work has been influential in postcolonial theory and increasingly in development theory. Kapoor, for example, refers to Spivak's consistently forceful examination of 'the proclivity of dominant discourses and institutions to marginalise the Third World "subaltern" ' and how she seizes on 'the question of representation of the third world' (2004: 627).

The Third World 'other' is often constructed and spoken about as though it bears no relation to the First World other than that of being less economically developed. This over-theorisation of the relations of dominance is often too general. While it is clear, for example, that disease is no respecter of political and social boundaries, it is also clear that the effects of epidemics are intricately bound up with 'precise geographical areas'. First and Third Worlds are intricately connected and research has major effects on the nature of the connections. This is clear for example in the literature of development, but it is also evident elsewhere.

For example, HIV/AIDS research often sets up a series of geo-political contrasts ('industrialised world'/'developing countries') and groups people cross-continentally through categories of race and gender, in order to address the urgency of HIV prevention. This happens in many ways, but here I address only two. First, the refereed journal networks relay protocols for approved methods of research that include configuring how 'prevention' itself is conceptualised behaviourally, cognitively and individually rather than socially (Bourdieu, 1999). These protocols predetermine the kinds of content possible in the generating of results. They are consistent with certain kinds of experimental and social research practices that are institutionally internationally sanctioned by various kinds of research and disciplinary traditions and their political contexts: on the one hand, methods accepted by disciplinary associations, refereed journals and peer review, and on the other hand, adopted by private and government research funding agencies and made conditions of prevention project design.

Second, there is the way sex becomes understood only in terms of gender and reproductive health. Dowsett has argued that though a focus on gender, for example, is crucial to understanding the growing HIV pandemic, when that focus becomes exclusive 'other equally structural ways in which HIV is transmitted are often overshadowed' (2003: 22). He instances several other structuring influences on HIV transmission, but his focus becomes the ways gender obscures sexuality. Two of the key problems he identifies with gender analysis are the emphasis on difference, rather than on similarity, and its constant linking with logics of reproduction. He argues that the problem with the latter in the HIV context has been that sexual expression 'does and does not intersect with human reproduction' – 'it is in these places that most of the patterns peculiar to HIV infection are to be found' (24). As a result, 'this reproductive health focus of gender glues the marginalisation of sex workers and gay and other homosexually active men back into the theorem of deviance' (24). What if, he asks, 'HIV/AIDS is actually an epidemic of desire?'(25).

Writing in 1984 the black American feminist bell hooks said:

> To be on the margins is to be part of the whole but outside the main body. As black Americans living in a small Kentucky town, the railroad tracks were a daily reminder of our marginality ...
>
> Living as we did – on the edge – we developed a particular way of seeing reality. We looked both from the outside in and from the inside out. We focused our attention on the centre as well as on the

margin. We understood both. This mode of seeing reminded us of the existence of ... a main body made up of both margin and centre. Our survival depended on an ongoing public awareness of the separation between margin and centre and an ongoing private acknowledgement that we were a necessary, vital part of the whole.

This sense of wholeness ... provided us an oppositional world view.

(Ferguson et al., 1990: 341)

Commenting on these remarks some years later, hooks said:

I was working in these statements to identify marginality as much more than a site of deprivation ... it is also the site of radical possibility, a space of resistance ... a central location for the production of a counter hegemonic discourse ... these margins have been both sites of repression and sites of resistance

(Ferguson et al., 1990: 341–342)

Fanon and hooks both speak to the difficulty of conceptualising the relations between margin and centre, though they do so very differently and each shifts around on this issue. It is likely, for example, that Fanon might be more at ease with the position taken by Stallybrass and White in 1986: 'what is socially peripheral is so frequently symbolically central' (Shields, 1991: 5). Here the figuring of the peripheral is done in relation to the central in a way which conceptually distinguishes symbolic power from social power and refuses the dominance of the social analytically. From this perspective, the centre is conceptually constituted in relation to the emergence of resistance.

An easy way to demonstrate this perspective is to point to how 'heterosexuality' only emerges historically as a social category once 'homosexuality' has been configured.[10] 'Homosexuality' as an analytic category emerges in the work of European medical sexologists in the later nineteenth century. It appears in dictionaries, as a result, well before 'heterosexuality'. Heterosexuality emerges consequently and subsequently as part of the discursification of 'normality'. It's not needed until the 'abnormal' is conceptualised (Katz, 1996; Sedgwick, 1990; Weeks, 1977).

Being perceived as 'hard to reach'

For purposes of empirical research, often quantitative in design, what are often referred to as marginal populations become in scholarly publications 'hard to reach' populations. 'Hard to reach' refers to difficulties in recruiting a methodologically sound sample, but it also involves a semiotic slide. A population-hard-to-reach-for-recruitment-purposes becomes simply a hard-to-reach-population. We might note two things here initially.

First, if you live within the social relations of what is referred to as 'a hard to reach' population then your perspective on the issue of who or what is hard to reach is quite different. For a street sex worker on a cold night, it may be the client who is hard to reach. He is simply not there. In a South African township, hard to reach is when friends would not answer their mobile phone or have not appeared in the club where you gather or are emotionally withdrawn for some reason or you cannot easily travel to where you want to go. If you live in a culture of like-minded or similarly identified people then questions of access are about you and your social networks, not researchers' difficulties with finding enough of you for purposes of recruitment and reliability of sampling.

So, and this is my second point here, 'hard to reach' sometimes signifies a deficit in the social relations between the researcher and the researched. Let us be very clear. The problem is a function of the point of view of who is speaking and a technical difficulty. From another point of view, the researcher is marginal to the researched. While this claim of researcher marginality may be read as a glib oversimplification of what it means to do socially useful research by those funded to do so, I would suggest that the issue of point of view is also germane to the issue of how social utility is determined and the relation between that utility and research as a practice. Useful from whose point of view? The researcher, the funder or the researched? What are the relations between them?

For the researcher engaged in developing a large random sample, it may seem as though what I am saying is irrelevant. For that researcher it is a question of how to reach the sample (printed survey, web-based survey, telephone sampling), and it is this issue that determines the social relations. However, what are the questions asked in the survey and why? Who had input into their determination? What kinds of thinking produced the questions? How are the answers to be discussed?

As suggested, the category of 'hard to reach' populations often emerges instrumentally as an issue in the recruitment of a pre-selected 'sample' population. The sample is itself a function of method, and in health-focused research at least, is formulated frequently in terms of groups of people being 'at risk' of a disease. That formulation is often developed in relation to epidemiological data used to identify 'at risk groups' or modes of transmission of a disease. On my reading, in an increasing proportion of social research, the categories built into the epidemiology are transferred into social research as though they are unproblematic. So for example, we might see not only the notion that men who have sex with men (MSM) are automatically all at the same risk of HIV and sexually transmitted infections (STIs), but also the notion that sex between men is itself a risky activity.

There is an implicit slide here that has two components. Sex itself becomes risky and risk remains tightly linked to notions of disease. Any notions of sex as pleasurable or as implicated in a wide range of emotional and social capacities or of having implications for how sense is made of and in everyday life disappear, along with understandings of risk as exciting. These matters are ignored or sidelined or problematised.

Such research both constructs the populations involved as marginal and stigmatises them. It pushes them to the margins by continuing to construct them as deviant.

Perhaps more importantly, the categories set up for the collection of the data create both a field and a subsequent series of analytic moves. If the categories of research design and data collection are granted an operational, axiomatic status in the description and/or discussion of the results, the consequence is sometimes an unproblematic use of quite specific examples as exemplary instances 'representative' of the category as a whole. The effect is a conceptual circularity. The closedness of the results confirms the category used to collect the data. As Halperin (2002) pointed out in relation to certain kinds of historical research into same sex practices, quite specific instances are then generalised over to the extent that they function as markers of the concept (homosexuality) as a whole, without regard for the intricacies of the phenomena under investigation. Stigmatised instances become definitive of groups or populations.

A standard move at this point is to say, but the researcher pointed out the limits of the method and is not responsible for how the results are represented by others. To the extent that the results are an artefact of the research design (the questions asked), and the design itself has ignored the relation between the concepts and the contextual social relations of the groups being researched, this is an unacceptable abrogation of responsibility. It is simply a new form of clerical scholasticism. The researcher becomes a faithful monk or a nun responsible only to the order as represented by technical protocols governing method. It also chooses to stay silent on the relations between the researcher and their funding sources. Researchers are often part of, and influential in, the government apparatuses that identify the issues requiring action, determine strategic funding priorities and influence service delivery outcomes. The ethics of dealing with governments in that sense have similarities with the necessary considerations of what it means to accept funding from pharmaceutical companies.

Another move might be to claim that there is a 'preciousness' inherent in what I am saying that makes the doing of research impossible.

Margins and 'the mainstream' II

One of the logics flowing through some of the preceding discussion forces the following question: how can we do research in which the margin can be repositioned outside of the centre's construction of the margin as 'other'? If we were to turn that into a research question it would be something like: 'is it possible to speak usefully of margins without falling into an implicit acceptance of the centre?' and we would look for empirical evidence of practices in which this occurred. However, it is also possible to argue that 'marginality' is not conceptually adequate to this task and that we need different ways of investigating relations of inequality, dominance and power.

We can see the tension between these two ways of proceeding in an article written by Mary Crewe, the Director of the Centre for the Study of AIDS, at the University of Pretoria, South Africa. Crewe (1997) argued that much of the work by marginalised groups was instructive because

it is this construction of themselves as (marginalised) social beings within the dominant power relations that determines how effectively public health practitioners, social welfare officers, educationalists, and community workers can make interventions which would lower the risk of HIV infection in those groups, as well as potentially transform the conditions under which these various defined groups of people live and understand the intervention process they are being asked to engage in.

(Crewe, 1997: 967)

Crewe's frustration is that much research work on marginality does not do the kind of critical analysis that allows the identification of how the social meanings are constructed within these groups:

crucial explanatory and interpretive issues such as power, sexuality, ideology, identity and the autonomous self are seldom adequately addressed ... what is our understanding of the autonomous self [as performed in these contexts-MH] – and what is the perception of marginalised groups such as IV drug users or street children in this regard?

(969)

What we get instead, she argued, is extended descriptive narratives that are positioned against purely bio-medical understandings of the social, but do not actually change anything. What happens, Crewe concludes, is that interventions are developed 'for' people in the margins that keep them there (969). In other words, the centre stays the centre.

Crewe is arguing several things. First, we need better social research that actually shows how marginalised groups built their own social capacities in spite of being marginalised, what they mean to them and how this relates to their understanding of HIV prevention. Second, we need research that links those capacities and understandings to wider issues of power and social intervention. Otherwise the research is simply another apparatus of power/knowledge that keeps people on the margins.

Like hooks, Crewe draws attention to the social relations within marginalised communities and configures them as a social resource. For Crewe, they are the pre-condition for successful social intervention. In this applied theoretical framework, critical marginality analyses suggest the following: first, that we research social capacity and symbolic capital as strategic opportunities for health care and social development; second, that we identify emerging opportunity structures and practices in relation to both existing social capacity and wider power structures (Wallis and Dollery, 2002).

There are signs here of conceptual robustness in that marginality is neither being configured only as a secondary effect of centralised power nor as a state defined only by deficit. Marginality is seen as having a constitutive force in its own right. This requires that researchers respect the integrity of these social relations, even as they explore the effects on them of wider structural forces. The risk is in romanticising the vibrancy of marginality. There are emerging parallels with Foucauldian analyses of the productivities associated with social power and the implication of social capacity in productive engagements with forms of governmentality and social technologies. It is at this intersection that we can move away from understanding the margins as either only suffering at the hands of or 'resisting' the centre and from understanding research as simply 'observing' the oscillations between them. A greater complexity of analysis in the name of marginality becomes possible.

Notes

1. I include page numbers for direct quotes, except where documents are accessed electronically.
2. There is no assumption here that change is permanent or always understandable as 'progress'. Often what happens is that the political field shifts in ways that reposition the issues under discussion and, in that sense, new agendas emerge (Gane 2004; Hall 1996).
3. Note that this is different from a more traditional account of the distinction between subject (researchers) and object (the researched) in which distance is understood as requiring separation.
4. The size of gay and lesbian populations is difficult to estimate, much less their involvement in community. The *Australian Study of Health and Relationships* survey (n = 19,307) reported that 1.6% of men and 0.8% of women identified as homosexual, however '8.6% of men and 15.1% of women were not exclusively heterosexual in either attraction or experience or both' (Smith et al., 2003: 141).
5. de Certeau (1988: xvii) suggestively remarked that 'Marginality is today no longer limited to minority groups, but is rather massive and pervasive'.
6. Willett (2000) makes a more substantive case for his claims of major social change.
7. Personal communication, Rachel Thorpe, Data Manager, *HIV Futures* surveys.
8. Indigenous Australians position themselves outside of 'ethnicity' because inclusion as another 'ethnic' group hides their status as the original inhabitants. 'Ethnicity' refers to the cultural origins of subsequent immigrants to Australia: English, Irish, Italian, Greek, Vietnamese etc. See, Bottomley, de Lepervanche and Martin, 1991; Langton, 1993.
9. In anthropological literatures 'marginality' has been used to refer to transitional states – rites of passage – and in that sense closely linked to what it means to live within those states as experiences of social liminality.
10. In case I need to say it, this is not a claim about human sexual behaviours and the order of their emergence (though it could be).

Bibliography

Adorno, T. *The Positivist Dispute in German Sociology*. Trans. Glyn Adey and David Frisby (London: Heinemann, 1976).

ANCARD. *The National Indigenous Australians' Sexual Health Strategy 1996–97 to 1998–99. A Report of the ANCARD Working Party on Indigenous Australians' Sexual Health* (Canberra: ANCARD, 1997).

Andron, L. and Tymchuk, A. 'Parents who are mentally retarded'. In A. Craft, (ed.), *Mental Handicap and Sexuality: Issues and Perspectives* (Tunbridge Wells: DJ Costello, 1987) 238–262.

Atkinson, D. 'Research and empowerment: Involving people with learning difficulties in oral and life history research', *Disability and Society*, 19: 7 (2004) 691–702.

Australian Federation of AIDS Organisations (AFAO). *HIV/AIDS Resource Manual* (Sydney: AFAO, 1998).

Australian Injecting and Illicit Drug Users League (AIVL). *National Statement on Ethical Issues for Research Involving Injecting/Illicit Drug Users* (Canberra: AIVL, 2003).

Australian Institute of Health and Welfare (AIHW). *Older Australians at a Glance*. AIHW Catalogue no. AGE 25 (Canberra: AIHW, 2002).

Australian Institute of Health and Welfare (AIHW). *The 2004 National Drug Strategy Household Survey* (Canberra: AIHW, 2005) 141.

Baker D., Williamson M., Kendig H., and Quine S. 'The 1999 NSW older persons' health survey: An opportunity to monitor the health and well-being of older people in the community', *NSW Public Health Bulletin*, 10: 9 (1999) 113.

Bailey, S. L., Camlin, C. S. and Ennett, S. T. 'Substance use and risky sexual behavior among homeless and runaway youths', *Journal of Adolescent Health*, 23: 6 (1998) 378–388.

Baltes P. and Smith J. 'New frontiers in the future of aging: From successful aging of the young old to the dilemmas of the fourth age', *Gerontology*, 49 (2003) 123–135.

Barnes, C. 'The social model of disability: A sociological phenomenon ignored by sociologists'. In T. Shakespeare (eds), *The Disability Reader: Social Science Perspective* (London: Cassell, 1998) 56–78.

Barnes, C., Oliver, M. and Barton, L. (eds) *Disability Studies Today* (Cambridge: Polity Press, 2002).

Baron, S. W. 'Street youths and substance use', *Youth and Society*, 31: 1 (1999) 3–26.

Bartos M. 'Community v. population: The case of MSM'. In P. Aggleton, P. Davies and G. Hart, (eds), *AIDS: Foundations for the Future* (London: Taylor and Francis, 1994).

Bernstein, B. *Class, Codes and Control* (London, Routledge Kegan Paul, 1971).

Biklen, S. K. and Moseley, C. ' "Are you retarded?" "No I'm Catholic": Qualitative methods in the study of people with severe handicaps', *Journal of the Association for Persons with Severe Handicaps*, 13: 8 (1988) 155–162.

Bird, S. M. and Brown, A. J. L. 'Criminalisation of HIV transmission: Implications for public health in Scotland', *British Medical Journal*, 323: 7322 (2001) 1174–1177.

Bishop, R. *Whakawanaungatanga: Collaborative Research Stories* (Palmerston North, Dunmore Press, 1996).

Blanchard, M., McKnight, A., Lui-Chivizhe, L., Wray, D., French, K., Sherwood, J., Galleguillos, S., and Smith, A. Creating an Optimistic Future for Indigenous Research in Education: Re-Visioning Both Outcome and Process. *Australian Association for Research in Education* (2000). http://www.aare.edu.au/00pap/bla00530.htm, 29 September 2005.

Booth, R. E. and Zhang, Y. 'Conduct disorder and HIV risk behaviors among runaway and homeless adolescents', *Drug and Alcohol Dependence*, 48 (1997) 69–76.

Booth, T. and Booth, W. *Growing Up with Parents Who Have Learning Difficulties* (London: Routledge, 1998).

Booth, T. and Booth, W. *Parenting Under Pressure: Mothers and Fathers With Learning Difficulties* (Buckingham: Open University Press, 1994).

Bottomley, G., de Lepervanche, M. and Martin, J. (eds) *Intersexions: Gender, Class, Culture, Ethnicity* (North Sydney: Allen & Unwin, 1991).

Bourdier, F. 'Shadowing the facts: the rise and collapse of a controversial trial in Cambodia', *HIV Australia*, 5: 1 (2005) 23–24.

Bourdieu, P. *Outline of a Theory of Practice* (Cambridge: Cambridge University Press, 1999).

Bowsher J., Bramlett M., Burnside I. M. and Gueldner S. H. 'Methodological considerations in the study of frail elderly people', *Journal of Advanced Nursing*, 18 (1993) 873–879.

Bradford, J., Ryan, C. and Rothblum, E. D. 'National lesbian health care survey 1984–85', *Journal of Consulting and Clinical Psychology*, 62: 2 (1994) 228–242.

Brown, H. and Turk, V. 'Defining sexual abuse as it affects adults with learning disabilities', *Mental Handicap*, 20 (1992) 44–55.

Browning C., Minichiello, V. and Kendig, H. 'Research methods in gerontology'. In V. Minichiello, L. Alexander and D. Jones, *Gerontology: A Multidisciplinary Approach* (Sydney: Prentice-Hall, 1992).

Butler, J. *Bodies that Matter: On the Discursive Limits of 'Sex'* (New York and London: Routledge, 1993).

Ca'ceres, C., Konda, K., Pecheny, M., Chatterjee, A., and Lyerla, R. 'Estimating the number of men who have sex with men in low and middle income countries', *Sexually Transmitted Infections*, 82 (2006) 3–9.

Cambridge, P. 'How far to gay? The politics of HIV in learning disability', *Disability and Society*, 12: 3 (1997) 427–453.

Cameron I. D. 'Recruiting older people for clinical trials and health promotion programs', *MJA*, 167 (1997) 441.

Cameron I.D. and Quine S. 'External hip protectors: likely non-compliance among high risk elderly people living in the community', *Archives of Gerontology and Geriatrics*, 19 (1994) 273–281.

Chalmers, A. *What is This Thing Called Science?* (Brisbane: University of Queensland Press, 1999).

Chamberlain, C. and Mackenzie, D. *Youth Homelessness: Early Intervention and Prevention* (Sydney: Australian Centre for Equity through Education, 1998).

Chandler, J., Davidson, A. and Harootunian, H. (eds) *Questions of Evidence: Proof, Practice, and Persuasion Across the Disciplines* (Chicago and London: University of Chicago, 1994).

Cohen-Mansfield J. 'Recruitment rates in gerontological research: the situation for drug trials in dementia may be worse than previously reported', *Alzheimer Disease and Associated Disorders*, 16: 4 (2002) 283–284.

Coleman, A. *Sister, it Happens to Me Every Day: An Exploration of the Needs of, and Responses to, Indigenous Women in Brisbane's Inner City Public Spaces*. Brisbane, Brisbane City Council, Department of Families, Department of Aboriginal and Torres Strait Islander Policy. (Department of Premier and Cabinet, Office of Women, 2000).

Coomber, R. 'Protecting out research subjects, our data and ourselves from respective prosecution, seizure and summons/subponea', *Addiction Theory and Research*, 10: 1 (2002) 1–5.

Corbett, J. 'A proud label: Exploring the relationship between disability politics and gay pride', *Disability and Society*, 9: 3 (1994) 343–357.

Couch, M. and Pitts, M. 'The positioning of bisexuals' and 'Men who have sex with men'. In *Sex, Sexuality and Sexual Health Research, 1990–2004. Health Sociology Review*, 15: 3 (2006) 269–276.

Coultan, M. 'Uncle Sam looks for all the world like the bad guy', *The Age*, 28: June (2005) 9.

Crewe, M. 'How marginal is a "Marginalised Group"?', *Social Science and Medicine*, 45: 6 (1997) 967–970.

Crossmaker, M. 'Behind locked doors: Institutional sexual abuse', *Sexuality and Disability*, 9: 13 (1991) 210–219.

Crow, L. 'Including all of us: Renewing the social model of disability'. In C. Barnes and G. Mercer (eds) *Exploring the Divide: Illness and Disability* (Leeds: The Disability Press, 1996).

Day, C., Degenhardt, L., Gilmour, S. and Hall, W. 'Effects of reduction in heroin supply on injecting drug use: Analysis of data from needle and syringe programmes', *British Medical Journal*, 329: 7463 (2004) 428–429.

de Certeau, M. *The Practice of Everyday Life* (Berkeley: University of California Press, 1988).

de Kock, Leon. 'Interview with Gayatri Chakravorty Spivak', New Nation Writers Conference in South Africa. *A Review of International English Literature*, 23: 3 (1992) 29–47.

de Lepervanche, M. and Bottomley, G. (eds) *The Cultural Construction of Race* (Annandale, N.S.W. Sydney Association for Studies in Society and Culture, 1988).

Dennis, R. *Marginality, Power and Social Structure: Issues in Race, Class, and Gender Analysis* (Amsterdam and London: Elsevier Science, 2005).

Denzin, N. and Lincoln, Y. S. (ed.) *Handbook of Qualitative Research*: Second Edition (London: Sage, 2000).

deVisser, R., Hillier, L., Horsley, P., Kavanagh, A., Pitts, M., Tong, B., et al. *Young Lesbian and Bisexual Women in the Women's Health Australia Study* (Melbourne: Paper presented at the Lesbian Health Day, 2003).

Dodson, M. The end in the beginning: re(de)finding Aboriginality. In M. Grossman, *Blacklines: Contemporary Critical Writing by Indigenous Australians* (Carlton, Victoria: Melbourne University Press, 2003) 25–42.

Dollimore, J. *Sexual Dissidence. Augustine to Wilde, Freud to Foucault* (Oxford: Clarendon Press 1991).

Dowsett, G. 'Some Considerations on Sexuality and Gender in the Context of AIDS', *Reproductive Health Matters*, 11: 22 (2003) 2–29.

Dowsett, G. W., Turney, L., Woolcock, G., Rance, A. and Thomson, N. *Hepatitis C Prevention Education for Injecting Drug Users in Australia: A Research Report* (Canberra: Commonwealth Department of Health and Aged Care, 1999).

Dura J. R. and Kiecolt-Glaser. 'Sample bias in care-giving research', *Journal of Gerontology*, 45: 5 (1990) 200–204.

Dyson, S. *Gender and Diversity: A Workbook for an Equity Approach to Practice* (Melbourne: Women's Health in the South East, 2001).

Ensign, J. 'Health issues of homeless youth', *Journal of Social Distress and the Homeless*, 7: 3 (1998) 159–174.

Fanon, F. 'Racism and Culture'. In Fanon, F. *Toward the African Revolution: Political Essays* (1956), trans. Haakon Chevalier (New York: Grove, 1967).

Feldman, M. A. 'Parenting education for parents with intellectual disabilities: A review of outcome studies', *Research in Developmental Disabilities*, 15 (1994) 299–332.

Ferguson, R., Gever, M., Minh-Ha, T. and West, C. (eds) *Out There. Marginalization and Contemporary Culture* (New York: The New Museum of Contemporary Art and MIT Press, 1990).

Fethers, K., Marks, C., Mindel, A. and Estcourt, C. S. 'Sexually transmitted infections and risk behaviours in women who have sex with women', *Sexually Transmitted Infections*, 76 (2000) 345–349.

Fitzgerald J. L. and Hamilton M. A. 'The consequences of knowing: Ethical and legal liabilities in illicit drug research', *Social Science and Medicine*, 43: 11 (1996) 1591–1600.

Foucault, M. 'Two Lectures', (1976). In C. Gordon (ed.) *Michel Foucault. Power/Knowledge. Selected Interviews and Other Writings 1972–1977* (Brighton, UK: Harvester Press, 1980) 78–108.

Foucault, M. *The History of Sexuality*, Vol. 1 (New York: Vintage Books, 1978).

Frawley, P., Johnson, K., Hillier, L. and Harrision, L. *Livings Safer Sexual Lives: A Workshop Manual* (Brighton: Pavilion Publishing, 2003).

Fry, C. and Dwyer, R. 'For love or money?: an exploratory study of why injecting drug users participate in research', *Addiction*, 96: 9 (2001) 1219–1225.

Gallagher, S. 'One Size Doesn't Fit All', *National AIDS Bulletin*, 12: 15 (1999) 14–15.

Gandhi, L. *Postcolonial Theory: A Critical Introduction* (St Leonards, NSW: Allen and Unwin, 1998).

Gane, N. *The Future of Social Theory* (London and New York: Continuum, 2004).

Gibson, D. *Aged Care: Old Policies, New Problems* (Cambridge: Cambridge University Press, 1998).

Gifford, S. and O'Brien, M. 'Bad blood, bad livers, bad women? Women's experiences of living with hepatitis C', *Australian Hepatitis Chronicle*, Issue 8: (2001) 9–13.

Gifford, S. M., O'Brien, M. L., Bammer. G, Banwell C. and Stoové. M, 'Australian women's experiences of living with hepatitis C virus: Results from a cross-sectional survey', *J Gastroenterol Hepatol.*, 18 (2003) 841–850.

Gifford, S. M., O'Brien, M. L., Smith, A. M. A., Temple-Smith, M., Stoové, M., Mitchell, D., et al. 'Australian men's experiences of living with hepatitis

C virus: Results from a cross-sectional survey', *J Gastroenterol Hepatol.*, 20 (2005) 79–86.

Goodley, D. 'Tales of hidden lives: A critical examination of life history research with people who have learning difficulties', *Disability and Society*, 11: 3 (1996) 333–348.

Greene, J. M. and Ringwalt, C. L. 'Youth and familial substance use's association with suicide attempts among runaway and homeless youth', *Substance Use and Misuse* 31: 8 (1996) 1041–1058.

Grierson, J., Thorpe, R., Saunders, M. and Pitts, M. *HIV Futures 4: State of the [Positive] Nation* (Melbourne: Australian Research Centre in Sex, Health and Society, La Trobe University, 2004).

Grulich, A. E., de Visser, R. O., Smith A. M. A., Rissel, C. and Richters, J. 'Injecting and sexual risk behaviour in a representative sample of adults', *ANZJPH*, 27: 2 (2003) 242–250.

Gubrium J. F. and Sankar A. *Qualitative methods in aging research* (Thousand Oaks: Sage, 1994).

Guillemin, M. and Gillam, L. 'Ethics, reflexivity and "ethically important moments" in research', *Qualitative Inquiry*, 10 (2004) 261–280.

Gunew, S. *Framing Marginality: Multicultural Literary Studies* (Melbourne: Melbourne University Press, 1994). Accessed at http://faculty.arts.ubc.ca/ sgunew/FRAMARG/TWO.HTM, accessed 27/04/2007.

Gwandz, M. *Antecedents and Consequences of Pregnancy and Parenthood among Adolescent Runaways in Shelters* (Unpublished dissertation, New York University, 1998).

Hall, S. 'The Meaning of New Times'. In D. Morley and K-H, Chen (eds) *Stuart Hall: Critical Dialogues in Cultural Studies* (London and New York: Routledge, 1996) 223–237.

Halperin, D. *How to Do the History of Homosexuality* (Chicago: University of Chicago Press, 2002).

Haraway, D. *Simian, Cyborgs, and Women* (New York: Routledge, 1991).

Harrison, L., Johnson, K., Hillier, L. and Strong, R. 'Nothing about us without us: The ideals and realities of participatory action research with people with an intellectual disability', *Scandinavian Journal of Intellectual Disability Research*, 5: 2 (2002) 56–70.

Harwood, V. 'Telling truths: Wounded Truths and the activity of truth telling', *Discourse: Studies in the Cultural Politics of Education*, 25: 4 (2004) 467–476.

Health Canada. 'Achieving health for all: A framework for health promotion, 2003' (from http://www.hc-sc.gc.ca/english/care/achieving_health.html2003), accessed 12/02/2003.

Henderson, L., Reid, D., Hickson, F., McLean, S., Cross, J. and Weatherburn, P. *First, Service: Relationships, Sex and Health among Lesbian Women* (London: Sigma research, 2002).

Higgs, P., Hellard, M., Walsh, N. and Maher, L. 'Careful data analysis required' (Rapid Response for Day et al. 329: 7463): *BMJ*, 7 (2004) 428–429. Accessed 8/12/2004.

Hillier, L. Johnson, K. and Harrison, L. 'Sex secrets and desire; people with an intellectual disability living safer sexual lives', *Network: Journal of the APS College of Community Psychologists*, 14: 1 (2003) 45–52.

Hillier, L. Turner, A. and Mitchell, A. *Writing Themselves In Again – Six years on: The Second National Report on the Sexuality, Health and Well-Being of Same Sex Attracted Young People in Australia.* Monograph Series Number 50 (Melbourne: Australian Research Centre in Sex, Health and Society, La Trobe University, 2005).

Hillier, L., Dempsey, D., Harrison, L., Beale, L., Matthews, L. and Rosenthal, D. *Writing Themselves In: A National Report on the Sexuality, Health and Well-Being of Same Sex Attracted Young People* (Carlton: National Centre in HIV Social Research, La Trobe University, 1998).

Hillier, L., Harrison. D. and Dempsey, D. 'Whatever happened to duty of care?: Same sex attracted young people's experiences of discrimination and abuse at school', *Melbourne Studies in Education*, 40: 2 (1999) 59–74.

Hillier, L., Matthews, L. and Dempsey, D. *A Low Priority in a Hierarchy of Need: A Profile of the Sexual Health of Young Homeless People in Australia.* Monograph Series Number 1 (Melbourne: Australian Research Centre in Sex, Health and Society, La Trobe University, 1997).

Hillier, L., Warr, D. and Haste, B. *The Rural Mural: Sexuality and Diversity in Rural Youth* (Carlton: National Centre in HIV Social Research, La Trobe University, 1996).

Hirtle, P. *Broadsides vs. Grey Literature.* Available: http://www-cpa.stanford.edu/byform/mailing-lists/exlibris/1991/11/msgOO02O.htm1991(June 15, 1997).

Hooks, B. 'Talking Back'. In R. Ferguson, M. Gever, T. Minh-ha and C. West (eds) *Out There: Marginalisation and contemporary cultures* (Massachusetts and London: The New Museum of Contemporary Art and MIT Press, 1990) 337–340.

Horsley, P. 'Lesbians and cancer'. In M. Q. Heffernan (ed.) *The Gynaecological Cancer Guide – Sex, Sanity and Survival* (South Yarra: Michelle Anderson Publishing, 2003).

Horsley, P. *Cancer – An Incredible Journey. Stories of lesbians living with cancer* (Melbourne: Lesbian Cancer Support Group, 2002).

Horsley, P., McNair, R. and Pitts, M. *Women's Health and Well-Being Strategy, Population Group – Lesbians* (Paper prepared for Department of Human Services, Victoria, February 2001).

Hough, M. 'Balancing public health and criminal justice interventions', *International Journal of Drug Policy*, 12 (2001) 429–433. http: /www.nhmrc.gov.au/publications/_files/ethicsbro.pdf

Huggins, J. 'Always was always will be'. In M. Grossman, M. *Blacklines: Contemporary Critical Writing by Indigenous Australians* (Carlton, Victoria, Melbourne University Press, 2003) 60–65.

Hurley, M. 'Contemporary gay cultures in Australia'. In G. Hawkes and J. Scott (eds) *Perspectives In Human Sexuality* (Melbourne: Oxford University Press, 2005).

Inciardi, J. A. and Surratt, H. L. 'Children in the streets of Brazil: Drug use, crime, violence, and HIV risks', *Substance Use and Misuse*, 33: 7 (1998) 1641–1480.

Israel, M. ' "Strictly confidential?" Integrity and the disclosure of Criminological and Socio-legal research', *British Journal of Criminology*, 44 (2004) 715–740.

Johnson, C. 'Visiting the margins: Revenge, transgression or incorporation – An Australian engagement with theories of identity', e-journal, *Theory and Event*, 1: 3 (1997). Accessed at http://www.press.jhu.edu/journals/theory_and_event/, accessed 10/08/2004.

Johnson, K. Hillier, L., Harrison, L. and Frawley, P. *People with Intellectual Disabilities: Living Safer Sexual Lives* (Melbourne: Australian Research Centre in Sex, Health and Society, Latrobe University, 2001).

Johnson-Eilola, J. 'Just Information: The politics of decontextualization in technical communication', Presentation CCCC (Phoenix, Arizona, March 13, 1997). Accessed at http://people.clarkson.edu/~johndan/read/just/welcome. html, accessed 27/04/2007.

Julien, I. and Mercer, K. 'Introduction – De Margin and De Centre', *Screen*, 29: 4 (1988) 2–10.

Kaldor, J. and Millwood, I. 'Consent and approval in medical research: The place of communities', *HIV Australia*, 4: 2 (2005) 23–24.

Kapoor, I. 'Hyper-self-reflexive development?' Spivak on representing the Third World "other", *Third World Quarterly*, 25: 4 (2004) 627–647.

Katz, J. *The Invention of Heterosexuality* (New York: Plume, 1996).

Kelly, J. *Zest for Life: Lesbians' Experiences of Menopause* (Melbourne: Spinnifex, 2005).

Kendig, H., Helme, R., Teshuva, K., Osborne, D., Flicker, L. and Browning, C. 'Health status of older people project: Preliminary findings of a survey of the health and lifestyles of older Australians', *Occasional Papers. Victorian Health Promotion Foundation* (La Trobe University and the University of Melbourne, 1996).

Kennedy, E., Davis, M. D. *Boots of Leather, Slippers of Gold: The History of a Lesbian Community* (New York: Penguin, 1994).

Kim S. Applebaum P., Jeste D. and Olin J. 'Proxy and surrogate consent in neuropsychiatric research: Update and recommendations', *The American Journal of Psychiatry*, 161 (2004) 797–806.

Kipke, M. D., Montgomery, S. and MacKenzie, R. G. 'Substance use among youth seen at a community-based health clinic', *Journal of Adolescent Health*, 14 (1993) 289–294.

Kipke, M. D., Montgomery, S., Simon, T. R. and Iverson, E. F. '"Substance abuse" disorders among runaway and homeless youth', *Substance Use and Misuse*, 32: 7–8 (1997) 969–986.

Kirkman, M. 'I didn't interview myself: The researcher as participant in narrative research', *Annual Review of Health Social Science*, 9 (1999) 32–41.

Klausner, J., Wolf, W., Fischer-Ponce, L., Zolt, I. and Katz, M. 'Tracing a Syphilis Outbreak through Cyberspace', *JAMA*, 284: 4 (2000) 447–449.

Kral, A. H., Molnar, B. E., Booth, R. E. and Watters, J. K. 'Prevalence of sexual risk behaviour and substance use among runaway and homeless adolescents in San Francisco, Denver and New York City', *International Journal of STD & AIDS*, 8 (1997) 109–117.

Kureishi, H. *My Beautiful Laundrette* (London: Faber & Faber, 1986).

Labov, W. *The Social Stratification of English in New York City* (Washington, DC, Center for Applied Linguistics, 1972).

Lakatos, I. and Musgrave, A. *Criticism and the Growth of Knowledge* (Cambridge: Cambridge University Press, 1970).

Langton, M. *'Well, I heard it on the radio and I saw it on the television': An Essay for The Australian Film Commission on the Politics and Aesthetics of Filmmaking by and about Aboriginal People and Things* (North Sydney, NSW: Australian Film Commission, 1993).

Latour, B. and Woolgar, S. *Laboratory Life: The Social Construction of Scientific Facts* (Los Angeles, USA: Sage, 1979).

Laumann, E. O., Gagnon, J. H., Michael, R. T. and Michaels, S. *The Social Organization of Sexuality* (Chicago: University of Chicago Press, 1994).

Lawrence, C., Prestage, G., Leishman, B., Ross, C., Muwadda, W., Costello, M., et al. *Queensland Survey of Aboriginal and Torres Strait Islander Men who have Sex with Men. 2004* (Sydney: National Centre in HIV Epidemiology and Clinical Research, 2006).

Lenton, S. and Tan-Quigley, A. *The Fitpack Study: A Survey of 'Hidden' Drug Injectors with Minimal Drug Treatment Experience* (Perth, Western Australia: National Centre for Research into the Prevention of Drug abuse, Curtin University of Technology, 1997).

Lewin, E., Leap, W. (eds) *Out in the Field: Reflections of Lesbian and Gay Anthropologists* (Urbana and Chicago: University of Illinois Press, 1996).

Lindsay, J, Smith, A. and Rosenthal, D. *National Survey of Australian Secondary Students HIV/AIDS and Sexual Health 1997* (Melbourne: National Centre in HIV Social Research: Program in Youth/General Population, Centre for the Study of Sexually Transmissible Diseases, 1998).

Lindsay, J., Smith A. M. A. and Rosenthal, D. A. *Secondary Students, HIV/AIDs and Sexual Health*, Monograph Series 3 (Melbourne: Centre for the Study of STDs, 1997).

Llewellyn, G. 'People with intellectual disabilities as parents: Perspectives from the professional literature', *Australian and New Zealand Journal of Developmental Disability*, 16: 4 (1990) 369–380.

Llewellyn, G. 'Relationships and social support: Views of parents with mental retardation/intellectual disability', *Mental Retardation*, 33: 6 (1995) 349–363.

Lo, B. and Bayer, R. 'Establishing ethical trials for treatment and prevention of AIDS in Developing Countries', *BMJ*, 327: 7410 (2003) 337–339.

Lorde, A. *Sister Outsider* (New York: The Crossing Press, 1984).

Machon, K. 'Preparing the facts', *HIV Australia*, 4: 3 (2005) 6–8.

Madden, A. *Peer Education among Illicit Drug User* (Canberra: Australian Injecting & Illicit Drug Users League (AIVL), 2005).

Maher, L. and Dixon. D. 'Policing and Public Health', *British Journal of Criminology*, 39: 4 (1999) 488–512.

Mallett, S., Edwards, J., Keys, D., Myers, P. and Rosenthal, D. *Disrupting Stereotypes: Young People, Drug Use and Homelessness* (Melbourne: The University of Melbourne, 2003).

McCarthy, M. *Sexuality and Women with Learning Disabilities* (London: Jessica Kingsley, 1999)

McCarthy, M. 'Consent and choices: Women with intellectual disabilities and sexuality'. In R. Traustadóttir and K. Johnson (eds) *Women with Intellectual Disabilities: Finding a Place in the World* (London: Jessica Kingsley, 2000) 135–168.

McCarthy, M. and Thompson, D. 'Sexual abuse by design', *Disability and Society*, 11: 2 (1996) 205–217.

McCarthy, M. and Thompson, D. 'No more double standards: Sexuality and people with learning difficulties'. In T. Philpot and L. Ward (eds) *Values and Visions: Changing Ideas in Services for People with Learning Difficulties* (Oxford: Butterworth-Heinemann, 1995) 278–289.

McKeganey, N. 'To pay or not to pay: respondents' motivation for participating in research', *Addiction*, 96 (2001) 1237–1238.

Mercer, K. 'Skin Head Sex Thing. Racial difference and the homoerotic imaginary'. In Bad Object-Choices (eds) *How Do I look? Queer Film and Video* (Seattle: Bay Press, 1991).

Michaels, E. 'A model of teleported texts (with reference to Aboriginal Television)', *Continuum*, 3: 2 (1990) 8–31.

Moore, H. A. Passion for difference: essays in anthropology and gender (Cambridge: Polity Press, 1994).

Moreton-Robinson, A. *Talkin' Up to the White Woman: Indigenous Women and Feminism* (St Lucia, Queensland: University of Queensland Press, 2000).

Motzafi-Haller, P. 'Writing birthright: on native anthropologists and the politics of representation'. In D. Reed-Danahay (ed) *Auto/Ethnography – Rewriting the Self and the Social* (New York: Berg, 1997) 195–222.

Muecke, S. 'Aboriginal literature and the repressive hypothesis', *Southerly* 48: 4 (1988) 405–418.

Murnane, A., Smith, A., Crompton, L., Snow, P. and Munro, G. *Beyond Perceptions: A Report on Alcohol and Other Drug Use Among Gay, Lesbian, Bisexual and Queer Communities in Victoria* (Melbourne: Australian Drug Foundation, ALSO Foundation, 2000).

New South Wales Health Department NSW Older *People's Health Survey (OPHS)* (Sydney: NSW Health Department, 2000).

NHMRC. *Human Research Ethics Handbook – Commentary on the National Statement on Ethical Conduct in Research Involving Humans* (Canberra: Commonwealth of Australia, 2001a).

NHMRC. *National Statement on Ethical Conduct in Research Involving Humans, 2005*, from http://www7.health.gov.au/nhmrc/publications/humans/contents.htm (Canberra: Commonwealth of Australia, 1999).

NHMRC. *Statement on Consumer and Community Participation in Health and Medical Research* (Canberra: Commonwealth of Australia, 2001b).

Nilles, B., Tripathi, R., Meienberg, F. and Sharma, S. *TRIPS on Trial: The Impact of WTO's Patent Regime On the World's Farmers, the Poor and Developing Countries* (J. Lewis. London, Action Aid, 2001).

O'Brien M. 'Governing risk and drug use in juvenile justice settings', *Contemporary Drug Problems*, 28: Winter (2001) 625–649.

O'Brien M. L. and Greenwood Z. 'Managing blood borne viruses and other health risks for juvenile offenders', *Youth Studies Australia*, 22: 3 (2003) 25–31.

O'Brien, M. and Gifford, S. 'A survey of women's experiences of living with hepatitis C', *Australian Hepatitis Chronicle*, Issue 9: (2001) 20–25.

Official Committee Hansard *Official Committee Hansard*. Select Committee on the Administration of Indigenous Affairs, 7899: Friday, 27 August 2004. Senate, Canberra, Commonwealth of Australia. http://wopared.aph.gov.au/hansard/senate/commttee/S7899.pdf, accessed 04/05/2007.

Ohnuki-Tierney, E. 'Native anthropologists', *American Ethnologist*, 11: 3 (1984) 584–586.

Ory M. G., Lipman P. D., Karlen P. L., Gerety, M. B., Stevens, V. J., Singh, M. A. F., Buchner, D. M., Schechtman, K. B. and the FICSIT Group. 'Recruitment of older participants in the Frailty/Injury Prevention Studies', *Prevention Science*, 3: 1 (2002) 1–22.

Owen, D. 'Equality, Democracy, and Self-Respect: Reflections on Nietzsche's Agonal Perfectionism', *Journal of Nietzsche Studies*, 24: Fall (2002) 113–131.

Park D., Cherry K. E. 'Human subjects and cognitive ageing research: a unique solution to a perennial problem', Special issue: cognitive ageing – issues in research and application, *Educational Gerontology*, 15: 6 (1989) 563–571.

Pitts, M. K., Couch, M. A. and Smith, A. M. A. 'Men who have sex with men (MSM): how much to assume and what to ask?', *Medical Journal of Australia*, 185: 8 (2006) 450–452.

Pitts, M., Smith, A., Mitchell, A., and Patel, S. *Private Lives. A Report on the Health and Wellbeing of GLBTI Australians*, Monograph Series Number 57 (Melbourne: Australian Research Centre in Sex, Health and Society, La Trobe University, 2006).

Platzer, H. and James, T. 'Methodological issues conducting sensitive research on lesbian and gay men's experience of nursing car', *Journal of Advanced Nursing*, 25 (1997) 626–633.

Plunkett A. and Quine S. 'Difficulties experienced by carers from non-English speaking backgrounds in using health and other support services', *Australian and New Zealand Journal of Public Health*, 20: 1 (1996) 27–32.

Poole M. and Feldman S. (eds) *A Certain Age: Women Growing Older* (Sydney: Allen & Unwin, 1999).

Quine S. 'Practical aspects of organising and conducting focus groups with older people', *Generations Review: Journal of the British Society of Gerontology*, 8: 4 (1998a) 4–6.

Quine S. 'Focus groups: the role of the scribe and procedures for transcription', *Australian Journal of Health Promotion*, 8: 3 (1998b) 214–216.

Quine S. 'Health concerns and expectations of Anglo and ethnic older Australians', *Journal of Cross-Cultural Gerontology*, 14 (1999a) 97–111.

Quine S. 'How do older immigrants view volunteer work, and do they have different training and support needs?' Chapter 13. In P. Rice (ed.) *Living in a New Country: Understanding Migrants' Health* (Melbourne: Victoria, Ausmed Publications, 1999b) 228–242.

Quine S. and Cameron I. D. 'The use of focus groups with the disabled elderly', *Qualitative Health Research*, 5: 4 (1995) 454–462.

Quine S. and Chan Y. 'A role for older volunteers in the health care system: Views of health professionals', *Education and Ageing*, 13: 3 (1998) 229–240.

Radicalesbians. 'The woman-identified woman'. In Linda Nicholson (ed.) *The Second Wave: A Reader in Feminist Theory* (New York: Routledge, 1997) 153–157.

Reinharz, S. and Rowles, G. D. (eds) *Qualitative Gerontology* (New York: Springer Publishing Company, 1988).

Reinharz, S. and Davidman, L. *Feminist Methods in Social Research* (New York: Oxford University Press, 1992).

Resnick, B., Concha, B., Burgess, J. G., Fine, M. L., West, L., Baylor, K., et al. 'Recruitment of older women: lessons learned from the Baltimore Hip Studies', *Nursing Research*, 52: 4 (2003) 270–273.

Rice, D. and Ezzy, D. *Qualitative Research Methods – A Health Focus* (South Melbourne: Oxford University Press, 1999).

Rissel, C., Richters, J., Grulich, A., de Visser, R. and Smith, A. 'Sex in Australia: First experiences of vaginal intercourse and oral sex amongst a representative sample of adults', *Australian and New Zealand Journal of Public Health*, 27: 2 (2003) 131–137.

Rissel, C., Richters, J., Grulich, A., De Visser, R. and Smith, A. 'Attitudes towards sex in a representative sample of adult', *Australian and New Zealand Journal of Public Health*, 27: 2 (2003) 118–123.

Ristock, J. *No More Secrets: Violence in Lesbian Relationships* (New York, London: Routledge, 2002).

Ristock, J., and Pennell, J. *Community Research as Empowerment: Feminist Links, Postmodern Interruptions* (Toronto: Oxford University Press, 1996).

Ritter, A. J., Fry, C. L. and Swan, A. 'The ethics of reimbursing injecting drug users for public health research interviews: what price are we prepared to pay?', *International Journal of Drug Policy*, 14 (2002) 1–3.

Rosaldo, R. *Culture and Truth: The Remaking of Cultural Analysis* (Boston: Beacon Press, 1989).

Rosier, P. 'Lesbians in front, up front and out front'. In S. Kedgeley (ed.) *Heading Nowhere in a Navy Blue Suit: And Other Tales from the Feminist Revolution* (Wellington NZ: Daphne Brasell Associates Press, 1993).

Rossiter, B., Mallett, S., Myers, P. and Rosenthal, D. 'Living well? Homeless young people in Melbourne', *Parity*, 16: 2 (2003) 13–14.

Rossiter, B., Mallett, S., Myers, P. and Rosenthal, D. *Living Well? Homeless Young People in Melbourne* (Melbourne: Australian Research Centre in Sex, Health & Society, La Trobe University, 2003).

Rowles, G. D. and Schoenberg N. E. *Qualitative Gerontology: A Contemporary Perspective* (New York: Springer Publishing Company, 2002).

Roy, E., Haley, N., Leclerc, P., Boivin, J.-F., Cedras, L. and Vincelette, J. 'Risk factors for hepatitis C virus infection among street youth', *Canadian Medical Association Journal*, 165: 5 (2001) 557–560.

Roy, M. and Roy, A. 'Sterilisation for girls and women with mental handicaps: Some ethical and moral considerations', *Mental Handicap*, 16 (1988) 97–100.

Russell, S. 'Beyond Risk: Resilience in the Lives of Sexual Minority Youth', *Journal of Gay & Lesbian Issues in Education*, 2: 3 (2005) 5–18.

Scott, J. W. 'The evidence of experience'. In H. Abelove, M. Aina Barle, and D. M. Halperin (eds) *The Lesbian and Gay Studies Reader* (New York: Routledge, 1993) 397–415.

Sedgwick, E. *Epistemology of the Closet* (Berkeley and Los Angeles: University of California Press, 1990).

Sell, R. L. and Petrulio, C. 'Sampling homosexuals, bisexuals, gays and lesbians for public health research: a review of the literature 1990–92', *Journal of Homosexuality*, 30: 4 (1996) 31–47.

Shields, R. *Places on the Margin: Alternate Geographies of Modernity* (London: Routledge, 1991).

Sigurjónsdóttir, H. B. and Traustadóttir, R. 'Motherhood, family and community life'. In R. Traustadóttir and K. Johnson (eds) *Women with Intellectual Disabilities: Finding a Place in the World* (London: Jessica Kingsley, 2000) 253–270.

Sigurjónsdóttir, H. B. and Traustadóttir, R. *Ósýnilegar fjölskyldur: Seinfærar/throskaheftar mæður og börn þeirra* (Invisible families: Mothers with intellectual limitations and their children) (Reykjavík: University of Iceland Press, 2001).

Sleegers, J., Spijker, J., van Limbeek, J. and van Engeland, H. 'Mental health problems among homeless adolescents', *Acta Psychiatrica Scandinavica*, 97 (1998) 253–259.

Smallacombe, S. 'What is ethical indigenous research?' In M. Langfield (ed.) *A Question of Ethics* (Carlton, The History Institute, Victoria, Inc, 1999) 13–24.

Smith, K. 'Pushing the boundaries: the exclusion of disability rights groups from political influence in Victoria', *Australian Geographer*, 34: 3 (2003) 345–354.

Smith, A., Agius, P., Dyson, S., Mitchell, A. and Pitts, M. *Secondary Students and Sexual Health 2002: Results of the Third National Survey of Australian Secondary Students, HIV/AIDS and Sexual Health* (Melbourne: Australian Research Centre in Sex Health and Society, La Trobe University, 2003).

Smith, A., Rissell, C., Richters, J., Grulich, A., and de Visser, R. 'Sexual identity, sexual attraction and sexual experience among a representative sample of adults', *Australian and New Zealand Journal of Public Health*, 27: 2 (2003) 138–145.

Smith R., Quine S., Anderson J., Black K. 'Assistive devices: Self-reported use by older Victorians', *Australian Health Review*, 25: 4 (2002) 169–177.

Smith, D. *The Everyday World of the Problematic: A Feminist Sociology* (Milton Keynes: Open University Press, 1987).

Solarez, A. L. *Lesbian Health: Current Assessment and Directions for the Future* (Executive Summary) (Washington: Committee on Lesbian Health Priorities, Neuroscience and behavioural health program, health sciences policy program, health sciences section, Institute of Medicine, 1999).

Spivak, G. 'Can the subaltern speak?' In C. Nelson and L. Grossberg (eds) *Marxist Interpretations of Culture* (Basingstoke, Macmillan Education, 1988) 271–313.

Spivak, G. 'Post-structuralism, marginality, post-coloniality, and value', *Sociocriticism*, 5: 2 (1989) 43–81.

Stevens, P. 'Lesbian health care research: A review of the literature from 1970 to 1990', *Health Care for Women International*, 13: 2 (1992) 291–307.

Stevens, P. and Hall, J. M. 'A critical historical analysis of the medical construction of lesbianism', *International Journal of Health Services*, 21: 2 (1991) 291–307.

Tapper, M. 'Ressentiment and Power: Some reflections on feminist practices'. In P. Patton (ed.) *Nietzsche, Feminism and Political Theory* (Sydney: Allen and Unwin, 1993).

Taylor, S. and Bogdan, R. *Introduction to Qualitative Research Method: A Guidebook and Resource*. Third Edition (New York: John Wiley & Sons, 1998).

Thompson P. G., Somers R. L. and Wilson R. 'Recruiting older people to a home safety program', *MJA*, 167 (1997) 439–440.

Thomson, N. and Morgan, K. *The Victorian Community Methadone Program, An Investigation into Consumer Complaints and Grievances* (Victoria: VIVAIDS, 1999).

Tiefer, L. 'The emerging global discourse of sexual rights', *Journal of Sex and Marital Therapy*, 28: 5 (2002) 439–444.

Tjamiwa, T. and Willis, J. 'Tjunguringkula waakaripai: Joint management of Uluru National Park'. In J. Birkhead, T. deLacy and L. Smith. *Aboriginal Involvement in Parks and Protected Areas* (Canberra, Aboriginal Studies Press, 1992).

Tomsen, S. *Hatred, Murder and Male Honour. Anti-homosexual Homicides in New South Wales, 1980–2000* (Canberra: Australian Institute of Criminology Research and Public Policy Series No.43, 2002).

Traustadóttir, R. 'Research with others: Reflections on representation, difference and Othering', *Scandinavian Journal of Disability Research*, 3: 2 (2001) 7–26.

Traustadóttir, R. and Sigurjónsdóttir, H. B. 'Adult children of mothers with intellectual disabilities: Three life histories'. In A. Gustavsson, J. T. Sandvin, R. Traustadóttir and J. Tøssebro. *Resistance, Reflection and Change: Nordic Disability Research* (Lund: Studentlitteratur. 2005).

Traustadóttir, R. and Sigurjónsdóttir, H. B. 'Tre generasjoner utvecklingstörda mödrar og deras familjenätverk' (Three generations of mothers with intellectual disabilities and their family support networks). In K. Barron (ed) *Genus och funksjonshinder* (Gender and disability) (Lund: Studentlitterature, 2004) 83–101.

Tremellen, S. 'What do we need to quit? Lesbians and smoking', *Healthsharing Women*, Issue 12–14 (1996–1997).

Trent, J. Inventing the Feeble Mind. *A History of Mental Retardation in the United States* (Berkeley: University of California Press, 1994).

Tribal Contract Support Cost Technical Amendments of 2000. Oversight Hearing: H. R. 946, H. R. 2671, and H. R. 4148 (Young, R-AK) *To make Technical Amendments to the Provisions of the Indian Self-Determination and Education Assistance Act Relating to Contract Support Costs, and for Other Purposes* (Committee on Resources, Second Session: 16 May 2000). House of Representatives, Washington, US Government Printing Office. http://commdocs.house.gov/committees/resources/hii68434.000/hii68434_0.HTM

Tuhiwai Smith, L. *Decolonising Methodologies: Research and Indigenous People* (London: Zed Books, 1999).

VicHealth Koori Health and Community Development Unit. *We Don't Like Research … but in Koori Hands it Could Make a Difference*. (Melbourne: VicHealth Koori Health and Community Development Unit, University of Melbourne, 2001).

VicHealth Koori Health and Community Development Unit. *Research – Understanding Ethics*. (Melbourne: VicHealth Koori Health and Community Development Unit, University of Melbourne, 2001).

Waite, H. 'Researching Lesbian Health'. Paper presented at the *Health in DIfference 1* (Melbourne 1996).

Wallis, J. and Dollery, B. 'Social Capital and Local Government Capacity', *Australian Journal of Public Administration*, 61: 3 (2002) 76–85.

Walmsley J. and Johnson, K. *Inclusive Research with People with Learning Disabilities: Past, Present and Futures* (London: Jessica Kingsley Publishing, 2003).

Walsh-Bowers, R. and Parlour, S. 'Researcher-participant relationships in journal reports on gay men and lesbian women', *Journal of Homosexuality*, 23: 4 (1992) 477–499.

Waples-Crow, P. and Pyett, P. *The Making of a Great Relationship: A Review of a Healthy Partnership between Mainstream and Indigenous Organisations* (Melbourne: Victorian Aboriginal Community Controlled Health Organisation, 2005).

Ward, L. *Seen and Heard: Involving Disabled Children and Young People in Research and Development Projects* (New York: Joseph Rowntree Foundation, 1997).

Weeks, J. *Coming out. Homosexual Politics in Britain from the Nineteenth Century to the Present* (London: Quartet Books, 1977).

Weeks, W. and Gilmore, K. 'How violence against women became an issue on the national policy agenda'. In T. Dalton, M. Draper, W. Weeks and J. Wiseman (eds) *Making Social Policy in Australia* (Sydney: Allen and Unwin, 1996).

Wells Y., Petralia W., De Vaus D., Kendig H. 'Recruitment for a panel study of Australian retirees', *Research on Aging*, 25 (2003) 36–64.

Weston, K. 'Requiem for a street fighter'. In E. Lewin and W. Leap (ed.), *Out In the Field: Reflections of Lesbian and Gay Anthropologists* (Chicago: University of Illinois Press, 1996) 274–285.

Wihongi, H. *The Process of Whakawhanaungatanga in Kaupapa Maori Research*. Sixth Biennial Conference: Doing Well, Auckland (Australia and New Zealand

Third Sector Research, 2002). http://www.anztsr.org.au/02conf/anztsrpapers/ Wihongi,%20Helen.pdf, accessed 24/01/2006.

Willett, G. 'Man of History', *B News*, 106 (2005) 4.

Willett, G. *Living Out Loud. A History of Gay and Lesbian Activism in Australia* (Sydney: Allen and Unwin, 2000).

Willis, J. Romance, Ritual and Risk: Pitjantjatjara Masculinity in the Era of AIDS. *Australian Centre for International and Tropical Health and Nutrition* (Brisbane: University of Queensland, 1997).

Willis, J., McDonald, K., Saunders, M. and Grierson, J. *HIV Futures 11: Aboriginal and Torres Strait Islander People Living with HIV*, Monograph Series Number 30 (Melbourne: Australian Research Centre in Sex, Health and Society, La Trobe University, 2002).

Wilton, T. 'Lesbian and Gay Health: power, paradigms and bodies'. In D. Richardson, and S. Seidmann (ed.) *Handbook of Lesbian and Gay Studies* (London: Sage, 2002). 253–270.

Wood, L. A. and Ryan E. B. 'Talk to the elders: social structure, attitudes and forms of address', *Ageing and Society*, 11 (1991) 167–187.

Woodruff-Pak, D. *Psychology and Aging* (Englewood Cliffs, NJ: Prentice Hall, 1988).

World Health Organisation (WHO). *Declaration of Alma-ATA, 2003*, from http://www.who.int/hpr/NPH/docs/declaration_almaata.pdf (1978).

Worth, A. and Tierney, A. J. 'Conducting research interviews with elderly people by telephone', *Journal of Advanced Nursing*, 18 (1993) 1077–1084.

Worth, S. and Adair, J. *Through Navajo Eyes* (Bloomington: Indiana University Press, 1972).

Index